Identities, Nations and Politics after Communism

This book focuses on questions of identity that have confronted the countries of Central and Eastern Europe after the collapse of the communist system that had previously provided them with an identity.

This development both facilitated and necessitated a reassessment of the now independent nations' history, orientation, symbols and identity. In some cases, new states were created without a clear national identity, while in others the nation was regaining statehood, but not always within borders that had an historical association with the nation concerned. The multiethnic character of the space of the former Soviet Union and its erstwhile "satellites," and the long historical legacy of complex relations, boundary changes, population migration, and economic and social changes presented different challenges to the various nations and states concerned.

The essays in this volume attempt to elucidate and understand these issues of ethnic and national identity, and their relationship to the emerging statehood in various regions of the post-communist world. This study makes clear that some nation-states were far better prepared to handle these issues than others, and that the longer-term impact of the communist experience has varied.

This book was previously published as a special issue of *Nationalities Papers*

Roger E. Kanet is Professor of International Studies at the University of Miami, Coral Gables. He has published widely on communist and postcommunist Europe.

T0293234

Nations and Nationalism of Eastern Europe and the Former USSR

The Association for the Study of Nationalities General Monograph Series

The Association for the Study of Nationalities (ASN) is the only scholarly association devoted to the study of ethnicity and nationalism from Europe to Eurasia. With hundreds of members in more than fifty countries, ASN brings together the world's leading scholars, and policy analysts interested in the politics, economics, social relations, culture, and history of central and southeast Europe, Russia, Central Asia, and adjacent regions. Its publications, annual convention, sponsored panels, and conferences provide a unique resource for understanding the ongoing processes of nation-building and state-building in these lands. ASN publishes two peer-reviewed journals: *Ethnopolitics* and *Nationalities Papers*. Its flagship publication, *Nationalities Papers*, is the premier journal in nationalities studies that concentrates upon the geographic sphere of the former Soviet Union and Eastern, Central, and Southeastern Europe. *Nationalities Papers* is a multidisciplinary journal that publishes original and innovative scholarly articles in both the humanities and social sciences and is designed to provide a serious forum for scholars, policy makers, journalists, and others working in the broadly defined field of nationalities studies. *Ethnopolitics* is an authoritative, peer-reviewed journal that provides a forum for serious debate and exchange on the topics of ethnicity and conflict-resolution. This series is the product of special issues published by the journals and represents a critical link between the journals and the broader scholarly community.

Identities, Nations and Politics after Communism

Edited by Roger E Kanet

Routledge
Taylor & Francis Group

LONDON AND NEW YORK

First published 2008 by Routledge

2 Park Square, Milton Park, Abingdon, Oxon OX14 4RN
711 Third Avenue, New York, NY 10017, USA

Routledge is an imprint of the Taylor & Francis Group, an informa business

First issued in paperback 2016

Copyright © 2008 Edited by Roger E Kanet

Typeset in Times-Roman (screen) by Techset, Salisbury, UK

British Library Cataloguing in Publication Data
A catalogue record for this book is available from the British Library

ISBN 978-0-415-46022-4 (hbk)
ISBN 978-1-138-97225-4 (pbk)

CONTENTS

Contributors

Aurora Álvarez Veinguer, Research Lecturer, Department of Social Anthropology, University of Granada, Spain.

Alina Curticapean, Research Fellow, Finnish Graduate School in Political Studies and Tampere Peace Research Institute, University of Tampere, Finland

Krzysztof Fedorowicz, Associate Professor of Political Science, Institute of Eastern Studies, Adam Mickiewicz University in Poznan, Poland

Roger E. Kanet, Professor of International Studies, University of Miami, United States

Rosalind Marsh, Professor of Russian Studies, University of Bath, England, President of British Association for Slavonic and East Euroean Studie

Søren Jacob Riishøj, Associate Professor, Department of Political Science and Public Management, University of Southern Denmark

Harlow Robinson, Professor of Modern Languages and History, Northeastern University, Boston, MA, USA

Triin Vihalemm, Associate Professor, Department of Journalism and Communication Faculty of Social Sciences, University of Tartu, Estonia

Claudia Weiss, Member of the Seminar für Geschichtswissenschaft Helmut-Schmidt-Universität der Bundeswehr, Hamburg, Germany

Introduction

Identities, Nations and Politics after Communism

Roger E. Kanet

This collection of essays focuses on questions of identity that have confronted the various countries of Central and Eastern Europe as a result of the collapse of the communist system that had provided them with an identity for several decades of the twentieth century (and in the case of much of the Soviet Union, three decades before that).

As part of the "communist world," these nations had an identity thrust upon them by their ruling communist parties, led by the Communist Party of the Soviet Union under successive authoritarian leaders. The dominant ideology gave an identity to these nations that were deemed to be engaging in the construction of socialism, to be followed by a communist society based on Marxist principles. They were also distinguished by a developed welfare system, a centralized command economy run by the state, and a political system that was based on control of varying degrees of severity. The system styled itself as the antithesis of the "capitalist countries" with the economic free-for-all that favored the owners of wealth at the expense of the working class and peasantry, and was in turn seen by those ideological opponents as a different world, characterized by lack of freedom, atheism, an overbearing state and other negative features that reflected a rejection of liberal democracy.

The collapse of the communist regimes in the late 1980s and early 1990s, entailing loss of power by the ruling parties and abandonment of the ideology, led also to the disintegration of the Soviet Union and Yugoslavia into their constituent republics. These now became independent states, in some cases for the first time in their history, joining those countries that had cast off communist rule and rejected Soviet "leadership." These developments both facilitated and necessitated a reassessment of the now independent nations' history, orientation, symbols and identity. In some cases, new states were created without a clear national identity, while in others the nation was regaining statehood, but not always within borders that had an historical association with the nation concerned. The multiethnic character of the space of the former Soviet Union and its erstwhile "satellites," and the long historical legacy of complex relations, boundary changes, population migration, and economic and social changes, presented different challenges to the various nations and states concerned.

The essays in this collection explore a number of cases in attempting to elucidate and understand the issues of ethnic and national identity and their relationship to the emerging statehood in various regions of the post-communist world. It is clear that some nation-states were far better prepared to handle these issues than others, and that the longer term impact of the communist experience has varied. Moreover, the choices made by the elites in consultation with their peoples (or simply on their behalf), or in a reflection of the clearly enunciated national mood, have been different, and different factors have been at play in promoting particular new identities and political orientations, in place of the half-century or more in which all roads led, metaphorically speaking, to Moscow.

In the first essay that follows, which raises important theoretical points that draw from a constructivist perspective, Alina Curticapean examines how collective identities—and especially national and ethnic identities—have been conceptualized in the field of international relations and how the theoretical concepts have been deployed in the study of Central and Eastern European identities. It claims that the *naturalization* of national identity is a phenomenon more pronounced in studies of Central and Eastern Europe than in studies of Western Europe. Arguing that the conceptualization of identity has political consequences, as reading national or ethnic identities as natural constructs rather than imaginings already forecloses certain political options, this article calls for a *softening* of the understanding of group identity as applied to Central and Eastern Europe.

In the first of the substantive examinations of identity, Harlow Robinson notes that the ballets of Aram Khachaturian occupy a special place in the history of Soviet ballet and of Soviet music and reflect diverse identities. An Armenian, brought up in Georgian Tbilisi and later trained in Moscow, the musically cosmopolitan Khachaturian was entirely a creation of the Soviet musical and dance establishment. Yet his ballets reflect diverse identities: the ethic of Soviet ideology, including the heroism of the working class and peasant builders of socialism, and friendship between Russians and ethnic minorities; the folk music traditions of Armenia and the Caucasus; and the new Soviet patriotism embracing multiple ethnic cultures. The Armenian identity of the music has never been challenged, and even *Spartacus* reflects the question of relations between a ruling group and a small ethnic minority, despite its "ideological" subject. Khachaturian's ballets therefore offer conflicting interpretations, allowing them to reflect and support conflicting identities: Soviet and nationalist.

Claudia Weiss's examination of the place of Siberia in imperial Russia's efforts in the late nineteen century to project an image of imperial grandeur and as justification for Russia's inclusion among the great powers of Europe is an interesting study of an early example of state-sponsored propaganda or public relations. She focuses on the role of a series of international expositions as the venue for Russia's efforts to project an imperial identity that would instill in others an appreciation of Russia's newly gained importance in world affairs. The incorporation of Siberia into Russian identity patterns freed Russia from the pressure to

2

be more European than it actually was. Thus, it helped the Russian Empire to overcome an old sense of inferiority in relation to the West and to place itself self-confidently as a Eurasian state. This important role of Siberia in Russian identity patterns has continued to this day.

The next study of national identity is Aurora Álvarez Veinguer's examination of the multidimensional relationship and the complex dialectic in the process of identity (re)presentation that emerges in the Republic of Tatarstan (Russian Federation) among three different areas: political discourse, institutional praxis, and everyday life. There is a dialogue between a formal rhetoric of inclusion, a rigid discourse and primordial understanding of identities transmitted by some institutions (i.e. national gymnásias) that aim to reinforce particular practices of segregation, as well as personal transgression in everyday life. Tatar national gymnásias create and reinforce static notions of ethno-Tatar identity (ethno-national representations), reproducing and supporting ethno-cultural Tatar segregation which consolidate strong mechanisms of differentiation between Tatar and Russian populations.

In the third substantive examination of identity, Triin Vihalemm notes that the Russian population in post-Soviet Estonia faced a trauma, as their Soviet identity was removed and they became an unwelcome, alien community in the Western-oriented, individualistic state in which they lived. They were confronted with a dilemma of choice over their identity. Research shows that in the past some had considered themselves "Soviet persons" or inhabitants of the Baltic region, while others' identity was of "Russians" or "Russian-speakers"; today their identity focuses on Russianness or language use, or on their residence in Estonia; fewer consider themselves citizens of Estonia, but the identity of "Baltic inhabitant" survives, and has been joined by other broad categories: "northerner," "European" and even "world citizen." The patterns of identity development reflect these dilemmas.

The final three articles concern the impact of identity on international relations. In the first of these, Søren Jacob Riishøj notes that the collapse of communism forced Central European nations to reassess their orientation: after several decades of enforced orientation towards the East they could "return to Europe." However, strains of pro-European sentiment combine with Euroskepticism and strong national feelings to underline mutually overlapping multiple identities. These sentiments are related in part to social factors and to political currents, parties and individual politicians. The examples of Poland and the Czech Republic illustrate these trends and suggest the emergence of "soft" and "hard" versions of Euroskepticism.

Krzysztof Fedorowicz deals with the emergence of a new, national interest-based foreign policy in Poland. The year 1989 marked the beginning of the system transformation in Poland. Its effect was the change of the principal aims of Polish foreign policy based on Polish conceptions of their national identity and their national interest. The process of the vivid changes in Poland after the end of the socialist period coincided with the changes in Europe's geopolitical situation. The collapse of the Eastern Bloc, the democratization of the countries of Central-Eastern Europe, the

3

unification of Germany, the process of Soviet disintegration and the struggle of the Soviet republics for independence presented a totally new challenge for Polish diplomacy.

The main purpose of this article is to explain the complex formation and evolution of Poland's eastern policy in the context of a changing international reality. A new geopolitical situation forced Polish diplomacy to consider international affairs in a different way, as well as to create a new element in its policy—an eastern policy. The essence of this eastern policy was, initially, to establish and set diplomatic relations that would meet Poland's interests, as well as to create the grounds for political dialogue with new countries in the east that border on Poland (Ukraine, Russia, Belarus, and Lithuania).

The third and final essay on the impact of identity on international affairs is Rosalind Marsh's overview of the treatment in the post-Soviet media and culture, especially in literature and film on historical themes, of certain aspects of the perennial debate about "Russia and the West." It traces a shift from the expression of significant pro-Western sentiments in the late 1980s and early 1990s to the increased manifestation of anti-Western and Russian nationalist sentiments in the late 1990s and the early years of the new century. Issues include writer's exploration of messianic attitudes and the search for a "new Russian idea," the similarities and differences between Russia and the West, and the harmful impact on Russia of Western-style capitalism. Is the West still regarded as Russia's "Other," or at a time when Western and Russian tastes in historical fiction are apparently converging, is such a polar opposition now fundamentally dated?

These articles were selected for publication here from papers on issues of national identity that were originally presented at the VII World Congress of Central and East European Studies, held in Berlin in July 2005. The editor wishes to express his sincere appreciation to all the authors for making their essays available for inclusion in this special issue of *Nationality Papers* and for the time and effort that they have put into revising their original papers. He also wishes to thank those authors whose articles were not selected for inclusion for making those papers available. Finally, he wishes to express his special appreciation to Professor Ronald Hill of Trinity College, Dublin, who was instrumental in the initial selection of these papers for possible publication.

"Are you Hungarian or Romanian?" On the Study of National and Ethnic Identity in Central and Eastern Europe

Alina Curticapean

Introduction

A personal note frames this essay. In recent years I have travelled with my Finnish colleagues from the University of Tampere to a number of international seminars and conferences organized in various European locations. While socializing with the other participants, my self-identification as Romanian has, on several occasions, prompted the question "are you Hungarian or Romanian ...?" No other options were ever offered, even though Romania has a quite sizeable Roma minority and a number of Saxons, though ever declining, still live in the country. At the same time, the ethnicity of my Finnish colleagues has never been questioned. True, Finns describe their country as a homogeneous place, yet Finland is a country with two official languages—Finnish and Swedish—ever praised for the treatment of its Swedish-speaking minority. And some other ethnicities—for instance, Roma and Sami—also live in Finland. Nobody interested? Or maybe there is more to it than simply a question of curiosity (or a lack of it). That the ethnicity of the Finnish participants was deemed irrelevant, whereas my ethnic identity seemed a topical issue for informal discussions during coffee breaks or conference lunches elicited my interest in the issue of national and ethnic identity. I have started to ask how collective identities, and especially national and ethnic identities, have been conceptualized and how those theoretical concepts have been deployed in the study of Central and Eastern European identities. Are there any differences in how Central and Eastern European identities are studied compared with Western identities?

This article addresses such issues. It relies mainly, but not exclusively, on material from the field that is closest to me, that is, international relations. It investigates scholarly works on national and ethnic identity and adds a normative flavour by claiming that the big risk and temptation when studying collective identities is that of reifying these identities. This article shows that this risk and temptation have been even higher when research has concerned national and ethnic identity in Central and Eastern Europe. Arguing that the conceptualization of identity has political consequences, and that reading national or ethnic identities as natural constructs rather than imaginings already forecloses certain political options, this article opts for theoretical approaches that challenge the naturalization of group identity. It argues that the subject of identity in Central and Eastern Europe should be approached with the same sophistication with which is has been dealt in the case of Western Europe.

The argument proceeds by highlighting the persistent distinction in the social sciences between "strong," "hard" or essentialist understandings of identity, on the one hand, and "weak," "soft" or anti-essentialist conceptualizations, on the other. I then discuss each of these ways of theorizing identity and I follow how these different understandings have been applied to studies of group—national, ethnic and regional—identities in Central and Eastern Europe. In a call for a *softening* of the understanding of identity in relation to the Central and Eastern European region, the article subsequently explores the possibilities opened by understanding identity as continuously performed rather than a natural construct.

"Strong" and "Weak" Conceptualizations of Identity

As is the case with many key terms in the social sciences, "identity" is both a *category of practice* and a *category of analysis*. As a category of practice identity is used by "lay" actors "to make sense of themselves, of their activities, of what they share with, and how they differ from, others."[1] Identity as a category of analysis refers, here, to the ways in which it is used in the social sciences. To be sure, identity is a very rich concept, and the conceptual and explanatory work that it does depends on the context of its use and the theoretical tradition from which the use in question derives. The most general distinction that one can make, however, is between a strong (hard, essentialist) and weak (soft, anti-essentialist, constructivist) understanding of the term identity.

Strong conceptions of identity underscore sameness over time or across persons. In this case the line between the practical and the analytical uses of identity is blurred and a series of problematic assumptions is in place. Thus, it is postulated that identity is something that all people or groups (such as ethnic, racial or national groups) *have*, or *ought to have*, or *are searching for*. Second, it is presumed that identity is something people and groups can have without being aware of it and, therefore, identity is something to be *discovered* and something about which one can be *mistaken*. Third, as strong conceptions of identity emphasize sameness among group members they also imply a clear-cut distinctiveness from non-members, a sharp *boundary* between inside and outside.[2]

We all know that even objects change constantly, as revealed by microscopic examinations if not otherwise obvious. Could it be, then, that identities remain unchanged over time? No, many theorists have answered, and they have broken consciously with the strong understandings of the concept. Such scholars have emphasized the *processual*, interactive development of "groupness" and have presented identity both as a contingent product of social and political action and as a basis of further action. Weak or soft understandings of identity, moreover, highlight the unstable, multiple, fluctuating and fragmented nature of identity.

Breaking with the everyday, hard uses of identity is by no means simple. Sliding into essentialist argumentation is favoured by the uneasiness of language to accommodate hybridity.[3] Then, the fact that we often encounter an amalgam of constructivist language and essentialist argumentation comes to testify to the dual nature of academic identitarians as both *analysts* and *protagonists* in social and political life. As Ernesto Laclau puts it:

> you cannot simply say "I'm outside essentialism," in the same way that one cannot say that one is entirely outside metaphysics. The only thing that one can do is to play new and different games with metaphysical and essentialist categories, games that both posit them and weaken them, and thus make possible language games far more complicated than those that were possible in the past.[4]

By inventing and playing these games the researcher should avoid reifying identity (racial, ethnic, national). To be sure, reification is central to the politics of ethnicity, race, nation and more often than not people feel that their identity is natural, not chosen. With all factors taken into consideration, the task of the analyst is to account for these processes of reification. Research should aim to explain the ways in which such imaginings as nation, ethnic group and race crystallize, at certain moments, in powerful, compelling "realities" for which some are ready to sacrifice their lives. To focus on how particular representations come to be, and on the political consequences of their being imagined in a certain way, already opens a space for alternative imaginings.

The researcher's choice for one or another way to conceptualize identity is, certainly, more that a personal option. Following David Campbell, I suggest that it is ultimately an *ethical* choice. What consequences the reification of ethnic identities can have is brilliantly demonstrated by Campbell in his *National Deconstruction: Violence, Identity, and Justice in Bosnia*. As stated in the preface, *National Deconstruction* is "concerned primarily with 'metaBosnia', the array of practices through which Bosnia (indeed, competing 'Bosnias') comes to be."[5] Campbell argues that the dominant narratives of the media and the academy alike have presented Bosnia as an ethnically ordered world of Croats, Muslims, and Serbs, in which no other conceptions of identity had political significance, and where group relations could not be other than mutually exclusive and conflictual.[6] Partition seemed the inevitable result. But he wants to impress upon us that this did not need to be—indeed, should not have been—the case. As he puts it, different problematizations encourage different political options. Indeed, if the international community, the media, and the academy had not failed to heed the plurality of political positions and the non-nationalist voices that contested the identity politics of those prosecuting the war, partition would have been no more than one political option among others.

7

"Strong" Understandings of Identity in Context

It should be said here that the strong and weak understandings of identity represent the very extremes of the spectrum of identity conceptualizations and most of the recent scholarship on identity tries to walk a fine line between the essentialization of identity, on the one hand, and its complete diffusion, on the other. In relation to the region of Central Eastern Europe, this essay reviews scholarly works situated closer to the hard and soft extremes on the continuum of identity conceptualizations. It argues that the position of the harder understandings in writing on collective (national, ethnic) identity in the region of Central and Eastern Europe is strong enough to demand careful consideration.

To start from the strong edge, in what follows I will highlight three problematic aspects in the study of Central Eastern European identities. The first aspect, and the first kind of essentialization of identities, is constituted by the explanation—in newspaper articles and academic contributions alike—of the post-communist resurgence of nationalism in the beginning of the 1990s in the region by the idea of the "lid being taken off the boiling pot." That is, that old hatreds and enmities which were suppressed under communist rule are now free to find their expression. This is what Brubaker calls the "return of the repressed" stereotype.[7]

Consider first Ronald Linden's surprise at the lack of conflict between Romania and Hungary after the end of the Cold War. The introduction to his article explains why the emergence of a conflict between the two countries would have been the "natural" situation, while its absence "is nothing short of astonishing."[8]

> Consider the following scenario: two states, immediate neighbors, have in this century been part of different empires and independent. They have fought wars against each other twice and invaded and occupied each other's territory. To this day significant *terra irredenta* remains, along with a sizable population of one on the territory of the other. After the Second World War these two states' politics, economics, and international relations were dominated by an outside power, which enforced compliance—and good neighborliness—through hegemony. After a time that hegemony collapsed, and soon after the hegemon itself. The two states thus approach the twenty-first century free to determine their own forms of government, domestic policies, and international relations ... Given the nature of these two states' relations with each other and the world in which they operate, what might be expected? "Conflict" would be a reasonable answer. Add further the fact that these two states are located in East Europe, a region long associated with territorial demands, forced exchanges, and, by some accounts, *ancient* ethnic hatreds ... and you have an almost *overdetermined* path toward conflict.[9]

Consider, then, another example from the former Soviet Union. Raimo Väyrynen states that: "*Due to historical reasons*, the Baltics *cannot but "securitize"* their relations with Russia, from which it follows that the intra-ethnic conditions within the countries and their relations with the West are also understood in security terms."[10]

Notice the strong terms used by both authors! Linden appreciates that following the end of the Cold War a conflict between Hungary and Romania would have been a "natural" occurrence. He further explains that "the path toward conflict" between the two states was "almost *overdetermined*" also because the two states are located in a region characterized by "*ancient* ethnic hatreds." Väyrynen, for his part, contends that the Baltics "*cannot but* securitize their relations to Russia." Such a choice of words makes us appreciate that both of the above examples operate with an understanding of group identity which is situated closer to the hard extreme of the spectrum of identity conceptualizations. In both Linden's and Väyrynen's arguments identity is conceptualized as a construct which remains largely unaffected by the passing of time. Used as a relatively static idea, the concept suggests (wrongly, in my mind) that, because of a specific history, the groups must be determined to act in a certain way: for instance, Romania and Hungary to engage in conflict with each other or the Baltics to securitize[11] their relations with Russia. The apex of this kind of essentialism is attained in the description of the Balkan area.[12]

In relationship to conceptualizing collective identities in Central and Eastern Europe as continuous in time, a second kind of essentialism is evident when nationalism in this region is cast as "ethnic" nationalism. Such a conceptualization follows the influential distinction drawn by Anthony Smith between "civic" and "ethnic" nationalism, in which the latter is regarded as being prevalent in a non-Western context where, it is argued, the birth community and native culture are emphasized to the detriment of contractual notions of citizenship said to characterize Western communities. According to Nira Yuval-Davis, recent contributions to the literature on nationalism and ethnicity have added a clear moralistic flavour to this dichotomous classification in the sense that civic nationalism has been deemed good and ethnic nationalism bad.[13]

Third, the eastern part of Europe is sometimes represented as a distinct area that demands a tailor-made theoretical and methodological approach, different from the one that can be applied in studies of Western states. Or at least this is what we are led to believe when Ruth Wodak, Rudolf de Cellia, Martin Reisigl and Karin Liebhart state in the introduction to their book *The Discursive Construction of National Identity* (1999): "This book is about the manifold attempts to imagine and construct national identity. Although our study focuses on Austria, it is by no means restricted to it. Many of its insights, especially its theoretical and methodological approach, which was specially developed for this investigation, are equally applicable to other *western European* states."[14] As enlightening as the book is, it still leaves us wondering why the discursive method cannot be equally applied to other states, such as *East European* states.

Each of the above-listed kinds of essentialization of ethnic, national or regional identities in Central and Eastern Europe and the Balkans can be, and has already been, critically investigated. First, anyone who considers "history" as the cause of a conflict in the region of Central and Eastern Europe or the Balkans should become aware that an historical explanation can always be "cooked up" to explain a conflict in Western Europe (which has not been so "conflict free" as some like to pretend). As some scholars have pointed out,[15] there is still very little reflection on the habitual practices of explaining contemporary events in the region of Central and Eastern Europe by reference to past centuries.[16] Perhaps even less attention is paid to the political effects of such academic, journalistic and political practices.

Second, seeing civic and ethnic nationalisms as mutually exclusive concepts—the former as an attribute of the West and the latter characterizing the East—obscures the extent to which both forms are implicated in any nationalist project. A classification of different states and societies according to these two types of nationalism would constitute an ahistorical, impossible and misleading mission. "The distinction between the two models is highly problematic," explains Silverman,[17] "and it is (if they are different modes at all) not easily applicable to the difference between individual countries (for example, France and Germany in the past, France and the USA or Great Britain now), but rather to differences in the countries themselves." Any serious analysis should, hence, look at how these "types" of nationalism are combined in different ways in specific historical cases.[18] Banal as this observation may seem, it has not become self-evident in scholarship on nationalism.[19]

Third, I appreciate that the study of identity in Eastern Europe would benefit from the new theories and methodologies applied to analysing identity in the West, namely the weak conceptualizations of identity. To my mind it is just as possible to analyse the *discursive* construction of national or ethnic identities in Central and Eastern Europe as it is to use such a theoretical and methodological approach in a study of, for example, Austrian, or any other, national identity. It is a banal statement to say that the way (or *how*) Austrian national identity is imagined is different from the way Bulgarian identity is created, but this does not mean that Bulgarian national identity is *less discursively* constructed than Austrian identity. In fact, taking notice of the strong position of essentialism in the study of group identities in Central and Eastern Europe, this chapter pleads openly for a *weakening* of the concept of identity in relation to this region.

The essentialization of collective identities in Central and Eastern Europe has a strong enough position in Western scholarship to demand careful consideration.[20] However, the Western discourse on Central and Eastern Europe is far from monolithic. One can easily identify an (increasing) number of (interdisciplinary) studies which attempt to weaken, to different degrees, the strong understanding of collective identity in the region of Central and Eastern Europe.[21] This article both draws on and attempts to add to this already existing group of studies by proposing that collective identity be understood as continuously "performed" rather than "fixed." It what follows, I introduce the notion of "performativity" and show how it has been linked with the study of state and national identity in the West. With the next section the discussion moves from exploring strong understandings of group identity towards investigating weak conceptualizations.

Performed Identities and Discourse

At the other extreme of the spectrum of identity conceptualizations, the weak extreme, identity is understood as emerging within discourse. The categorization of identity as "what we are" (or internal) is exposed as "something entirely phantasmatic," as there is no ground to identity.[22] *Identity is not something that we have, nor something we achieve, rather identity is performed.*[23]

The notion of performativity was introduced and developed by Judith Butler in her work on sex and gender.[24] Understanding the gendered identity as performative means that it is regarded as having no ontological status apart from the various citational processes that constitute its reality. However, that identity is performed does not mean that the physical reality of the body is denied. Rather, it means that "the identity of any body, the ways we *understand* the materiality of the body, does not pre-exist all manners of performative expressions of sex and gender."[25]

Performances become more meaningful and more authoritative to the extent that they are repeated. Butler explains that: "[P]erformativity is ... not a singular 'act', for it is always reiteration of a norm or set of norms, and to the extent that it acquires an act-like status ... it conceals or dissimulates the conventions of which it is a repetition."[26] Repeated performances, then, have the cumulative effect of normalizing their own assertions. The less we question these norms the more successful they become at achieving authority as natural or ideal. The connection to normativity is the key to understanding the difference between performance (as referring to a singular or deliberate act) and performativity.[27] Normativity is the paradoxical element in the performative act as it provides both its beginning and its end. In other words, the performative subject cannot be engaged in the citation of norms without being herself created by them, while these norms cannot be resisted or rearticulated except by a subject who has been produced by the norms. This constitutive circle is what Butler calls "the paradox of subjectivation."

But where does this discussion on the performative constitution of gender leave the student of collective identity? As David Campbell has suggested, understanding the performative constitution of gender brings us one step closer to understanding the performative constitution of the state.[28] The sites of the performative constitution of state and national identity are many and varied, and equally varied is the body of scholarship that tackles them. Thus, some have addressed the performative constitution of state and national identity in foreign and security practices in general,[29] while others have gone to more specific sites and have investigated the production of national identity through, for instance, missile crises,[30] interventionist actions,[31] and immigration strategies.[32] For exemplification, I will discuss in some detail Campbell's *Writing Security* and Weber's *Simulating Sovereignty*.

Relying explicitly on Butler's notion of the performative, in his pathbreaking *Writing Security* (1992), David Campbell challenges the traditional narrative of asking how foreign policy serves the national interest. Instead, he develops a theory

11

of foreign policy as discursive practices that help constitute and reconstitute the identity of the community in whose name it is said to operate. Campbell starts by articulating a non-essentialistic conceptualization of danger. Thus, "[D]anger is not an objective condition. It is not a thing which exists independently of those to whom it may become a threat."[33] As "danger is an effect of interpretation" (2), nothing is more or less dangerous than something else, except when interpreted as such. In terms of the non-essentialistic character of danger, the objectification and externalization of danger need to be understood as an effect of political practices rather than the condition of their possibility. As danger is never objective, Campbell's argument continues, neither is the identity which it is said to threaten. Rather, the contours of this identity are subject to constant (re)writing, and foreign policy is an integral part of the discourses of danger which serve to discipline the state. Campbell's theory—a declared challenge to conventional approaches which assume a settled nature of identity—is, thus, that state identity can be understood as the outcome of practices associated with a discourse of danger.

Campbell's argument, however, should not be understood as a denial of the existence of the material world. Drawing on Ernesto Laclau and Chantal Mouffe, he is careful to underline:

> [t]he fact that every object is constituted as an object of discourse has *nothing to do* with whether there is a world external to thought, or with the realism/idealism opposition . . . What is denied is not that . . . objects exist externally to thought, but the rather different assertion that they could constitute themselves as objects outside of any discursive condition of emergence.[34]

We speak about the foreign policy of state x or state y, thereby indicating that the state is prior to the policy, but Campbell's creative insights come to challenge such a position. He explains that national states are "paradoxical entities which do not possess prediscursive stable identities" (11). As states are always in the process of becoming, "for a state to end its practises of representation would be to expose its lack of prediscursive foundations" (11). Ironically, the inability of the state project of security to succeed is the guarantor of the state's continued success as an impelling identity. "The constant articulation of danger through foreign policy is thus not a threat to a state's identity or existence: it is its condition of possibility" (12).

Another scholar who has aimed at linking the notion of performativity to the subject of the nation-state is Cynthia Weber in her *Simulating Sovereignty* (1995). While Campbell is concerned with security, Weber sets up the task to discuss another central concept in international relations, namely the notion of sovereignty. She starts by arguing that "[I]t is not possible to talk about the state as an ontological being—as a political identity—without engaging in the political practice of constituting the state."[35] Weber, furthermore, deplores what she sees as the historically uncontested nature of sovereignty and intervention. Sovereignty, she suggests, is "as a site of political struggle" (3). From here, Weber begins to tackle historically the

12

representational practices by which intervention is legitimated and collective understandings of state secured.

In fact, Campbell and Weber analyse different aspects of how state identities are "written" in foreign policy.[36] While the former is mainly concerned with how state identity is constituted through the identification of enemies, the latter examines how the sovereignty/intervention boundary discursively constructs the state as well, as the meaning of sovereignty and intervention. They suggest that nation-states are not pre-given subjects but subjects in process and that all subjects in process (be they individual or collective) are the *ontological effects* of *discursive practices* that are *performatively enacted*. Both examples work with a weak conceptualization of identity and they both testify to the complexity and sophistication displayed by recent approaches to national and state identity in the West.

The Critique of Balkanism

On the other hand, the weak conceptualization of identity as performed in various discursive practices is not very common in studies of Central and Eastern Europe. However, a preoccupation with discursive practices is apparent in a handful of recent (mainly historical) studies of Southeastern Europe.[37] Such works are directed at the *meanings* and *power* of the term Balkan, but they can be easily connected with studies of group identity (understood, of course, in a weak sense). These studies share a view of political and cultural discourse as an articulatory practice that constitutes and organizes social relations. Approaching the discourse on the Balkans (so-called Balkanism[38]) from this standpoint, they view it as a very effective method of setting the Balkans apart, of making them a subaltern place. In other words, most of these works see Balkanism as a *power discourse*—and an extraordinarily powerful one—which not merely describes but in fact *structures* and *constrains* both insider and outsider responses to the Balkans.

The most fervent critique of the Balkanist discourse, Maria Todorova, argues in her highly influential *Imagining the Balkans* (1997) that the term Balkan has become "one of the most powerful pejorative designations in history, international relations, political science, and, nowadays, general intellectual discourse."[39] The rhetoric in this view amounts to "a persistent hegemonic discourse from the West, continuously disparaging about the Balkans, which sends out messages about the politicization of essentialized cultural differences" (59). Todorova also treats Balkanism as a discourse that severely constrains the options of the people in the Balkans. Confronted with the hegemonic Western construction imposed on them, she writes, it is hardly realistic to expect the Balkans to create a liberal, tolerant, all-embracing identity celebrating ambiguity and a negation of essentialism (59). In a similar vein, Milica Bakic-Hayden and Robert M. Hayden present Balkanism as a discourse that relies on the apparent naturalness of the categories it employs to acquire an almost unshakeable stigmatizing effect. "Indeed," these scholars write, "the unfavorable normative import of adjectives such as byzantine and balkan is so pronounced as to make orientalism axiomatic in regard to peoples and societies so labelled."[40] They argue that the Balkanist discourse is interiorized by the people in the former Yugoslavia and present this situation as an argument of the hegemonic quality attained by Balkanism.

The critique of Balkanism, as Patrick Hyder Patterson observes, "typically treats it not just as a remarkably powerful discourse, but as a remarkably *pervasive, persistent*, and *uniform* mode of thought as well."[41] Writings *on* Balkanism, concludes Patterson, leave us

> with a grim image of western writing and thinking about the Balkans, a discourse portrayed as unremittingly myopic and distressingly uniform in its prejudices—not only highly programmatic but also largely programmed, with the limited range of possible expression virtually foreordained by the structural power of the categories involved.[42]

Patterson's study leads him towards a rather different conclusion. He sets the task of investigating how the concepts of the Balkans, Central Europe and Europe figured in Slovenian public discourse in the late 1980s and early 1990s, on the one hand, and how Slovenia and Slovenes have been depicted in Italian and Austrian accounts, on the other. His analysis suggests that approaches to the Balkans may be rather more nuanced and plural than the critique of Balkanism admits.

Patterson's analysis shows Slovenia's rejection of the Balkans which, in Slovenian rhetoric, was more often than not associated with Yugoslavia. Indeed, admits Patterson, in its most radical variant Slovenia's rejection of the Balkans portrayed Slovenia as one of the borderlands of European civilization and claimed that at the south of Slovenia starts the land of "chaos, violence, and Balkan emotionalism" (119). But, he continues, it is important to note that such extreme positions by no means typified Slovenian commentary on Yugoslav affairs. In Slovenian analyses of Yugoslav politics and interethnic relations, *Balkanism* might have been an important and recurring motif, but there is clear evidence that not all Slovenian accounts fell into the trap of Balkanist rhetoric. Then, Austrian and Italian observations on Slovenian society present an even more mixed record, claims Patterson. While some Austrian and Italian observers did engage in harsh Balkanist stereotyping, this in no way represented a dominant or unique tendency.

Patterson's analysis problematizes one of the fundamental conclusions of the critique of Balkanism, that is, that Balkanism functions as a *power discourse* that has attained a *hegemonic position*. Instead, Patterson's study illuminates some instances in which the power of the discourse proved limited. This evidence serves us as a strong warning not to divert from an understanding of *discourse-as-power* to an understanding of *discourse-as-straitjacket*. If we are to work with a weak conceptualization of identity as performed in discourse, and there are good reasons to do so, we must still be careful not to reduce the plurality of discourses (and associated identities) to a single, dominant one.

The critique of Balkanism reviewed in this section exemplifies the application of the soft conceptualization of identity to the region of Eastern Europe. To be sure, there are other studies that attempt to weaken the understanding of identity vis-à-vis this region, but the critique of Balkanism is closer to the soft extreme of the spectrum of identity conceptualizations and that is why this section has described it in more detail.

In this paper I advocate *softening* the understanding of collective identity in relation to Central Eastern Europe. In what follows I will highlight three problematic aspects related to a strong understanding of identity and the way that they can be addressed by weakening the understanding of identity. First, when a hard conceptualization of identity is embraced, the danger is that the researcher starts her or his analysis with predefined concepts and images. For instance, some recent scholarly contributions regarding Central and Eastern Europe and the Balkans have followed the now almost classic distinction between civic and ethnic nationalism. If such a distinction represents the premise of the study then the conclusions are not difficult to anticipate. I argue that if a soft understanding of identity is preferred then such assumptions are put under critical scrutiny and the research is likely to have an empirical and contextualized character and aims to explicate, rather than assume or take for granted, what type of nationalism characterizes a particular society at a certain point in time.

Second, a soft conceptualization of identity is likely to challenge the appearance of neutrality and objectivity typically embedded in master narratives or dominant discourses. Instead of reifying the master narratives of the state, or of one dominant group—which often happens when hard conceptions of identity prevail—the research will pin down the plurality of stories existent in any society. Research should draw attention to the extent to which identity is shaped with and by others. Thus, the focus on one site alone should be excluded and the multitude of sites from which the definition of identity emerges taken into analysis. For the societies of Central and Eastern Europe and the Balkans, where, sometimes, the ideal of nationalism proves to be the dominant narrative, the unveiling of alternative, multicultural, even if marginal, narratives is of critical relevance. A soft understanding of identity underscores that neither multicultural nor monoculturalist identities are natural, pre-given. Both are materialized through an array of practices, and these practices can be directed towards the nurturing of multicultural identities.

In relation to this, the third point is that narrative and discourse analysis are helpful in making the researcher aware of the contingent nature of her/his own explanations as well as those of other researchers. Science differs from other narratives because it commits the success of its story to the criterion of truth.[43] Narrative explanatory analysis guides us, as researchers, to construct and to believe in "the best possible account" at the same time that we are aware that what counts as "best" is itself historical and that research criteria will change and change again. Together with Laclau,[44] I suggest that by confessing the contingent nature of her/his explanation, the researcher should give the audience a choice that is in her/his power to grant: that of stepping outside of her/his discourse.

Conclusion: The Central East European Identity Theme

Two main ways of theorizing collective identity—strong, hard or essentialist, on the one hand, and weak, soft, constructivist or anti-essentialist, on the other—have been investigated in (mainly Western) studies of identities in the Central and Eastern European region. Interestingly enough, this chapter reveals that hard conceptualizations hold a strong position—or at least strong enough to demand careful consideration—in academic writings on national identity in Central and Eastern Europe. But here, Fleming warns us,[45] we must view the term academic with caution. Referring to the Balkans, he expresses the opinion that the vast majority of such writings is in fact produced not by academicians in the strictest sense of the term but rather by what he calls experts whose expertise derives from their experience as journalists, travellers or political strategists. The work of these specialists, continues Fleming, is targeted at "a nonspecialist, non-academic audience and purports to explain and unravel the intricacies of Balkan history and politics for lay readers" (1226). He claims that within Western Europe, and even more so in North America, the number of such specialists outnumber academic ones (such as historians, scholars of literature, political scientists who are housed in universities). It may be that the essentialization of collective (ethnic and national) identities is more widely spread in studies of the Balkans than in analyses of identities in other Central and Eastern European societies. Or, as Fleming claims, that it is more often used by so-called Balkan (or, for that matter, Central and Eastern European) experts or specialists rather than by academics. This is not so important. Important is the fact that these kinds of essentializations exist and have significantly negative effects.

This study has suggested that the way we understand identities is not without political consequences. When strong understandings of identity are in place and concepts such as nation or ethnic group are addressed as natural constructs, rather than imaginings, some political options are already foreclosed. After all, different problematizations mandate different political options. Aligning to this argumentation, this article has overtly pleaded for *softening* the approach to national identity in Central and Eastern Europe. There is one thing, though, that I have not tried to do. I do not argue that national identity in Central Eastern Europe is the same as national identity in Western Europe, nor that it should be. In other words, I do not have any political project of colonizing Eastern identity according to a Western model. Rather, what I do argue is that national identity in Central Eastern Europe should be approached with the same theoretical sophistication that is applied to Western European identity.

To return to the question from the title, "Are you Hungarian or Romanian?," this article claims that the *relevance* of ethnic belongingness in today's Romania or any other Central Eastern European society, for that matter, should be a subject of thoughtful investigation rather than the premise of the study. Of course, I do not mean to imply that those asking the question were operating with an essentialist understanding of identity. It could equally be that some people were more interested in my professional affiliation with a Finnish research institute—and because of a certain linguistic affinity, but also institutionalized co-operation, a Hungarian background could have offered a plausible explanation—than in any ethnic divisions in Romania. To put it differently, I do not take the question "Are you Hungarian or Romanian?" for more that it actually was, namely the spark for my interest in the study of national identities in Central Eastern Europe and the preliminary catalyst for this very paper.

NOTES

1. Brubaker and Cooper, "Beyond 'Identity,'" 4.
2. Ibid., 10.
3. For instance, David Campbell (*National Deconstruction* 258, n. 52) contests the mapping of Bosnia as a place populated by the coherent and settled identities of Serbs, Croats and Muslims. Despite this, in a number of places, his book reluctantly persists—even as it wants to problematize them—with national categorizations. As Campbell himself acknowledges, the difficulty of imagining alternative representations testifies to the way language cannot easily accommodate hybridity and to the power of the national imaginary.
4. Laclau, "Universalism, Particularism and the Question of Identity," 131.
5. Campbell, *National Deconstruction*, x.
6. Ibid., 157.
7. Brubaker, "Myths and Misconceptions in the Study of Nationalism."
8. Linden, "Putting on their Sunday Best," 122.
9. Ibid., 121, emphasis added.
10. Väyrynen, "The Security of the Baltic Countries", 216, emphasis added. My concern here is not with whether or not the Baltics securitized their relations with Russia, but rather with Väyrynen's argument that this securitization is unavoidable because of historical reasons.
11. The notion of "securitization" was introduced by Ole Wæver and subsequently developed by the so-called Copenhagen School of security studies. It refers to the understanding of security as a speech act (i.e. a special kind of discursive practice). According to Wæver ("Securitization and Desecuritization"), by "saying security" a particular case is characterized as extraordinarily important, and it is moved into a specific area where extraordinary means can be used. When an issue is securitized, one says that this is of existential importance, and if we do not react immediately against this threat we might cease to exist.
12. See Campbell, *National Deconstruction*, esp. 49–81, for an overview of political, journalistic and academic accounts of the war in Bosnia.
13. Yuval-Davis, *Gender & Nation*, 20.
14. Wodak et al., *The Discursive Construction of National Identity*, 2, emphasis added.
15. Neumann, *Uses of the Other*; Lieven, "Against Russophobia."
16. Lagerspetz ("Postsocialism as a Return") has noted that much of social science in Central and Eastern Europe also operates with a naturalized conception of the past.
17. Silverman, cited in Wodak et al., *The Discursive Construction of National Identity*, 19.
18. Cf. Yuval-Davis, *Gender & Nation*; Wodak et al., *The Discursive Construction of National Identity*; Brubaker, "Myths and Misconceptions in the Study of Nationalism"; Campbell, *National Deconstruction*.
19. See Dungaciu, "East and West and the 'Mirror of Nature.'"
20. Operating with strong understandings of collective identities in Central and Eastern Europe is not limited to Western academia. According to Dungaciu (ibid.), self-essentialization is a

local phenomenon in the Central and Eastern European region, and especially in the Balkans.

21. See, for example, Kuus, "European Integration in Identity Narratives in Estonia"; Drulak, *National and European Identities in EU Enlargement*; White, *Nationalism and Territory*; Prizel, *National Identity and Foreign Policy*; Neuburger, "Bulgaro-Turkish Encounters and the Re-imagining of the Bulgarian Nation (1878–1995)"; Holy, *The Little Czech and the Great Czech Nation*; Hansen, "Slovenian Identity"; Pynsent, *Questions of Identity*; Lehti and Smith, *Post-Cold War Identity Politics*; Hosu, "Post-Cold War Romania," etc. This list is by no means comprehensive. It includes only a number of scholarly works which, in one way or another, touch on the discipline of international relations, the main discipline on which this paper relies and to which it aims to contribute.

22. Lloyd, "Performativity as Politics," 1399.

23. Note that many poststructuralists prefer to use concepts such as "subject" and "agency" instead of "identity." Brubaker and Cooper ("Beyond 'Identity'") even argue that, because of its sheer ambiguity and contradictory meanings, identity fails to perform the analytical work it is supposed to do and it should be replaced with some other, less ambiguous, concepts. Identity is, to be sure, a contested concept, yet I think that it can be used if it is made clear *how* it is used (or what meaning is assigned to it).

24. Butler, *Gender Trouble*; idem, *Bodies that Matter*; idem, *Excitable Speech*.

25. Cf. Weber, "Performative States," 80, emphasis in original.

26. Butler, *Bodies that Matter*, 12.

27. Cf. Weber, "Performative States," 81.

28. Campbell, *Writing Security*, 9.

29. Campbell, *Writing Security*.

30. Weldes, "Constructing National Interests"; idem, "The Cultural Production of Crises."

31. Weber, *Simulating Sovereignty*; Doty, "Foreign Policy as Social Construction"; Milliken, "Intervention and Identity."

32. Doty, "Sovereignty and the Nation."

33. Campbell, *Writing Security*, 1.

34. Laclau and Mouffe, quoted in Campbell, *National Deconstruction*, 25.

35. Weber, *Simulating Sovereignty*, 3.

36. Campbell, *Writing Security*; Weber, *Simulating Sovereignty*.

37. See, for example, Todorova, "The Balkans"; idem, *Imagining the Balkans*; Bakic-Hayden and Hayden, "Orientalist Variations on the Theme 'Balkans'"; Bakic-Hayden, "Nesting Orientalisms"; Guzina, "Inside/Outside Imaginings of the Balkans"; Iordanova, "Are the Balkans Admissible?"

38. To varying extents these critiques of *Balkanism* have drawn on Edward Said's influential *Orientalism* (1978). However, some of them modify or depart in important respects from Said's analysis. For a convincing argument that it is "unnecessary or even counterproductive to make explicit use of the Saidian critique" in studies of Southeastern Europe see Fleming, "*Orientalism*, the Balkans, and Balkan Historiography."

39. Todorova, *Imagining the Balkans*, 7.

40. Bakic-Hayden and Hayden, "Orientalist Variations on the Theme 'Balkans,'" 2.

41. Patterson, "On the Edge of Reason," 140, emphasis added.

42. Ibid., 141.

43. Somers and Gibson, "Reclaiming the Epistemological 'Other,'" 84, n. 41.

44. Laclau, "Universalism, Particularism and the Question of Identity," 95.

45. Fleming, "*Orientalism*, the Balkans, and Balkan Historiography."

REFERENCES

Bakic-Hayden, Milica. "Nesting Orientalisms: The Case of Former Yugoslavia." *Slavic Review* 54, no. 4 (1995): 917–31.

Bakic-Hayden, Milica, and Robert M. Hayden. "Orientalist Variations on the Theme 'Balkans': Symbolic Geography in Recent Yugoslav Cultural Politics." *Slavic Review* 51, no. 1 (1992): 1–15.

Brubaker, Rogers. "Myths and Misconceptions in the Study of Nationalism." In *The State of the Nation: Ernest Gellner and the Theory of Nationalism*, edited by John A. Hall. Cambridge: Cambridge University Press, 1998.

Brubaker, Rogers, and Frederick Cooper. "Beyond 'Identity.'" *Theory and Society* 29, no. 1 (2000): 1–47.

Butler, Judith. *Gender Trouble: Feminism and the Subversion of Identity*. New York and London: Routledge, 1990.

———. *Bodies that Matter: On the Discursive Limits of "Sex."* New York and London: Routledge, 1993.

———. *Excitable Speech: A Politics of the Performative*. New York and London: Routledge, 1997.

Campbell, David. *Writing Security: United States Foreign Policy and the Politics of Identity*. Minneapolis: University of Minnesota Press, 1992.

———. *National Deconstruction: Violence, Identity, and Justice in Bosnia*. Minneapolis and London: University of Minnesota Press, 1998.

Doty, Roxanne Lynn. "Foreign Policy as Social Construction: A Post-Positivist Analysis of US Counterinsurgency Policy in the Philippines." *International Studies Quarterly* 37, no. 3 (1993): 297–320.

———. "Sovereignty and the Nation: Constructing the Boundaries of National Identity." In *State Sovereignty as Social Construct*, edited by Thomas J. Biersteker and Cynthia Weber. Cambridge: Cambridge University Press, 1996.

Drulak, Petr, ed. *National and European Identities in EU Enlargement: Views from Central and Eastern Europe*. Prague: Institute of International Relations, 2001.

Dungaciu, Dan. "East and West and the 'Mirror of Nature.' Nationalism in the West and East Europe—Essentially Different?" In *A Decade of Transformation*, IWM Junior Visiting Fellows Conferences, vol. 8, Vienna, 1999, <http://www.iwm.at/publ-jvc/jc-08-03.pdf> (accessed 25 February 2004).

Fleming, K. E. "*Orientalism*, the Balkans, and Balkan Historiography." *American Historical Review* 105, no. 4 (2000): 1218–33.

Guzina, Dejan. "Inside/Outside Imaginings of the Balkans: The Case of the Former Yugoslavia." *Balkanistica* 12 (1999): 39–66.

Hansen, Lene. "Slovenian Identity: State-Building on the Balkan Border." *Alternatives* 21, no. 4 (1996): 473–96.

Holy, Ladislav. *The Little Czech and the Great Czech Nation*. Cambridge: Cambridge University Press, 1996.

Hosu, Alina. "Post-Cold War Romania: A Study in the Construction of Security and Identity." In *Routing Borders between Territories, Discourses and Practices*, edited by Eiki Berg and Henk van Houtum. Aldershot: Ashgate, 2003.

Iordanova, Dina. "Are the Balkans Admissible? The Discourse on Europe." *Balkanistica* 13 (2000): 1–36.

Kuus, Merje. "European Integration in Identity Narratives in Estonia: A Quest for Security." *Journal of Peace Research* 39, no. 1 (2002): 91–108.

Laclau, Ernesto. "Universalism, Particularism and the Question of Identity." In *The Identity in Question*, edited by John Rajchman. New York and London: Routledge, 1995.

Laclau, Ernesto, and Chantal Mouffe. *Hegemony and Socialist Strategy*. London: Verso, 1985.

Lagerspetz, Mikko. "Postsocialism as a Return: Notes on a Discursive Strategy." *East European Politics and Societies* 13, no. 2 (1999): 377–90.

Lehti, Marko, and David Smith. *Post-Cold War Identity Politics: Northern and Baltic Experiences*. London and Portland, OR: Frank Cass, 2003.

Lieven, Anatol. "Against Russophobia." *World Policy Journal* XVII, no. 4 (2000/01), <http://www.worldpolicy.org/journal/lieven.html> (accessed 12 May 2007).

Linden, Ronald H. "Putting on their Sunday Best: Romania, Hungary, and the Puzzle of Peace." *International Studies Quarterly* 44, no. 1 (2000): 121–45.

Lloyd, Moya. "Performativity as Politics: Contesting the Boundaries of Identity?" In *Contemporary Political Studies*, Proceedings of Political Studies Association Conference, edited by Jeffrey Stanyer, Iain Hampsher-Monk, Joni Lovenduski, and Delphine Jones. Oxford and Cambridge: Blackwell, 1996, http://www.psa.ac.uk/journals/pdf/5/1996/lloy.pdf (accessed 12 May 2007).

Milliken, Jennifer. "Intervention and Identity: Reconstructing the West in Korea." In *Cultures of Insecurity*, edited by Jutta Weldes, Mark Laffey, Hugh Gusterson, and Raymond Duvall. Minneapolis and London: University of Minnesota Press, 1999.

Neuburger, Mary. "Bulgaro-Turkish Encounters and the Re-imagining of the Bulgarian Nation (1878–1995)." *East European Quarterly* 31, no. 1 (1997): 1–20.

Neumann, Iver B. *Uses of the Other: "The East" in European Identity Formation*. Manchester: Manchester University Press, 1999.

Patterson, Patrick Hyder. "On the Edge of Reason: The Boundaries of Balkanism in Slovenian, Austrian, and Italian Discourse." *Slavic Review* 62, no. 1 (2003): 110–41.

Prizel, Ilya. *National Identity and Foreign Policy: Nationalism and Leadership in Poland and Ukraine*. Cambridge: Cambridge University Press, 1998.

Pynsent, Robert B. *Questions of Identity: Czech and Slovak Ideas of Nationality and Personality*. Budapest: Central European University, 1994.

Somers, Margaret R., and Gloria D. Gibson. "Reclaiming the Epistemological 'Other': Narrative and the Social Constitution of Identity." In *Social Theory and the Politics of Identity*, edited by Craig Calhoun. Oxford and Cambridge: Blackwell, 1994.

Todorova, Maria. "The Balkans: From Discovery to Invention." *Slavic Review* 53, no. 2 (1994): 453–82.

——. *Imagining the Balkans*. New York and Oxford: Oxford University Press, 1997.

Väyrynen, Raimo. "The Security of the Baltic Countries: Co-operation and Defection." In *Stability and Security in the Baltic Sea Region: Russian, Nordic and European Aspects*, edited by Olav Knudsen. London and Portland, OR: Frank Cass, 1999.

Wæver, Ole. "Securitization and Desecuritization." In *On Security*, edited by Ronnie D. Lipschutz. New York: Columbia University Press, 1995.

Weber, Cynthia. *Simulating Sovereignty: Intervention, the State, and Symbolic Exchange*. Cambridge: Cambridge University Press, 1995.

——. "Performative States." *Millennium: Journal of International Studies* 27, no. 1 (1998): 77–95.

Weldes, Jutta. "Constructing National Interests." *European Journal of International Relations* 2, no. 3 (1996): 275–318.

Weldes, Jutta. "The Cultural Production of Crises: U.S. Identity and Missiles in Cuba." In *Cultures of Insecurity*, edited by Jutta Weldes, Mark Laffey, Hugh Gusterson, and Raymond Duvall. Minneapolis and London: University of Minnesota Press, 1999.

White, George W. *Nationalism and Territory: Constructing Group Identity in Southeastern Europe*. Lanham, MD: Rowman & Littlefield, 2000.

Wodak, Ruth, Rudolf de Cillia, Martin Reisigl, and Karin Liebhart. *The Discursive Construction of National Identity*, translated by Angelika Hirsch and Richard Mitten. Edinburgh: Edinburgh University Press, 1999.

Yuval-Davis, Nira. *Gender & Nation*. Thousand Oaks, CA: Sage, 1997.

The Caucasian Connection: National Identity in the Ballets of Aram Khachaturian

Harlow Robinson

The ballets of Aram Khachaturian (1903–1978) occupy a special place in the history of Soviet ballet and of Soviet music. Considered along with Dmitri Shostakovich and Sergei Prokofiev as one of the leaders of Soviet music, Khachaturian devoted many years to the creation of ballet, although in the end he produced only three ballet scores: *Schast'e* [Happiness], completed in 1939; *Gayane*, completed in 1942; and *Spartak* [Spartacus], completed in 1954. Of these three, *Gayane* and *Spartacus* (both repeatedly revised) were notably successful, both immediately acclaimed as important new achievements in the development of an identifiably Soviet ballet style. Taken on tour abroad by the Bolshoi Ballet in a revised version, *Spartacus* also became one of the most internationally successful ballets written by a Soviet composer, although it never came close to equaling the international recognition eventually achieved by Prokofiev's Soviet ballets *Romeo and Juliet* or *Cinderella*. *Gayane* was not widely staged outside the USSR, but some of the music from the ballet, arranged into three orchestral suites by the composer, became very popular internationally—particularly the "Sabre Dance," which became the single most recognized piece of Khachaturian, recycled repeatedly in Hollywood film scores.

Unlike Prokofiev, who spent nearly 20 years after the Bolshevik Revolution living in the West, and who worked extensively with Western dance companies and choreographers, Khachaturian was entirely a creation of the Soviet musical and dance establishment. And unlike both Prokofiev and Shostakovich, whose personal and cultural origins were Russian, and whose education took place chiefly in the former imperial capital of St. Petersburg, Khachaturian was an Armenian born and raised in an Armenian milieu in the Georgian capital of Tbilisi, just before and after the 1917 Revolution. Only in the 1920s did Khachaturian gravitate to Moscow, where he pursued systematic musical training at the Gnessin Institute and the Moscow Conservatory. Because of his proletarian origins, non-Russian ethnic origins and Soviet training, Khachaturian became a powerful symbol within the Soviet musical establishment of the ideal of a multinational Soviet cultural identity, an identity which the composer enthusiastically embraced and exploited both at home and abroad. It is also worth noting that as an Armenian, Khachaturian felt particular gratitude to the Soviet regime because it had "rescued" the Armenian nation after the disastrous genocide carried out against ethnic Armenians by the government of the neighboring Turkish Ottoman Empire during World War I.

In his music Khachaturian made extensive use of the non-Russian and non-Western musical techniques and traditions with which he had become intimate during his formative years in the cosmopolitan Caucasian capital of Tbilisi (Tiflis), a vibrant crossroads of Armenian, Georgian, Azerbaijani, Turkish and other influences. Like the members of the *moguchaya kuchka*, especially Borodin and Rimsky-Korsakov, whose works to some extent served him as a model, Khachaturian drew heavily upon "Eastern" or "Oriental" material in creating compositions in various classical genres and styles of European origin. But Khachaturian's cultural identity and rigorous musical training within the Soviet establishment allowed him to penetrate more deeply to the essence of Eastern and Caucasian music and to incorporate it more fully in his mature work, including the ballets.

In an article published in *Sovetskoye iskusstvo* in June 1953, Khachaturian's admirer and friend Dmitri Shostakovich observed that Khachaturian was "the first among our composers who has succeeded with unquestioned authority in revealing the many-faceted possibilities of the 'symphonization' of the music of the Soviet East, to express strong dramatic experiences, patriotic ideas and deep spiritual currents."[1] Other scholars who have written about Khachaturian's music and career also stress his special status as a multinational artist who was uniquely formed by the aspirations of Soviet culture to be international, to absorb and project the utopian communist ideal of transcending narrow national or ethnic identity in the service of a greater cause. "In his works," writes Georgii Tigranov in his important 1960 study *The Ballets of Aram Khachaturian*,

> Khachaturian ecstatically and passionately exalts the free, happy life, creative labor, the heroic struggle of the Soviet people, the beautiful spiritual outlook of the new man, he praises the indestructible fraternal friendship of the peoples of our country, love and loyalty to the socialist way of life. In Khachaturian's compositions we see colorful genre portraits and scenes of folk celebrations, all illuminated by the sunny light of the landscape of his native country.[2]

My focus in this paper is the representation of nationality and national characters in Khachaturian's ballets. When Khachaturian first undertook to compose a ballet in the late 1930s he chose a narrative of present-day Soviet life in Armenia. The project was a commission from the Spendiarov Theater of Opera and Ballet in Erevan in connection with an upcoming festival of Armenian art to be held in Moscow. In order to familiarize himself with the atmosphere, Khachaturian spent the spring of 1939 in Armenia, where he had previously spent little time. The ballet's libretto was written by G. A. Ovanesyan and deals with issues treated in many other works of Soviet literature and art of the 1930s: "the theme of labor, the defense of the country, the patriotism of the Soviet people."[3] The action takes place in an Armenian collective farm village, in the Ararat valley near the border with Turkey—defense of the border from potential invaders is a dominant issue, a reflection of the Soviet concern with national security in the late 1930s, and a familiar feature of Soviet literature and film of the period. It is spring, and the members of the collective farm are seeing off their sons who are joining up with the Red Army. One of those enlisting is Armen, our hero, who bids farewell to his sweetheart. He is sent to guard the border and is gravely wounded in a skirmish with "violators of the frontier." Meanwhile, back home, his sweetheart Karine is dancing with her comrades to celebrate the gathering of the harvest. When she is told of Armen's wound she runs off to find him at the border, but he has already returned home. The scene of their joyful wedding follows, with the presentation of dances of the various peoples of the region: a Ukrainian gopak is followed by Georgian, Armenian, and Russian dances. For the finale, the stage darkens, then the lights come up to illuminate a *tableau vivant* of two border guards who "proudly stand watch, casting a watchful glance over the borders of the Great Motherland. The ballet concludes with an apotheosis—a chorus of collective farmers and border guards, praising the socialist homeland."[4]

The score for *Schast'e* includes numerous Armenian folk songs and dances, as well as a Lezginka, a Ukrainian gopak and a Russian folk dance, in order to represent the multinational character of the region and of the USSR. Particularly noted at the time were Khachaturian's use of unusual non-Western rhythmic patterns typical of Armenian music and his imitation of the sounds of traditional Caucasian instruments.

Schast'e was performed for the first time by the Erevan Opera and Ballet Theater at the Bolshoi Theater on 24 October 1939. Although most of the reviews complained about the dramatic weaknesses of the libretto, many hailed the ballet from the 36-year-old composer (already recognized for his Piano Concerto and a few chamber works) as an important experiment in setting a "contemporary theme on the material of national folklore."[5] At this time very few ballets on contemporary life had been written by Soviet composers. In the late 1920s and early 1930s Shostakovich created three—*Zolotoi vek, Bolt* and *Svetlyi ruchei*—but all had vanished from the repertoire for various reasons, and after the denunciation of Shostakovich's opera *Lady Macbeth of the Mtsensk District* in 1936, Shostakovich's dramatic works could hardly be used as a model. (*Zolotoi vek* deals with a Soviet athletic team on tour in the capitalist West; *Bolt* with industrial efficiency and machinery; and *Svetlyi ruchei* with collective farm life.) In his *Red Poppy* (1927), Gliere had made some use of "national folklore," both Russian and Chinese, but the setting was China, not the USSR. After being harshly criticized by Soviet critics for his topical industrial ballet *Le Pas d'acier*, which was produced in Paris by Diaghilev in 1927, Prokofiev avoided ballet libretti on contemporary themes, and instead turned to Shakespeare for his first Soviet ballet, *Romeo and Juliet*. Boris Asafiev also preferred in his ballets to use subjects taken from Russian classical literature (especially Pushkin) or from historical revolutionary events that had occurred in the West (*Flames of Paris*).

In 1940 Khachaturian received a commission from the Kirov Theatre to write a new ballet. The libretto, by K. N. Derzhavin, was based on *Schast'e*, but introduced new characters and conflicts, and centered on the character of a young Armenian woman named Gayane, after whom the ballet was titled. The score for *Gayane* contains most of the music written for *Schast'e*, much of it heavily revised, but Khachaturian also composed a significant amount of new music. The first version of *Gayane* was finished by late 1942, in Perm, where Khachaturian was living in evacuation with the Kirov Ballet troupe during the first years of World War II. (Prokofiev was also there working on *Cinderella*.)

The original libretto for *Gayane*, also set in Armenia, revolves around the heroine Gayane, a virtuous member of a Soviet collective farm village, and her relationship with her destructive drunk husband Giko, who neglects his work and "shames the family." When he demands that Gayane leave the collective farm with him, she refuses, and an argument follows between Giko and Gayane's brother Armen, also a positive character. Now the Russian commander of the border patrol, Kazakov, appears on the scene with two of his soldiers, and they are happily greeted by the villagers. Kazakov gives a rose to Gayane in admiration of her beauty and virtue. Seeing this from behind the tree where he is hiding, Giko becomes enraged and demands again that Gayane leave with him, but she continues to refuse and Giko is banished from the village. Thus, Act I establishes a conflict of "action" and "counteraction." Musically, Khachaturian sets up a sharp contrast between the themes of Gayane and Giko, giving Gayane two themes that are both lyrical and strong and conveying her "steadfast behavior in struggle."

Act II takes place in Gayane's house, where carpet weavers are working, accompanied by an Armenian folk melody. Gayane sings a lullaby, also based on a folk song, to her child. But Giko returns to interrupt the peaceful atmosphere. He is joined by three "strangers who turn out to be criminals, and they share some plunder with Giko." Giko plans to flee with them and burn down the collective farm. When Gayane tries to stop him, he pushes her away, locks her up and flees with the criminals.

For Act III the scene changes to a mountain village inhabited by Kurds, and is filled with Kurdish dances. Here, Gayane's brother Armen meets his sweetheart, the Kurdish maiden Aisha—their romance also illustrates the peaceful relations between the various peoples of the Caucasus region under Soviet control. Armen has a rival for Aisha's affections, however, the Kurdish youth Ismail, who attacks Armen. At that very moment, the criminals reappear, searching for the escape route to the border. Armen pretends to help them, but sends word back to the village about the impending danger. To the rescue comes the Russian officer Kazakov with his men. In the distance is seen the glow of a fire at the collective farm, set by the criminals and Giko. (In an earlier version of the libretto, the fire was set by "foreign saboteurs.") The villagers manage to extinguish the fire, Gayane seizes Giko and exposes him publicly; he stabs her in fury but is led away by guards. It is worth noting that one of the heroic themes heard in this scene was later used by Khachaturian in the music he wrote for the anthem of the Armenian Soviet Socialist Republic.[6]

Act IV is an extended divertissement with little dramatic action. Kazakov and Gayane are joyfully reunited and profess their love. The Russian officer Kazakov will replace the drunken Armenian law-breaker Giko as Gayane's husband, a resolution that, in Tigranov's words, "is not only the ballet's lyrical theme, but also a symbol of the idea of the friendship of the Russian and Armenian peoples."[7] Also to be joined in marriage are the Kurdish maiden Aisha and the Armenian Armen (Ismail has inexplicably disappeared), and Gayane's friends Nune and Karen. Blessing these unions are representatives of various military units of the Soviet Red Army representing different ethnic groups—Russian, Ukrainian, Georgian, Armenian.

For this scene, Khachaturian composed a new piece that had not been in *Schast'e*— the "Sabre Dance," celebrating the native Caucasian traditions of warfare as expressed in war dances, with wildly asymmetrical rhythms repeated with an elemental insistence and ferocity. It was this piece more than any other that would become associated in the future with Khachaturian's music and name. The entire act is a sort of competition of national dances, and modeled at least in part on similar scenes from the Russian classical ballet repertoire, such as the final act of Glazunov's *Raymonda*. (The plot of *Raymonda*, not incidentally, centers on the conflict between the Western and Eastern—that is, Muslim—world as represented by Raymonda's two suitors, Jean de Brienne and the Saracen knight Abderakhman.) In *Gayane*, however, these dances transcend the purely decorative function of "character dance" to assume a central dramatic, musical and ideological purpose. Khachaturian also makes extensive use of authentic folk songs of the various ethnic groups, and places the tar and the saz, Caucasian folk instruments, in the orchestra. Intervals of the diminished second, so characteristic of Armenian folk music, abound in the harmonies and melodic lines. Similarly, Khachaturian used the balalaika for the Russian folk dances.

For Soviet critics one of the most important aspects of *Gayane*, which received its premiere in Perm in 1942 and was restaged in 1945 and 1952, was the fact that the ballet dealt with contemporary characters in a contemporary and multinational setting. In particular, the vexing problem of the positive hero was addressed in the character of Gayane, a "typical" collective farm worker. Gayane's musical personality is very closely connected to Armenian folk song, reflecting her closeness to "folk"— *narodnye*—values. Indeed, Gayane was the first convincing model of a multi-ethnic Soviet heroine in the history of Soviet ballet. In his book, Tigranov also makes the claim that *Gayane* is a realistic portrait of Soviet life and the Soviet people, "about their new relationship to work, and their love and loyalty to the Motherland."[8]

Almost immediately, however, changes were made to the libretto of the 1942 version of *Gayane*. In some wartime productions topical details were added, such as the announcement on the radio of the German invasion of the USSR and the subsequent mobilization of recruits to the front. (At the time, the Caucasus was under imminent threat of German attack.) As the popularity of the music of *Gayane* continued to grow, so did attempts to create a more satisfying dramatic structure for the ballet. Many changes were made to the libretto and to the score for a new production at the Kirov in 1952. Khachaturian began to come under attack for agreeing so easily to changes, for failing to insist upon a single version. The head of the Union of Soviet Composers, Tikhon Khrennikov, even accused Khachaturian of "an extremely superficial understanding of the role of music in the theater."[9] Various different versions (both of *Gayane* and later of *Spartacus*) were also staged abroad. In a letter written in 1975, Khachaturian complained that most of these productions were full of "confused notation, confused libretti, everywhere the same arrogance and distortion."[10]

But the most significant changes to *Gayane* were made in 1957 for a new production at the Bolshoi Theater, choreographed by Vasily Vainonen. A new libretto was prepared by B. Pletnev that alters the plot and eliminates characters from the 1942 version, and Khachaturian revised about a third of the score. In a letter to the composer Kara Karayev, Khachaturian complained: "They have written an entirely new libretto for *Gayane*. I objected, but then agreed. What will come out of this enterprise, I do not know. It's terribly unpleasant and dirty work."[11] Later, Khachaturian admitted he was not even sure which of the many versions of the score and libretto of *Gayane* he himself preferred. It was this 1957 version of the score and libretto that was published in 1988 by Muzyka, the first publication of a complete score of the ballet. This has become the standard performing edition.

The Pletnev libretto for the Bolshoi 1957 version is in three acts (a prologue and seven scenes), rather than the four acts of the original 1942 production. The number of major characters is reduced to six: Gayane, Aisha, Nunne, Armen, Georgii and Karen. The Russian officer Kazakov is eliminated, as is Gayane's drunken husband Giko. The setting is no longer a collective farm but a village in the mountains where the main activity is hunting. The saboteurs and criminals of the earlier version have vanished, along with the preoccupation over the protection of the border. Obvious ideological references are nearly absent, and the enemies are the unforgiving elements—storm, wind, mountains—and rapacious animals, especially bears. The plot is a bland story of friendship, love and jealousy in a picturesque Caucasus mountain community.

Each of the scenes has a descriptive title: Friendship, Spring, Regaining Health, Jealousy, Crime, Love, Conscience, Repentance. In the prologue the close friends Armen and Georgii are hunting in the mountains. The mountain girl Aisha appears, looking for a lamb that has wandered away from the flock. She slips and falls as a storm approaches, and lies unconscious at the bottom of a cliff. When Armen and Georgii see her, they rescue her and return to their village. Scene One takes place in the garden next to Gayane's house. She and her friends are weaving and dancing for each other. She rejoices when she sees her sweetheart Armen (he was her brother in the 1942 version) and Georgii, bringing in the lifeless body of Aisha, who soon revives and is welcomed into the community. The scene ends with a *pas de deux* for Gayane and Armen. Scene Two, Regaining Health, also takes place in Gayane's garden. Georgii has fallen in love with Aisha, and tells her so, but she is too modest and shy to reply. Aisha's silence leads Georgii to suspect that Aisha prefers Armen, especially when Georgii sees Armen hand Aisha some flowers, not knowing that they are intended for Gayane. Scene Three shows the men preparing for the hunt. As they are setting off, again a misunderstanding arises between Georgii and Armen over Aisha, and the two men almost come to blows. Only Gayane can separate them. Aisha decides she must return to her home in the mountains. In Scene Four the men are hunting in the mountains. Georgii has gone off alone and is spying on Armen from behind a cliff. When Armen is attacked by a bear, Georgii is so overcome by his jealousy that he fails to come to his aid, and Armen falls down the mountainside. In the process, Armen is wounded and blinded. Georgii is horrified that he did not save his friend from this fate—"I am a traitor, I have committed a crime."[12]

Scene Five shows us Gayane caring tenderly for Armen, who is still unable to see. Georgii wants to confess his guilt, but is so shocked by the sight of his injured friend that he decides to run away forever. In Scene Six, Georgii encounters Aisha in her mountain village and she professes her love for him, finally overcoming her shyness. But Georgii feels unworthy of her love, and running off, vows to confess his guilt to Armen. The final scene takes place in the autumn. The festival of the harvest is in full swing. Armen longs to be healthy again, and removes his eye bandage—and suddenly he is able to see once again! The celebration intensifies until Georgii and Aisha run in. Georgii publicly confesses his crime in failing to aid Armen on the mountainside. After some hesitation, Armen forgives him. Aisha accepts responsibility as well, and vows to go away with Georgii to start a new better life. They leave under the approving eyes of their friends.

In the revised 1957 *Gayane* all elements of external conflict—intruding criminals, enemies threatening the border, saboteurs—are removed. This fact can be explained by a number of factors. In 1957 the official mood in the post-war USSR was one of pacifism, not the territorial paranoia of the Stalinist period. The militarism of the original libretto was suitable for 1942, but not for 1957. In its blandness, Pletnev's libretto contains little to offend, and becomes less identifiably Soviet. The treatment of the issue of the multinational fraternity of Soviet society is also minimized. As Tigranov writes, the revised libretto celebrates "love and friendship, loyalty and bravery, while deceit, egotism, and the failure to do one's duty are condemned." He also admits that "this libretto also suffers from a lack of internal dramatic logic, and insufficient motivation for the action."[13]

That the music Khachaturian wrote for *Gayane* has survived, and continued to grow in popularity, is remarkable in view of the persistent libretto problems. Its quality of "Armenian-ness" has never been questioned, and this has been one of the few constants in the ballet's troubled history. When Leningrad choreographer Boris Eifman staged *Gayane*, first at the Maly Theater in Leningrad in 1972 and in 1975 in Lodz, he was also troubled by the weak libretto. But he came to understand that the music was the key to a successful production. Khachaturian's music, he observed, moved him because of its

> spirit of nationalism. In my view Armenia is not only a riot of colors. In my view Aram Khachaturian is not only a feast of music. I have always perceived the Armenians to be a people whose tragic historical fate has been imprinted on the outlook and behavior of each individual. And when an Armenian smiles, you can always see in their eyes a shadow of sadness. I hear all of this in Khachaturian's music, including *Gayane*.[14]

Khachaturian's third and last ballet, *Spartacus*, also traveled a very bumpy road from conception to completion. Like *Gayane*, its libretto and score were revised and rearranged repeatedly. The idea of creating a Soviet ballet on the life of the historical figure of the slave Spartacus, leader of a famous Roman slave uprising in the years 74–71 BC, dates back to the 1930s, when the "heroic theme" was dominant in Soviet culture. It helped, of course, that both Lenin and Marx had praised Spartacus in their works as a forerunner of twentieth-century revolutionaries. Marx described Spartacus as "the most magnificent figure in all of ancient history,"[15] and Lenin called him "one of the most outstanding heroes of one of the most important slave rebellions."[16] Dancer-choreographer Igor Moiseyev, later famous as the director of the Moiseyev Dance Troupe, which presented dances of the different peoples of the USSR, wanted to choreograph the new ballet for the Bolshoi. Khachaturian was asked to write the music, and the experienced librettist Nikolai Volkov was commissioned to write the libretto for a planned production at the Bolshoi Theater. Volkov had worked extensively on ballets with Caucasian settings composed by Boris Asafiev, including *Kavkazskii plennik* and *Bakchisaraiskii fontan*, and also wrote the libretto for Prokofiev's *Cinderella*.

But many years went by before Spartacus took the stage. Khachaturian only began writing the score in 1951. This was a very delicate moment in his career. In early 1948, Khachaturian, previously immune to official censure, had been attacked publicly along with Prokofiev and Shostakovich at the Composers Congress called by Stalin, and fell into a deep personal and creative depression. He needed to find an ideologically appropriate project with which to rehabilitate himself, and *Spartacus* fit the bill nicely. In an interview on the project published in *Sovetskoe iskusstvo* in 1951, Khachaturian stressed its ideological relevance in the Cold War era. Spartacus, he said, was a

> symbol of the struggle of oppressed peoples for their freedom, against greedy masters. It seems to me that the theme of Spartacus is resonant and near to our era, when the freedom-loving peoples of Korea and Vietnam are shedding blood for freedom and independence, when all of progressive humanity is struggling for peace against imperialists and their greedy plans for the enslavement of peoples ... The theme of Spartacus is especially relevant today when colonialism is in its death throes.[17]

But the character of Spartacus also appealed to Khachaturian on a deep personal level. He could identify with Spartacus first of all as the member of a minority-group nationality within a multinational empire: Khachaturian was an Armenian in the Russia-dominated USSR and Spartacus a Thracian in the Rome-dominated Empire. Like

Spartacus, who was brought to Rome from the colonial periphery to be trained as a gladiator because of his physical and mental prowess, Khachaturian had come to the Soviet imperial capital of Moscow to be trained as a Soviet composer. While Khachaturian's life did not carry the obvious risk of death that Spartacus endured, he did come to learn in 1948 (if he hadn't realized it earlier) that he was not a free man, but a subject of the emperor, vulnerable to his whims. And the milieu of the Roman Empire around 70 BC appealed to Khachaturian's artistic imagination because it was multinational and in a real way "Eastern," with vast territories in the Eastern Mediterranean and stretching towards the Black Sea and the Caucasus.

It is beyond the scope of this essay to elaborate on the complicated evolution of *Spartacus* as a ballet, which, like *Gayane*, exists in several different versions. What I want to stress is the central role that the idea of nationality plays in the score and characterizations. One of the organizing principles of the score is the contrast made behind the musical world of the Roman masters (military fanfares, marches, decadent waltzes and bacchanals) and the musical world of the slaves (Oriental, lyrical, folk inspired). Since most of the slaves in the Roman Empire were non-Roman members of conquered ethnic and national groups, the music that accompanies their appearance on stage is strongly "ethnic"—Ethiopian, Egyptian, Thracian, Gallic, German, Syrian, Nubian. Khachaturian made this point clear in an interview on *Spartacus*: "Rome in that era was multinational."[18] So Khachaturian used his own "national style" in providing a portrait of Spartacus' Rome, without any attempt at accurate historical imitation or stylization. As we know, folk music occupied a privileged position in the official Soviet musical aesthetic, and it is the "positive characters" in *Spartacus* who are most closely associated with it—the slaves, the suffering gladiators, Spartacus and his wife Phrygia. The Roman lieutenant Crassus and his lover Aegina (even though she is a Greek dancer) are associated with a more neutrally "classical" style. Phrygia's music, in particular, is even reminiscent of the Armenian folk music given to Gayane, while the scenes of grief make abundant use of Armenian laments, and melodies associated with the traditional Caucasian poet-singers, the Ashug. Although Spartacus does meet his death in the end, crucified in the last scene by the Romans, his music and the music of his fellow slaves and gladiators from the Eastern Mediterranean vanquish the proud Roman fanfares.

Exactly what Khachaturian's intentions were in composing *Spartacus* have been the object of considerable speculation. On the surface, as we have seen, he claimed that the ballet offered an appropriate ideological lesson grounded in Marxism–Leninism, and asserted the rights of the oppressed minority peoples of the world against their more powerful majority rulers. And yet it is very tempting to see a different sort of identification occurring here: the Romans as the Russians within the USSR ("Moscow the Third Rome"!), arrogant and selfish, ruling over the non-Russian peoples of the realm and using them for their entertainment and economic advantage. Part of the success of *Spartacus* as a work of art is that it allows us to entertain both interpretations.

NOTES

1. Shostakovich, "Aram Khachaturian."
2. Tigranov, *Balety Arama Khachaturiana*, 7–8.
3. Ibid., 23.
4. Ibid., 24.
5. Katonova, *Muzyka sovetskogo baleta*, 140.
6. Tigranov, *Balety Arama Khachaturiana*, 57.
7. Ibid., 59.
8. Ibid., 70.
9. Iuzefovich, *Aram Khachaturian*, 138.
10. Ibid., 139.
11. Ibid., 140.
12. Khachaturian, *Gayane. Partitura*, t. 1, 12.
13. Tigranov, *Balety Arama Khachaturiana*, 91–92.
14. Quoted in Iuzefovich, *Aram Khachaturian*, 142.
15. Marx and Engels, *Works*, 15.
16. Lenin, *Sochineniia*, 444.
17. Khachaturian, "Balet 'Spartak."
18. Khachaturian, "O balete 'Spartak," 10.

REFERENCES

Iuzefovich, Viktor. *Aram Khachaturian*. Moscow: Sovetskii kompozitor, 1990.
Katonova, Svetlana. *Muzyka sovetskogo baleta*. Leningrad: Sovetskii kompozitor, 1980.
Khachaturian, Aram. "Balet 'Spartak'." *Sovetskoe iskusstvo* (1951).
——. "O balete 'Spartak'." In *Sbornik statei* "Spartak". Leningrad: Muzgiz, 1957.
——. *Gayane. Partitura*, t. 1. Moscow: Muzyka, 1988.
Lenin, Vladimir. *Sochineniia*. Vol. 29. Moscow.
Marx, Karl, and Friedrich Engels. *Works*. Vol. 23.
Shostakovich, Dmitrii. "Aram Khachaturian." *Sovetskoe iskusstvo*, 10 June 1953.
Tigranov, Gennadii. *Balety Arama Khachaturiana*. Moscow: Sovetskii kompozitor, 1960.

Representing the Empire: The Meaning of Siberia for Russian Imperial Identity

Claudia Weiss

Would you like to travel to outer space? Explore like real astronauts the slow, gentle movements characteristic of a weightless environment? The Houston Space Center offers its visitors such a trip through the ISS, the International Space Station. It presents America's space programme by using a simulator to create a compelling environment, complete with 3,000 accurately placed stars that mimic what the real astronauts experience in the ISS.[1] You can feel the glory of current-day American scientific progress, the power of the US, the world's number one power.

If you wanted to make an extraordinary virtual journey in 1900, the Universal Exhibition in Paris was the place to be. With the help of the very popular panoramas, dioramas or cosmoramas, many exotic virtual voyages were offered to the over 48 million visitors to the exhibition.[2] One of the most popular and successful panoramas was a virtual train journey from Moscow across the Siberian expanses to Beijing. It was placed in the gardens of the Trocadero, at the colonial section of the Universal Exhibition, where the Russian Empire had a pavilion, suitably impressive in both size and location, to exhibit Russian Asia. At "Moscow" station, visitors bought a train ticket and entered one of three original wagons—simulated rattling and shaking included—of the wagons-lits company, which were set up as a restaurant. While the "passengers" dined, a movable panorama painted on a 950 m long canvas passed by the windows at different speeds and with different motives to create the illusion of a voyage across Siberian landscapes. Forty-five minutes later, the passengers disembarked at "Beijing" station, welcomed by servants in traditional Chinese costumes.[3]

This panorama was one of the most popular attractions of its kind at the exhibition, and its painter, the Russian military doctor Pavel Iakovlevitch Piasetskii, who created it after his own sketches of Siberia, won a gold medal and the membership in the Legion of Honour for it.[4]

This virtual voyage created a certain image of Siberia: travellers were allowed to imagine a beautiful and, in a certain way, exotic landscape. They were made aware of the vast expanses of the region that somehow seemed to be have subdued by humans—at least thanks to the luxurious train that made travelling so comfortable and represented the economic power of the Russian Empire. Not only could they travel across vast expanses, exploited through agriculture and mining, but they also transgressed cultural borders, from Europe to Asia, from Russia to China, bound together by the technical prowess, political power and imperial dominance of the Russian Empire, the world's largest continental empire.

What was experienced here is the stylization of Siberia as a placeholder for the Russian Empire. To understand this stylization, we have to look at the meaning of Siberia for the development of Russia from the Muscovite state in the sixteenth century to the Russian Empire as it saw itself at the cusp of the twentieth century. For example, it was the conquering of Siberia in the late sixteenth century and the subsequent economic exploitation of it that provided Russia with the financial resources to wage war against Sweden.[5] By the late seventeenth century up to 160,000 per year Siberian fur pelts were passing through the Urals. They were Russia's most important export article and constituted up to 10% of the state's income.[6] The external success of Peter the Great in 1721 made possible the transition from the Muscovite tsardom to the All-Russian Empire (*vserossiiskaia imperiia*).[7] Thanks to Siberian wealth, Russia established its place among the European Powers. In the eighteenth and early nineteenth century Russia understood and treated Siberia as its colony, pretty much in the same way as other European colonial powers did their colonies. In this manner, Siberia provided Russia not only with the wealth needed to claim imperial status but also with the territory and consequential geopolitical position that was one of the characteristics of an empire.[8] During the first half of the nineteenth century, Siberia's role in Russian self-understanding changed as a result of a temporarily waning in the region's economic importance (most of the fur-bearing animals had been exterminated) as well as the emergence of nationalism. It also influenced interpretations of Russian nationalism, which were not easily pressed into the patterns of European nationalism. Out of this development grew one of the most common interpretations of the relationship between Russia and Siberia: to understand Siberia as the Russian "Other," as an opposition, an alternative to typical Russian identity patterns.[9] There are many good arguments and proofs that strengthen this interpretation. But they are all based on a perspective concerned with Russian national identity and, because of that, neglect Russia's imperial identity. The concept of understanding Siberia as the Russian "Other" evokes a rapprochement of Russia to Europe, its culture and traditions. The evident opposition to Asian Siberia seems to make Russia more European. This was already evident in Russia's treatment of Siberia as a colony. But one barrier always seemed to be insurmountable in making Russians feel at home with this European-stamped Russian national identity: it was not acknowledged by the other Europeans. For them, Russia always seemed to be different, exotic, a hybrid nation, or better: empire. By the first quarter of the sixteenth century Sigmund von Herberstein saw the Muscovite state "as differing from us enormously amongst all countries touched by the holy christening in its customs, facilities, church service and its trade of war."[10] And even almost 100 years after the Westernizing endeavours and reforms of Peter the Great, the French soldiers who arrived in Moscow in 1812 with Napoleon's Grande Armée were struck by the exotic appearance of the old Russian capital. "This capital looked to us like some fantastical creation, a vision from the thousand and one nights . . . This magnificent spectacle surpassed by far everything that our imagination had been able to conjure in terms of Asiatic splendour." But, at the same time, the Russians confirmed their otherness to the Europeans by leaving the city unconditionally and later burning it. "The barbarians," exclaimed Napoleon, "they really mean to abandon all this?"[11]

Siberia helped Russia to overcome this shortcoming and to be accepted fully by the other European states by giving her an even richer imperial identity. Siberia appeared as Russia in hyperbole: while Russia was cold, Siberia was freezing cold. While Russia was big, Siberia was vast. While Russian landscape appeared monotonous, Siberian landscape seemed to be even drearier. Russia had a lot of forests, Siberia had the taiga, Russian rivers were big, Siberian rivers were some of the biggest in the world. Much of Russia was sparsely populated, whereas much of Siberia was deserted. Russia always had the image of a cruel country, Siberia was called white hell. Russia already had multinational subjects, but Siberia enriched this diversity enormously. Thanks to the Tatar influence, Russia had an Asiatic touch. But Siberia *was* Asia. So, Siberia helped the Russian Empire to appear bigger, stronger, richer, more powerful, more exiting, more beautiful, more indomitable, and really special. By doing so, Siberia affected Russian identity, helped it in a way to free itself from the patterns formed by European national thinking and to create a more imperial identity, an identity that saw Siberia as an inseparable part of Russia, of the Russian Empire.[12]

The process of mentally appropriating Siberia started nearly at the same time as the influence of European nationalism reached the Russian Empire, and, to some degree, was connected to it. Nationalism produced nationalistic thinkers in the Russian Empire, who quickly saw themselves in conflict with state power and soon afterwards found themselves as political exiles in Siberia, convicted for their political intention to place the cause of the Russian people above tsarist and imperial interests. For many of the political exiles, who were recognized as representatives of the repressed Russians, Siberia was synonymous with their hopes for freedom or their suffering, and in this function became representative for all Russians and was mentally appropriated by them. Also, this transfer of intelligentsia to Siberia created a stronger mental connection between both parts of the Empire and increased the interest of Russian elites in the fate of Siberia and its population.

Apart from this mental appropriation through political exiles, another form of appropriation of Siberia developed in the middle of the nineteenth century. It grew out of a mixture of national and imperial interests and activities and involved geographical exploration. It combined the mental claim with imperial possession. With regard to foreign policy, and in the aftermath of the Crimean War, the Russian Empire turned its interests to Eastern Siberia, the Pacific coast and the Amur region, which was annexed in 1858 by the treaty of Aigun.[13] To confirm her imperial claim on Eastern Siberia, the Amur region and the Pacific coastline, Russia also put forward the argument that these regions had a "mental" connection to the Russian Empire. Here science, especially geography, helped. Military exploration often went hand in hand with geographical expeditions into these regions, mostly organized by the Imperial Russian Geographical Society and the St. Petersburg Academy of Science. The scientific explorations document the use of geography as an instrument of imperial appropriation. The land was surveyed, infrastructure problems were discussed, the regions were mapped. The customs of the natives were explored, which provided useful knowledge on how to handle and control them administratively. With their descriptions of the region, the Russian explorers created images and perceptions of Siberia that deepened the feeling of possession in their readers. They gave them the feeling that they understood Siberia. The explorers had a certain interest in agricultural utilization of the region as well as in its native population. They pointed out the good and friendly relationship between Russians and the native population. In this way, they created a strong reference, nearly a sense of belonging of these people to the Russian Empire that was passed on to the readers of their reports. With this documented reciprocal understanding they fortified the Russian claim of annexation—for the sake of the indigenous population.[14]

I would like to demonstrate to what degree this mental appropriation of Siberia by the Russian Empire, which led to an enriched imperial identity, was reflected in the Empire's self-portrayals at the great international exhibitions of the nineteenth century. International exhibitions, and especially the universal exhibitions, are considered to be a perfect stage for national or imperial self-portrayals.[15] As a result, the concepts behind several exhibits that presented nations or empires give a deep insight into particular identity concepts. Burton Benedict calls such exhibits "exercises in the imagery of nationalism," whereas Elfie Rembold understands the exhibitions as "a platform for the mutual creation of national images as being promoted by the organizers on the one hand and constructed by the visitors on the other."[16]

Exhibitions constituted a perfect space for encounters with the representation of the "Other" that creates national or imperial identities. Michael Wilson explains how an exhibition achieves this representation through two rhetorical tropes. On the one hand the synecdote—the substitution of the part for the whole, and the whole for the part, and on the other the metonymy—association by contingency.[17] To illustrate this in relation to the international self-portrayals of the Russian Empire, we shall have a closer look at four universal exhibitions, the Centennial Exposition in Philadelphia 1876, the Universal Exhibition in Paris 1889, the World's Columbian Exposition in Chicago 1893, and the Universal Exhibition in Paris 1900.

The Russian Empire began participating at the universal exhibitions shortly after the first one in London in 1851. Its exhibits always had a different appearance from those of the other imperial powers represented at these exhibitions, which were gaining importance as time-referenced exterritorial trials in cultural autonomy.[18] Russia's relations with the West were marked by a combination of the political power it held in Europe and by an ambivalent cultural and political position concerning modernization evidenced in relative economic backwardness.[19] The last point was very evident at the Universal Exhibition in Paris 1867, where the Russian Empire had not been able to show the world anything save examples of raw materials for which barely any processing facilities existed in the Russian Empire itself, and some ethnographic pictures of everyday life in the Caucasus, in Siberia, and in Central Asian regions.[20] Also, the exhibition in Vienna in 1873 did not foster very much international esteem for Russian industry.[21] When in the same year, the Russian Empire was invited to participate in the Centennial Exposition in Philadelphia in 1876, it first declined by arguing "the Russians consider America much farther off than Americans do Russia. They are neither a travelling or commission people, nor are they a manufacturing one to any considerable extent."[22] In the time after that answer was given, though, Russian priorities in foreign affairs changed. In October 1875 the new Russian Minister of Foreign Affairs, Baron Jomini, finally accepted the American invitation so as not to offend the Americans who intended to celebrate the centennial of American independence with this exhibition.[23] The fact that Russian participation was more a political than an economic decision was clearly visible in the way the Russian Empire was represented. It renounced a national pavilion and presented the main part of the exhibits in the main building of the exhibition. In this manner, it avoided a display of clearly national symbols that were typical of the national pavilions in universal exhibitions. All the more remarkable was the fact that the Russian exhibits were dominated by national elements. A Russian visitor, for example, was content to find so many masterly manufactured exhibits that distinguished Russian culture from that of the West.[24] Moreover, exhibits with a more international character as intended by the organizers of the Universal Exhibition were missing in the Russian exhibits.[25] The organizers of the Russian exhibition, mainly the Ministry of Finance, were particularly concerned to portray a rich and powerful image of the Russian Empire. On the one hand, opulent and valuable exhibits such as precious sables and gigantic stuffed bears, exquisite jewellery and tea services as well as decorative artworks made of silver and gold dazzled the visitors and created an overwhelming image of luxury and glamour. The Russian Empire owed this opulence to Siberia. On the other hand, many military exhibits dominated the Russian section and showed the military power and even dominance of the Russian Empire.[26] It was this military power that allowed the Russians to dominate the vast regions of Asia and finally integrate them into the Russian Empire. The reactions and commentaries of the observers of the Russian section in Philadelphia were accordant:

> No part of the Exhibition has more richly repaid careful study; and this chiefly from the fact that the Russian display differs from those of England and France, no matter how magnificent these may be, in that it comprises works in the arts and manufactures hitherto unknown to Americans.[27]

Another American critic stated: "The collection was of bewildering magnificence and of a splendour which, though the term is questionable, is best described as barbaric."[28]

So, while Americans judged the Russian display as different, exotic in comparison with the commonly known European canon, Russian visitors such as M. M. Vladimirov were disappointed by too many multiethnic influences that overshadowed a specific "ethnic Russian" character of the Russian presentation.[29] But it was precisely to this multiethnic base that the Russian Empire owed its imperial power, which was reflected as a part of its identity in its official self-portrayal.

If convincing the Russian government to participate in the Centennial Exposition in Philadelphia had been difficult, the task was even worse for the Universal Exhibition in Paris in 1889. In the same tradition as the Centennial Exposition, the Paris show was intended to celebrate the 100th anniversary of the French Revolution. The Russian Empire, as one of the last autocratic powers, had no intention of assisting a celebration that questioned its own political justification. Consequently, Russia did not participate officially at the Universal Exhibition in 1889, but, in contrast to Philadelphia, Russian exhibitors were allowed to display exhibits, but there was no official national representation. As a result, the Russian section was not as large as it had been at earlier exhibitions, with only 500 exhibits compared to the 1,179 at the Universal Exhibition in Paris in 1878.[30] One effect of this was that the Russian Empire's self-portrayal was not centrally managed, but evolved more or less accidentally out of the random selection of exhibits of the financially potent Russian exhibitors. Laurence Aubain divides the image of the Russian Empire that resulted into four characteristics:

1. A savage, barbaric character expressed in the architecture of buildings that combined massive semi-military and semi-religious elements with a certain mysticism and savagery. It was also found in the many stuffed fur animals that were exhibited.
2. An opulent mysticism intended to express the role of the Russian Empire as the new Byzantium.
3. The image of the "eternal Russia," expressed by an overwhelming richness, founded in her continental expansion, represented by big amounts of gemstones extracted from the Urals, the Altai or the Caucasus.
4. A munificent exotic appearance that was visible in an excessive use of velvet and silk creating a symbolic connection with the Orient that touched the borders of the Russian Empire.[31]

As seen at previous universal exhibitions, the showing of Russian Empire's economic power was comparatively weak.[32] So, again it was up to Siberia to bestow on the Russian Empire the image of being bigger, richer, wilder, and more exotic than the other European Powers. The awareness of Siberia as Russia's house of riches was growing for increasing numbers of observers, both Russian and foreign. And it was also up to Siberia to overcome Russia's lasting and evident backward image in the economic domain by providing the background for the most worthwhile infrastructural endeavour, the construction of the Great Siberian Railway.

The first major international presentation of the railway project was in 1893 at the Universal Exhibition in Chicago, the World's Columbian Exposition. Here again, the

Russian Empire renounced hosting its own national pavilion and preferred to present over 1,000 exhibits, split into 16 different departments, spread over the different main buildings of the exposition.[33] But unlike the exhibitions in Philadelphia or Paris, this time the Russian government was involved from the very beginning in the preparations of the exhibition and instructed the Minister of Finance to ensure a hitch-free execution.[34] Most of the exhibits were reminiscent of previous expositions. Again, there were many precious furs and other leather products, exquisite porcelain and crystal products, jewellery and minerals. But a new aspect that attracted a lot of attention was the Great Siberian Railway project.[35] This railway was supposed to become the longest railway in the world, with a total length of 9,280 kilometres. From an infrastructural point of view, it would open up the world's largest resource base for use by the Russian Empire, assisting it on its impressive industrial progress that had been ongoing for more than a decade. In the oil sector, the Russian Empire was already the second largest producer in the world after the US,[36] and a better transport connection to the Western Siberian plains would also prepare the ground for a serious concurrence in the agrarian sector. In order to present the Russian advancements in a beneficial light, the Russian Ministry of Finance brought out several volumes of books (in English) called "The Industries of Russia." One was dedicated exclusively to Siberia and the Great Siberian Railway.[37] The original Russian version was edited by V. I. Kovalevskii, the president of the Russian Commission of the Universal Exhibition in Chicago, together with the active help of P. P. Semenov, the vice president of the Imperial Russian Geographical Society. It was Semenov's job to deliver an appealing description of Siberia, containing a historical sketch as a geographical review of the area. In his report, Semenov created images of the region that were to influence perceptions of Siberia for many years to come. In a sober yet benevolent style he described the different regions, with special emphasis on Western Siberia, the most interesting part of Siberia from an economic perspective. He drew comparisons of its large river systems with other well-known systems such as the Nile, the Amazon and the Mississippi.[38] To illustrate the enormous dimensions of Eastern Siberia he compared it as "exceeding twice the extent of Germany, Austria and France taken together."[39] Unfavourable aspects like the harsh climate he mentioned soberly without greater detail. Further on, he pointed out the overwhelming majority of Russians in Siberia and mentioned the indigenous population only for statistical aspects without describing them in any detail.[40] The main part of the book was dedicated to Siberia's economy. Its efficiency and potential were highlighted and its deficiencies mentioned, but most of all the future was emphasized [or conjured up]. Finally, the last 27 pages of the book introduced the planning of the Great Siberian Railway project, emphasizing in particular its meaning for the economic development of Siberia, the future land of the Russian Empire:

> There is no occasion to dwell upon the political importance of the Great Siberian Railway. Its significance is clear from the fact that when the line is completed

Russia will not only nominally but actually occupy that position in the east of Asia which it holds among its friends and enemies in Europe. As the line shortens the distance from European Russia to the east of Asia, in a like measure will the power of Russia increase in the East. [...] Finally the opening of a railway line to the Pacific Ocean will enable Russia to carry on more direct intercourse with the United States of America, which in spite of being the great competitor of Russia in the grain trade of Europe, in consequence of the solidarity of its political and other interests, cherishes sincere sympathy for Russia.[41]

This book, in terms of content and form, was the basis of many subsequent publications on the Great Siberian Railway in the Russian as well as the international book market.[42] Therefore, it set not only the tone on how to report on Siberia but also the style and even the appraisal of the region. So, when Siberia found herself again in a central position to represent the Russian Empire at the Universal Exhibition in Paris in 1900, the audience was pre-programmed as a result of the stereotypes that had already become established.[43]

The Universal Exhibition in Paris in 1900 was the largest exhibition the world had seen up to that point. It was a nostalgic swan song to the nineteenth century as well as a triumphant celebration of modern spirit.[44] For Russia, this was the real first opportunity to present itself and its empire on an equal footing with the other Great Powers. Russia was finally able to demonstrate to the world an impressive image of its empire as a modern and promising imperial power. Being the most important ally of the host country, Russia was treated as France's guest of honour at the exhibition. To highlight the close and friendly Franco-Russian relations, a new bridge over the Seine was inaugurated and named after Tsar Alexander III, who had set the seal on the Franco-Russian alliance in 1892. Again, Russia was the only Great Power that did not have one of the very elaborate pavilions on the rue des Nations. But, in accordance with its special status and to demonstrate Franco-Russian friendship, it was provided with ample space for its exhibits in all the French sections.[45] On the whole, the Russian Empire presented about 2,400 exhibits that occupied more than 6,300 square metres, and won 1,589 of the 42,790 prizes awarded at the Universal Exhibition in 1900.[46] The Russian Empire also achieved the high appreciation of the other powers for its consolidated positioning as a front-row member of the Great Powers, a status that had been at least questionable after the Crimean War.

Not only in relation to the other powers did the Russian Empire reposition itself and fortify its claim as an imperial power. It also tried to reinvent itself, to enhance its imperial identity. Among all the exhibits of the Russian Empire there was one that seemed to have no other intention than to represent this new identity; an identity that interwove national and imperial traits: the Kasli cast iron pavilion—*Kaslinskii chugunnyi pavil'on*. Not being classified as an object of art, but as an exhibit of cast iron handcraft, the pavilion was placed in the XI group, mining and metallurgy, in the 65th class, fabrication of metal products.[47] It was a masterpiece of cast iron moulding, styled by a promising architect from St. Petersburg, executed by master craftsmen from Kasli, one of the oldest and most important Ural mining towns with a long tradition. The initiative of creating a pavilion for the Universal Exhibition in Paris was a private one, taken by Vasili Grigor'evich Druzhinin, one of the works' owners and secretary of the Imperial Russian Architectural Society in St. Petersburg.[48] This intention placed him in line with governmental interests to present the Russian Empire and its economic, industrial and cultural capabilities at their best.[49] The pavilion was designed with monumental decorative forms, typical of the new Russian style that had emerged in Russian architectural practice in the 1890s. It counted about 3,000 pieces, each artfully crafted first in wood, then in bronze, then in cast iron. The public in Paris was enthusiastic: the Kasli cast iron pavilion won a Grand Prix.[50] The new Russian style was an eclecticism that expressed itself by a free choice of decorative configuration. Hence the pavilion was swamped with Old Russian, Scandinavian, Byzantine, and Venetian motifs. In conjunction with these, the very popular art nouveau ornaments were also used extensively.[51] It was an advancement of the Russian style that had already shaped Russian architecture for about two decades.[52] The new Russian style combined the elements of the Russian style with those typical of art nouveau. It was immediately recognized abroad as Russia's "new decorative movement" and became, for a brief but influential moment, its most potent symbol of tradition reconciled with progress, of vernacular Russian forms integrated at last with the dominant Western style.[53] In this way, the new Russian style enhanced Russia's claim to modernity, and underlined its function as a marker of an imperial identity on the meridian of the Age of Empire.

But how was this reflected in the pavilion? We shall have a look at three of its constituent aspects, namely the material, its architecture, and its ornaments and relief.

The pavilion was made completely of cast iron, and bronze was used only as an underlay in the airy parts to accentuate the ornaments. Cast iron was *the* material of the nineteenth century. It was the symbol for progress par excellence. An important iron industry meant wealth for a state. But for Russia cast iron was absolutely atypical in architecture and building. Buildings were constructed of wood; rarely, and only in large towns, of stone. However, Russia was one of the world's most important exporters of iron.[54] Also, the location of the mining that provided the cast iron for the pavilion was meaningful: Kasli belonged to the most traditional and important mining towns in the Russian Empire. Geographically, Kasli was situated on the border of Europe and Asia. That made it a symbol of the Russian dichotomy that had shaped Russian thinking during the nineteenth century: being culturally located between these two continents. Hence, Kasli symbolized a synergy effect: Asian raw materials wrought with European mastery created Russian arts and crafts. But at the same time the Russian Empire demonstrated it possessed the knowledge to use its resources. It was no longer only a distributor of raw material but was also as modern as its imperial neighbours; it had mastered the material of the age.

As regards the architecture, the pavilion was built under the strong influence of the new Russian style.[55] Because of its decorative forms, borrowed from the Old Russian

41

art, the architectural composition of the pavilion seemed to be in a Byzantine style. But the form of the pavilion resembled a typical Ural abode. It had the same inside dimensions: 430 centimetres in length, width and height. The outside height was 5 metres.[56] The choice of a Ural dwelling again points to the intersection of Europe and Asia. The typical house of this region presents the archetype for this imperial pavilion: like the Russian Empire, the pavilion unites Europe and Asia, and both parts are reflected in its architecture.

The ornaments and relief, too, were inspired by old Russian art and reflected motifs of Russian history, religion, mythology as well as imperial reality. We find here, for example, the fabled prophetic birds Sirin and Alkonost, "Radost' i Pechal'," "Joy and Sorrow." They are often shown in Russian folkloristic art. These fabulous birds belong as much to Russian myth as to Greek mythology, the ancestor of Byzantium and the cradle of European culture.[57] Another relief shows a barque with billowing sail. The cut of the sail and the kind of oars immediately create an association with a Viking boat. The Vikings, as symbols of glorious warriors, are regarded as the founders of the old Rus', and as the ancestors of the old Russian nobility, including the tsar in pre-Petrine Russia. Thanks to his newly constructed fleet, Peter the Great vanquished Sweden, and thereby founded the modern Russian Empire. On the relief, the figurehead of the boat is an eagle, the heraldic animal of the Russian Empire.

There are also reliefs that show a falcon hunting a hare as well as an Asian lion (*panthera leo persica*) killing a sheep that is defended by a shepherd's dog. Animal forms in ornaments are considered to be a Northern European style. They are found especially in Scandinavian art from the eleventh to the fourteenth century, where animal motifs played an important role.[58] But here it is royal or, alternatively, Asian animals in attack mode. So, again, we see a subtle amalgamation of Europe and Asia as well as a demonstration of aggressive power. Finally, there are sculptures of dragons. They very much resemble the Russian folkloristic pictures of Simargol-Pereplut, a holy dog with wings, a Slavic goddess of drink and of changing fortunes. Simargol-Pereplut was venerated by drinking from a horn, usually formed like the wings of the pavilion's dragons.[59] At the same time dragons were associated with China and Chinese culture. It was into this very region of the Far East that the Russian Empire had already been gradually expanding for more than 40 years (since the treaty of Aigun in 1858 confirmed the Russian annexation of the Amur). The Great Siberian Railway was about to connect the Russian Empire even more strongly to China so that in the near future they might share more than only mythic dragons.

In the Kasli cast iron pavilion one can visualize how the Russian Empire saw itself: a Great Power amalgamating two continents in its imperial identity; an imperial power incorporating its colonies and its annexed peripheries, and in so doing, reinventing itself.

This image emerged even more explicitly in the presentation of the Great Siberian Railway, a project that was completely official and had the power of the state behind it.

After the success in Chicago, the planning of the presentation of the railway project was approached even more carefully. As early as October 1897, Finance Minister Sergei Witte personally asked Peter Semenov to participate in the Planning Commission for the Russian section of the Universal Exhibition in Paris.[60] His excellent support in the Chicago presentation qualified him for this responsible task. Semenov prepared and edited on behalf of the Imperial Russian Geographical Society a publication, with the Russian title *Okrainy Rossii* [Borderlands of Russia], which was published in 1900 by the Commission simultaneously in Russian and French for PR purposes. The book was understood as an accompanying reader for the visitors of the "*Russkii Okrainnyi Otdel*" (Russian section of border territories). They were to be given the correct impression of the natural wealth of Russia's Asian peripheries, of the cultures of its various peoples, and of the common methods of exploitation of the regions' resources.[61] These regions were in no way called colonies as the French or the British designated the remote parts of their empires. Here, once again, it was obvious that Russia understood its peripheries as an integral part of the Russian Empire. At the centre of interest, with 122 out of 287 pages, was Siberia, the biggest, richest and most important periphery of the Russian Empire. As in the Chicago publication, in *Okrainy Rossii* the indigenous population was rarely mentioned, the meaning of "ssylka" and "katorga"—exile and forced labour—for Siberia was downplayed, but the potential for economic growth was underlined from different points of view.

This image was also reflected in the Russian section itself. In the pavilion of Russian borderlands at the Trocadero in Paris, Siberia and the Great Siberian Railway occupied three halls with their exhibits. They showed the geographical conditions as well as the technical challenge of the railway project or its meaning and opportunities for an enforced colonization of the traditionally sparsely populated region. The exhibits were divided into three groups: (1) printed publications, (2) maps, and (3) different materials such as diagrams, cartograms, collections and photos. The Planning Commission for the Russian section made particular efforts regarding printed materials. They published a booklet entitled *The Great Siberian Railway* in Russian, French, English and German with a print run of 80,000.[62] Many of the exhibits were the result of the intensive exploration of Siberia, mostly promoted by the Imperial Russian Geographical Society, which in 1851 had already declared Siberia as one of its most important research fields.[63] So, the visitors could admire geological maps, fossils, samples of schist, of limestone, mineral oils, sediments of iron, fossil carbon, lead, mercury, zinc and gold.[64] All this was placed in a pavilion, designed by the architect Meltzer and decorated by the painter Konstantin Korovin in the tradition of the new Russian style that opened up to the restaurant in the wagons with the panorama of Siberian landscapes. Here, the visitors could continue their virtual journey across the land of the future of the Russian Empire.[65]

At the Universal Exhibition in Paris in 1900 the Russian Empire presented itself as a happy state: colossal, powerful, deeply rooted in its traditions, and still modern. It was a state that appropriated and integrated its peripheries, particularly Siberia, by upgrading its status from a former colony to an integral part of the Russian Empire that had enhanced its imperial identity, power and potential. It was Siberia, on the one hand, that brought the Russian Empire to where it was, and on the other intended to carry it on to a new sphere of economic and perhaps political domination of the world's largest continent—Asia. These images were evident not only in the self-portrayal of the Russian Empire in Paris but also in the comments and reactions published in the press.[66] They dominated the perceptions of the Russians as those of the other European Powers—at least as long as the Russian disaster in the Russian–Japanese war in 1904/1905 let the other images of Siberia again come to the fore: an untameable and insurmountable wilderness even for the Russians themselves. And also this went down as a pattern of Russian imperial identity: being more dominated by the soil than dominating it.

Siberia's important role in Russian identity patterns has continued to this day. In Soviet times it was Siberian resources that made the enormous efforts of Soviet industrialization possible. Today, 15 years or so after the breakdown of the Soviet Union with its ideological and military power, it is still Siberia that offers Russia its strength in energy resources and, consequently, in economic power. Without Siberia Russia would not have been able to repay its enormous foreign debts so quickly. It would not have become a member of the G8 states, nor regained its position as a worldwide economic and political partner. In the actual Forbes list of the World's Richest People there are 33 Russians, 22 within the top 200; and nine of those have made their money with Siberian oil or gas, nearly all the others in mining or lumber.[67] In the twenty-first century the control over energy resources defines power, and power nourishes identity. Here again we find Siberia in a crucial position in relation to Russian identity.

NOTES

1. International Space Center, 2007, <http://spacecenter.org> (accessed 3 February 2007).
2. On the development and importance of the panorama for mass entertainment in the nineteenth century, see von Plessen, "Der gebannte Augenblick."
3. Concerning the Trans-Siberian panorama at the Universal Exhibition in Paris in 1900, see Archives nationals de France; Remnev, "Uchastie komiteta sibirskoi zheleznoi dorogi vo vsemirnoi vystavke 1900 goda v Parizhe," 167–76; Poulsen, *Die Transsibirische Eisenbahn*, 58; and von Plessen, "Der gebannte Augenblick," 12, 17.
4. von Plessen, "Der gebannte Augenblick," 18.
5. Donelly, "Peter the Great and Siberia," 119–26.
6. Lincoln, *Die Eroberung Sibiriens*, 107, 111; Fisher, *The Russian Fur Trade*, 69, 119, 135, 230.
7. Stökl, *Russische Geschichte*, 362.
8. On characterizations and definitions of empires, especially the Russian Empire, see Münkler, *Imperien*: Motyl, *Imperial Ends*; Lieven, *Empire*; idem, "Dilemmas of Empire 1850–1918"; idem, "The Russian Empire and the Soviet Union as Imperial Polities."

9. Concerning the concept of Siberia, or Asia, as Russia's "Other," see O'Connell, "Constructing the Russian Other"; Bassin, "Imperialer Raum/Nationaler Raum"; Tolz, *Russia*; Fryer, "Heaven, Hell, Or ... Something in Between?"; Hellberg-Hirn, "Ambivalent Space"; idem, *Soil and Soul*; Diment and Slezkine, *Between Heaven and Hell*; Bassin, "Russia between Europe and Asia"; Riasanovsky, "Asia through Russian Eyes."
10. von Herberstein, *Das alte Russland*, 12.
11. Zamoyski, *1812*, 296–97.
12. Concerning the mental appropriation of Siberia, see Weiss (2007).
13. Concerning the annexation of the Amur and the mental claim to this area, see Bassim, *Imperial Visions*.
14. For example, in the report of the surveyor Peshchurov, "Peschtschuroff's Aufnahme des Amur-Stromes," 476.
15. On the meanings of international exhibitions for national identity, see Fuchs, *Weltausstellungen im 19. Jahrhundert*; Rembold, "Exhibitions and National Identity"; Benedict, "International Exhibitions and National Identity"; Wilson, "Consuming History."
16. Benedict, "International Exhibitions and National Identity," 5; Rembold, "Exhibitions and National Identity," 222.
17. Wilson, "Consuming History," 138.
18. Schriefers, *Für den Abriss gebaut?*, 29.
19. Fisher, "Westliche Hegemonie und russische Ambivalenz," 45.
20. Peshkova, "Parizh," 24.
21. Fisher, "Westliche Hegemonie und russische Ambivalenz," 51.
22. Cited in Saul, *Concord and Conflict*, 139.
23. The US was Russia's most viable partner against Great Britain, which had again started to undermine Russian interests in the Balkans. Fisher, "Westliche Hegemonie und russische Ambivalenz," 51.
24. Vladimirov, *Russkii sredi Amerikantsev*, 325–26.
25. Fisher, "Westliche Hegemonie und russische Ambivalenz," 54.
26. Ibid., 54–55.
27. Leslie, *Frank Leslie's Illustrated Historical Register of the Centennial Exposition, 1876, 1877*, 95–96.
28. Smith, *The Masterpieces of the Centennial International Exhibition*, 280.
29. Fisher, "Westliche Hegemonie und russische Ambivalenz," 57.
30. *Commission impériale de Russie*, p. V.
31. Aubain, "La Russie à l'exposition universelle de 1889," 356–58.
32. Ibid., 359.
33. Sokolov, "Rossiia na vsemirnoi vystavke v Chikago v 1893 g," 156.
34. In order to facilitate the organisation of the Russian section at the Universal Exhibition in Chicago the Ministry of Finance brought out a booklet with the most important references and all the groups listed. See *Archiv Russkogo Geograficheskogo Obshchestva* (ARGO), 1-1892, 1892.
35. Sokolov, 157.
36. Ibid., 161.
37. *Siberia and the Great Siberian Railway*.
38. Ibid., 24.
39. Ibid., 34.
40. Ibid., 42.
41. Ibid., 265.

42. For the Universal Exhibition in 1900 the committee of ministers published a small booklet in Russian and German entitled *Die Große Sibirische Eisenbahn* (St. Petersburg, 1900). The Ministry of Finance published two publications that reflected on the presentation of Siberia of the Chicago publication: Kovalevskii, *Rossiia v konce XIX veka*; and Semenov, *Okrainy Rossii*. In 1901 the Russian Ministry of Transport and Communication published a voluminous book that documented the actual state of the railway project. It was also translated into English and German: *Wegweiser der Großen Sibirischen Eisenbahn*. In Germany, several publications were produced that discussed the Great Siberian Railway, based on the same geographical descriptions. For example: Krahmer, *Sibirien und die große sibirische Eisenbahn*; Ruge, *Die Transsibirische Eisenbahn*.

43. On the impact of stereotypes and symbols for national identity, see Link and Wülfing, *Nationale Mythen und Symbole in der zweiten Hälfte des 19*.

44. Greenhalgh, *Ephemeral Vistas*; Kretschmer, *Geschichte der Weltausstellungen*.

45. Peshkova, "Parizh," 26.

46. Aubain, "La Russie à l'éxposition universelle de 1889"; Orlov, *Vsemirnaia Parizhskaia vystavka 1900 goda v illiustratsiakh i opisaniakh*, 223, 233.

47. *Rossiia na vsemirnoi vystavke v Parizhe v 1900 godu*, 99.

48. Gubkin, "Istoki ornamentiki Kaslinskogo chugunnogo pavil'ona," 8.

49. Schriefers, *Für den Abriss gebaut?*, 24.

50. Gubkin, "Istoki ornamentiki Kaslinskogo chugunnogo pavil'ona," 16. Overall, 2,827 Grands Prix were awarded at the Universal Exhibition in Paris in 1900; 212 of them went to exhibits of the Russian Empire.

51. Gubkin, "Istoki ornamentiki Kaslinskogo chugunnogo pavil'ona," 9.

52. Wortman, "The 'Russian Style' in Church Architecture as Imperial Symbol after 1881"; O'Connell, "A Rational, National Architecture."

53. Salmond, *Arts and Crafts in Late Imperial Russia*, 3.

54. By the turn of the century production had reached its peak in the extraction of pig iron: 179.1 million *pud* per annum, and of cast iron: 165.2 million *pud* per annum (Geyer, *Der russische Imperialismus*, 110). One *pud* equals 16.38 kilograms.

55. This style had two basic ideological assumptions: (1) a human aim, based on the devotion to sources of national culture, as an attempt to give a deeper sense to things by imagining how former generations lived. (2) The amalgamation of artistic energies from all artistic styles made it possible to create any object in the wholeness of the world's shape (Kriazheva, "Elementy stilia 'modern' v dekore Kaslinskogo pavil'ona," 54).

56. Ibid., 55.

57. Sirin is a legendary bird of paradise with a human form; it is a bird of joy, success. It entrances people with its singing. Its songs are a model of the divine word, which enchants humankind, and the singing elicits joy. Only a happy or lucky person can hear the song, and not everyone can see Sirin, for she flies away as quickly as do fame and success. Alkonost is also a bird of paradise; in apocrypha and legends the bird of sorrow and melancholy. The image of Alkonost is traceable to the Greek myth of Alcion, who threw himself into the sea and was transformed by the gods into a kingfisher (halcyon). Alkonost lays eggs on the sea-shore and, burying them in the depths of the sea, makes it calm for six days. Whoever hears Alkonost's song forgets about everything in the world.

58. Gubkin, "Istoki ornamentiki Kaslinskogo chugunnogo pavil'ona," 11.

59. Ibid., 12.

60. Archiv Russkoi Akademii Nauk (ARAN), fond 906, op. 1 n° 12, l. 98.

61. Semenov, *Okrainy Rossii*, unpaginated preface.

62. Remnev, "Uchastie komiteta sibirskoi zheleznoi dorogi vo vsemirnoi vystavke 1900 goda v Parizhe," 169.
63. 'Of the numerous regions of Russia, without a doubt, there is no other region in which studies would be of such practical interest, and even of state interest, than Siberia, which conceals in its depths such productive forces, waiting only for man's enterprising hands to transform them into a never-ending source of richness for the State and the Russian people. In addition, Siberia's geographical make-up constitutes one of the most important parts of the Asian continent, the study of which must be seen as one of the major tasks of Russian science, and for us as Russians, with our close ties to Asia, it is the object of great interest and importance' (*Otchet IRGO za 1851*, 6–7).
64. Aimone and Olmo, *Les Expositions universelles*, 202.
65. This was the title given to Fridtjof Nansens' book *Sibirien—ein Zukunftsland*, in which Nansen describes his experiences on a railway journey across Siberia.
66. Remnev ("Uchastie komiteta sibirskoi zheleznoi dorogi vo vsemirnoi vystavke 1900 goda v Parizhe," 172–75) gives a good overview of reactions in the international press.
67. Forbes, <http://www.forbes.com/lists/2006/10/Rank_1.html> (accessed 3 February 2007).

REFERENCES

Aimone, Linda, and Carlo Olmo. *Les Expositions universelles: 1851–1900*. Paris: Belin, 1993.
Archiv Russkogo Geograficheskogo Obshchestva (ARGO), 1-1892. op. 1, n° 12, 1892. Polozhenie o Russkom otdele na Vsemirnoi Vystavke 1893 g. v Chikago.
Archiv Russkoi Akademii Nauk (ARAN), fond 906, op. 1 n° 12, l. 98.
Archives nationals de France (ANF). F^{12} 4264, 4265.
Aubain, Laurence. "La Russie à l'exposition universelle de 1889." *Cahiers du Monde russe* 37, no. 3 (1996): 349–68.
Bassin, Mark. "Russia between Europe and Asia. The Ideological Construction of Geographical Space." *Slavic Review* 50, no. 1 (1991): 1–17.
Bassin, Mark. *Imperial Visions: Nationalist Imagination and Geographical Expansion in the Russian Far East, 1840–1865*. Cambridge: Cambridge University Press, 1999.
Bassin, Mark. "Imperialer Raum/Nationaler Raum. Sibirien auf der kognitiven Landkarte Russlands im 19. Jahrhundert." *Geschichte und Gesellschaft* 28 (2002): 378–403.
Benedict, Burton. "International Exhibitions and National Identity." *Anthropology Today* 7, no. 3 (1991): 5–9.
Commission impériale de Russie à l'Exposition Universelle de 1900, Catalogue général de la Section russe. Paris: Imprimeries Lemercier, 1900.
Diment, Galya, and Yuri Slezkine, eds. *Between Heaven and Hell: The Myth of Siberia in Russian Culture*. New York: St. Martin's Press, 1993.
Donelly, Alton S. "Peter the Great and Siberia: Russian Commercial Activities in Siberia during the Reign of Peter the Great." In *Sibérie II. Questions sibériennes. Histoires, cultures, litterature*, edited by Boris Chichlo. Paris: Institut d'études slave, 1999.
Fisher, David C. "Westliche Hegemonie und russische Ambivalenz. Das Zarenreich auf der Centennial Exposition in Philadelphia 1876." In *Weltausstellungen im 19. Jahrhundert*, edited by Eckardt Fuchs. Leipzig: Leipziger Universitätsverlag, 2000.
Fisher, Raymond. *The Russian Fur Trade: 1150–1700*. Berkeley: University of California Press, 1943.

47

Fryer, Paul. "Heaven, Hell, Or … Something in Between? Contrasting Russian Images of Siberia." In *Beyond the Limits: The Concept of Space in Russian History and Culture*, edited by Jeremy Smith. Helsinki: Suomen Historiallinen Seura (SHS), 1999.

Fuchs, Eckardt, ed. *Weltausstellungen im 19. Jahrhundert*. Leipzig: Leipziger Universitätsverlag, 2000.

Geyer, Dietrich. *Der russische Imperialismus. Studien über den Zusammenhang von innerer und auswärtiger Politik 1860–1914*. Göttingen: Vandenhoeck & Ruprecht, 1977.

Greenhalgh, Paul. *Ephemeral Vistas: The Expositions universelles, Great Exhibitions and World's Fairs, 1851–1939*. Manchester: Manchester University Press, 1988.

Gubkin, O. P. "Istoki ornamentiki Kaslinskogo chugunnogo pavil'ona." In *Kaslinskii chugunnyi pavil'on. Materialy nauchnoi konferencii posiashchennoi 100-letiiu Kaslinskogo chugunnogo pavil'ona 27 aprelia 2000*. Ekaterinburg: isdatel'stvo Uralskogo universiteta, 2001.

Hellberg-Hirn, Elena. *Soil and Soul: The Symbolic World of Russianness*. Aldershot: Ashgate, 1997.

——. "Ambivalent Space. Expressions of Russian Identity." In *Beyond the Limits: The Concept of Space in Russian History and Culture*, edited by Jeremy Smith. Helsinki: Suomen Historiallinen Seura (SHS), 1999.

Kovalevskii, V. I., ed. *Rossiia v konce XIX veka*. St. Petersburg: Brockhaus-Efron, 1900.

Krahmer, G. *Sibirien und die große sibirische Eisenbahn*. Leipzig: von Zuckschwerdt, 1897.

Kretschmer, Winfried. *Geschichte der Weltausstellungen*. Frankfurt and New York: Campus, 1999.

Kriazheva, N. G. "Elementy stilia 'modern' v dekore Kaslinskogo pavil'ona." In *Kaslinskii chugunnyi pavil'on. Materialy nauchnoi konferencii posiashchennoi 100-letiiu Kaslinskogo chugunnogo pavil'ona 27 aprelia 2000*. Ekaterinburg: isdatel'stvo Uralskogo universiteta, 2001.

Leslie, Frank. *Frank Leslie's Illustrated Historical Register of the Centennial Exposition, 1876, 1877*. Reprinted New York: Paddington Press, 1974.

Lieven, Dominic. "The Russian Empire and the Soviet Union as Imperial Polities." *Journal of Contemporary History* 30 (1995): 607–36.

——. "Dilemmas of Empire 1850–1918: Power, Territory, Identity." *Journal of Contemporary History* 34, no. 2 (1999): 163–200.

——. *Empire: The Russian Empire and its Rivals*. New Haven and London: Yale University Press, 2000.

Lincoln, W. Bruce. *Die Eroberung Sibiriens*. Munich and Zurich: Piper, 1994.

Link, Jürgen, and Wulf Wülfing, eds. *Nationale Mythen und Symbole in der zweiten Hälfte des 19. Jahrhunderts. Strukturen und Funktionen von Konzepten nationaler Identität*. Stuttgart: Klett-Cotta, 1991.

Motyl, Alexander J. *Imperial Ends: The Decay, Collapse, and Revival of Empires*. New York: Columbia University Press, 2001.

Münkler, Herfried. *Imperien: Die Logik der Weltherrschaft—vom Alten Rom bis zu den Vereinigten Staaten*. Berlin: Rowohlt, 2005.

Nansens, Fridtjof. *Sibirien—ein Zukunftsland*. Leipzig: Brockhaus, 1914.

O'Connell, Lauren M. "A Rational, National Architecture: Viollet-le-Duc's Modest Proposal for Russia." *JSAH (Journal of the Society of Architectural Historians)* 52 (1993): 436–52.

——. "Constructing the Russian Other. Viollet-le-Duc and the Politics of an Asiatic Past." In *Architectures of Russian Identity: 1500 to the Present*, edited by James Cracraft and Daniel Rowland. Ithaca and London: Cornell University Press, 2003.

Orlov, M. A. *Vsemirnaia Parizhskaia vystavka 1900 goda v illiustratsiiakh i opisaniiakh*. St. Petersburg, 1900.

Ory, Pascal. *Les Expositions universelles de Paris*. Paris: Editions Ramsay.

Otchet IRGO za 1851. (1982). pp. 6-7.

Peshchurov, A. "Peschtschuroff's Aufnahme des Amur-Stromes in Jahre 1855 und die russisch-chinesische Grenze im Amurlande von 1689 bis 1856, von A. Petermann." *Petermanns Mitteilungen* 2 (1856): 472–79.

Peshkova, I. M. "Parizh—Ekaterinburg. God 1900-i." In *Kaslinskii chugunnyi pavil'on. Materialy nauchnoi konferencii posiashchennoi 100-letiiu Kaslinskogo chugunnogo pavil'ona 27 aprelia 2000*. Ekaterinburg: isdatel'stvo Uralskogo universiteta, 2001.

Poulsen, John. *Die Transsibirische Eisenbahn. Die längste Eisenbahn der Welt*. Malmö: Stenvall, 1986.

Rembold, Elfie. "Exhibitions and National Identity." *National Identities* 1, no. 3 (2000): 221–25.

Remnev, Anatolii V. "Uchastie komiteta sibirskoi zheleznoi dorogi vo vsemirnoi vystavke 1900 goda v Parizhe." In *Khozjastvennoe osvoenie Sibiri. Istoriia, istoriografiia, istochniki*. Vol. 1. Tomsk: isdatel'stvo Tomskogo universiteta, 1991.

Riasanovsky, Nicholas V. "Asia through Russian Eyes." In *Russia and Asia: Essays on the Influence of Russia on the Asian Peoples*, edited by Wayne S. Vucinich. Stanford: Hoover Institution Press, 1972.

Rossiia na vsemirnoi vystavke v Parizhe v 1900 godu. Chap. 2. St. Petersburg, 1900.

Ruge, P. Sophus. *Die Transsibirische Eisenbahn*. Dresden: Zahn & Jaensch, 1901.

Salmond, Wendy R. *Arts and Crafts in Late Imperial Russia: Reviving the Kustar Art Industries, 1870–1917*. Cambridge: Cambridge University Press, 1996.

Saul, N. E. *Concord and Conflict: The United States and Russia, 1867–1914*. Lawrence: University Press of Kansas, 1996.

Schriefers, Thomas. *Für den Abriss gebaut? Anmerkungen zur Geschichte der Weltausstellungen*. Hagen: Ardenkuverlag, 1999.

Semenov, P. P., ed. *Okrainy Rossii. Sibir, Turkestan, Kavkaz i poliania chast' Evropeiskoi Rossii*. St. Petersburg: Brockhaus-Efron, 1900.

Siberia and the Great Siberian Railway (The Industries of Russia, vol. 5). Edited and translated by John M. Crawford. St. Petersburg, 1893.

Smith, Walter. *The Masterpieces of the Centennial International Exhibition, Philadelphia*. Vol. 2, *Industrial Art*. Philadelphia: Gebbie & Berrie, 1876.

Sokolov, A. S. "Rossiia na vsemirnoi vystavke v Chikago v 1893 g." *Amerikanskii ezhegodnik* (1984): 152–64.

Stökl, Günther. *Russische Geschichte. Von den Anfängen bis zur Gegenwart*. Stuttgart: Alfred Kröner, 1983.

Tolz, Vera. *Russia*. London and New York: Oxford University Press, 2001.

Vladimirov, M. M. *Russkii sredi Amerikantsev. Moi lichnye vpechatlenie kak tokaria chernorabochnogo, plotnika I puteshestvennika*. St. Petersburg, 1877.

von Herberstein, Sigmund. *Das alte Russland. In Anlehnung an die älteste deutsche Ausgabe aus dem Lateinischen übertragen von Wolfram von den Steinen. Mit einem Nachwort von Walter Leitsch*. Zürich: Manesse, 1985.

von Plessen, Marie-Louise, ed. "Der gebannte Augenblick. Die Abbildung von Realität im Panorama des 19. Jahrhunderts." In *Sehsucht. Das Panorama als Massenunterhaltung des 19. Jahrhunderts*. Basel: Stroemfeld/Roter Stern, 1993.

Wegweiser der Großen Sibirischen Eisenbahn. Herausgegeben vom Ministerium der Wegekommmunikationen und Redaktion von A. I. Dmitriiew-Mamonov, Berlin, 1901.

Weiss, Claudia. "Nash: Appropriating Siberia for the Russian Empire." *Sibirica: Interdisciplinary Journal of Siberian Studies* 5, no. 1 (2006): 141–55.

Weiss, Claudia. *Wie Sibirien "unser" wurde. Die Russische Geographische Gesellschaft und ihr Einfluss auf die Bilder und Vorstellungen von Sibirien im 19. Jahrhundert*. Göttingen: V&R Unipress, 2007.

Wilson, Michael. "Consuming History: The Nation, the Past, and the Commodity at l'-Exposition Universelle de 1900." *American Journal of Semiotics* 8, no. 4 (1991): 131–53.

Wortman, Richard. "The 'Russian Style' in Church Architecture as Imperial Symbol after 1881." In *Architectures of Russian Identity: 1500 to the Present*, edited by James Cracraft and Daniel Rowland. Ithaca and London: Cornell University Press, 2003.

Zamoyski, Adam. *1812: Napoleon's Fatal March to Moscow*. London: Harper Perennial, 2004.

(Re)Presenting Identities: National Archipelagos in Kazan[1]

Aurora Álvarez Veinguer

Introduction

The Republic of Tatarstan is located between Europe and Asia. It is important to emphasize geographical location, which is a key element in the processes of identities[2] formation and transformation. Tatarstan is located in the core of the Russian Federation, situated in the European part of Russia and 800 kilometres from Moscow, at the confluence of the Volga and the Kama Rivers. The capital of Tatarstan is Kazan. The economic potential of the republic is based mainly on raw materials (including oil and gas), industry and agriculture. According to the constitution of the republic (approved on 6 November 1992) Tatarstan (previously known as Tataria) is defined as a multi-ethnic republic, with two official languages, Russian and Tatar. The largest ethnic groups are Tatars and Russians; as a consequence it makes sense to talk in terms of a bicultural society with two main confessional groups, namely Muslim and Orthodox Christians.

Tatars are an ethnic group of Turkic origin, the largest ethnic minority group in Russia, and almost 75% of the Tatar population lives outside the republic. Russians and Tatars are often perceived as enemies, and numerous historic references and interpretations can be used to justify this perception. Since the Russian conquest of Kazan, Tatars have experienced numerous attempts at Russification and Tatar cultural annihilation, repression that provoked diverse rebellions and a massive migration to Central Asia.

On 30 August 1990 Tatarstan had issued its Declaration of State Sovereignty. On 15 February 1994, after three years of negotiations, Kazan and Moscow signed a bilateral treaty, an agreement granting Tatarstan more extensive autonomy, which gave the right to ownership to the Tatar government of land, mineral wealth and other resources. During this period a discourse of ethnic and cultural integration was promoted and presented as the new slogan of the republic. But some practices seem to illustrate that concrete measures have been adopted to promote ethno-cultural Tatar revival, instead of promoting a multiethnic society where all groups and cultures are represented equally. In other words, the rhetoric and the practice seem to be taking different paths.

In July 1992 a language law was adopted giving the Tatar and Russian languages equal rights. This law made concrete references to the use of both languages at the political and administrative level; simultaneously emphasizing the use of both languages in the media, industrial enterprises, public transport, and in general in any activity that involves interaction with the public. It also stressed the need to develop the Tatar language through concrete policies such as opening Tatar language schools and nurseries and promoting the Tatar language in the area of broadcasting.[3]

As a result of language and national policies during the Soviet period the majority of young people became uninterested in their mother tongue. Moreover, many non-Russians started to identify with Russian as their mother tongue, since it became their first language, and they declined to study their vernacular. Kharisov[4] defines this period as linguistic nihilism, because a considerable sector of the population did not want to learn their mother tongue because of its social unpopularity, and the preference for knowing Russian increased from year to year, since the knowledge of the vernacular did not represent any practical benefits.

After Tatarstan sovereignty was declared (August 1990), and the new law "on languages of the Republic of Tatarstan peoples" was approved, the situation in relation to the Tatar language began to change dramatically. Its marginality was swiftly exchanged for its incorporation into the mainstream institutional discourse. Tatar language instruction not only became compulsory in school for all pupils, regardless of their nationality, but the number of hours per week was made equivalent to those of Russian language instruction. For the past 10 years a substantial effort had been made by the authorities to situate both languages at the same level.

Presenting the Data

This work is based on an in-depth and long-term empirical exploration of the processes of identities construction in the specific institutional context of Tatar and non-Tatar gymnásias (secondary schools) in the Republic of Tatarstan, part of the Russian Federation. The research was conducted in two different districts in Kazan, one Tatar and one non-Tatar gymnásia in each district. In *Moskovskii raion* (district) the educational institutions were Tatar gymnásia No. 2 and a non-Tatar gymnásia No. 9, and in *Privolskii raion* (district) a Tatar gymnásia No. 16 and a non-Tatar gymnásia No. 52. Data generation consisted of semi-structured and unstructured interviewing and long-term participant observation in Kazan (the capital of Tatarstan) during a period of seven months (between 1999 and 2000) with the support of a pilot study conducted over six months during the winter of 1997–1998.

Nowadays Tatar gymnásias are effective instruments for Tatar culture and language rebirth, something that is detectable because of the strong encouragement and support that they receive from the political elite, which is expressed publicly. They are institutions that officially define the Tatar language and cultural revival, and the development of national culture and consciousness as their main purpose.

Process of Identities (Re)presentation: Integration–Segregation–Transgression

Throughout this work it will be claimed that the process of identities construction in Tatarstan involves a complex dialogue between the dialectic and interaction among at least three different areas in the process of identities representation, transformation, reproduction and formation, namely: (i) political discourse, (ii) institutional praxis, and (iii) everyday life, resulting in a complex dialectic and interrelation among all of them that has often been ignored. This is a multidimensional process that is affected by political, economic and social conditions, institutional discourses, enunciative strategies, popular (re)presentations, specific policies and mechanisms that are marking difference and exclusion, where personal and individual experiences are deeply implicated in the process.

Integration–segregation–transgression are the three different aspects embodied in these three coexisting areas, regardless of their apparent antagonism and opposition: integration, as an expression of the political discourse; segregation, as an institutional praxis; and transgression, as manifested in everyday life. Consequently, it is not a question of which dimension or area is most relevant, because all three of them are equally involved and indispensable in a multidimensional explanation.

Paradoxically, it is in the context of discontinuity, volatile relations and the unstable dynamics characteristic of rapid political and economic change, as well as lack of ideological references, or uncertainty and insecurity about the future, that ethnic and national discourses are more likely to be accepted and incorporated. They offer social cohesion and solidarity, a sense of belonging and being part of a society by answering such basic questions as "who we are?" and "where do we come from?" As Calhoun[5] has indicated, national identity, in particular, can easily be seen as natural and pre-political in our contemporary world.

Political Discourse of Integration

After more than a decade of sovereignty, ethno-national categorizations are more than alive in people's discourses and representations. Furthermore, it seems that the inclusive notion of *Tatarstantsy* makes reference to a political project, and it needs time to be able to embrace or to become part of everyday representations. At present, we can only speculate about the future of this concept, since in real terms it does not exist outside the inclusive formal rhetoric and might never become part of something more concrete.

The political discourse of integration, first expressed in terms of the Soviet people and later through the civic notion of *Tatarstantsy*, is often not in harmony or in step with actual institutional praxis where the idea of the others is promoted. Such practices reinforce difference and maintain segregation instead of the claimed plurality and diversity.

Officially (and according to the Tatarstan constitution) the republic represents a multiethnic society, where all the cultures and nationalities are equally supported and have the same status and recognition. In Tatarstan the advertised ideology of *Tatarstantsy* and its politics are based on cultural pluralism, which is recognized in all documents. It is presented by ideologists as a diversity of nationalities, not based on any principle of exclusion.[6] But the practice seems to illustrate that concrete measures are adopted to encourage ethno-cultural Tatar revival, instead of promoting a multiethnic society where all groups and cultures are represented equally. Once again, echoing what occurred during the Soviet years, the tension between the political discourse of integration and the institutional praxis of segregation has emerged as a reiterative reality.

Institutional Praxis of Segregation: National Archipelagos

It is not our purpose to generalize what is presented here to all institutional practices in the republic, since attention is focused on certain concrete and perhaps marginal institutions which can be called national archipelagos (Tatar gymnásias can be considered as islands in a sea of mainly Russian society and culture), and which may play a very significant role in the future. In any event they are closely involved in the process of identities construction in the republic. National archipelagos epitomize a mechanism to prevent the demise of the Tatar language and a place where pupils can learn about the history of Tatarstan and its traditions.

In the words of the then Minister of Education:

> National education centers are developed according to the principle of openness and democracy. [...] Dialogue between cultures contributes to positive and tolerant relations between people, education for citizenship. [...] We cannot forget that *natsiia* [people, nation] and the State—are geographically different notions. For example, outside Tatarstan there are living three quarter of Tatars. This is the reason why, one of the educational republic purposes is to offer them intellectual support. [...] The bases of a *natsiia* are—mother tongue, culture, the school where knowledge is embraced, moral and identity formation [...][7]

Five different themes or social dimensions are analysed in this paper, all of which have contrasting expressions in Tatar gymnásias: (i) attitude to the Tatar language, (ii) rhetoric of otherness, (iii) discourses of ethno-cultural segregation, (iv) religiosity, and (v) patriotism, referring to an exclusive perception of Tatarstan. All five dimensions can be correlated with the triadic dialectic among political discourse, institutional praxis and everyday life in the process of identities construction.

Promoting Primordial Understanding of the Tatar Language

In Tatar gymnásias Tatar was the dominant language,[8] even though occasionally one would hear some Russian. Generally, learning the Tatar language is one of the main reasons why parents want their children to study in a Tatar gymnásia.

Inside Tatar gymnásias there is a constant idealization and almost a mythical perception of the vernacular, often presented as something sacred. Everyone knows that there are explicit incentives because the current government is working insistently to promote the Tatar language by offering financial incentives to employees.

> I am Tatar by *natsional'nost* [...] and nowadays there is a demand in society to know your mother tongue. And I would like our son to know Tatar better than I do, so he will be able to speak, to read, he will not be determined enough, this is the main reason. And in the future, politics [...] to lead the republic, the Ministry of Education is working in that direction, they are developing national cadres. (Father of a male pupil)

Everything is presented almost as a simple mathematical equation, as a dream and an illusion, probably a self-justification for his choice and decision, a reason why this parent opted (as did many others) for a more innovative gymnásia. He stressed a direct correlation between the Tatar language and politics, assuming and anticipating that knowledge of the Tatar language brings access to the political arena, not to any specific administrative position, but to the national elite. In fact it is quite a common idea in the school because everyone (pupils, teachers and parents) is conscious that it is a prestigious gymnásia supported by the state benefactor.

Since the disintegration of the Soviet regime, the Tatar language has become an ideological symbol, representative of a specific reading of Tatar history, burdened with different historical interpretations and cultural nuances. Because a language is not an empty category its meaning as a whole is susceptible, like any cultural creation, to being negotiated and (re)defined from time to time. At given times languages can become ideological symbols with different meanings and connotations constructed through the accumulation of experiences and interests—an ideological symbol used by specific groups which can try to achieve a new relocation; or a process of revival, repossession and reclamation where the unity of the group plays an important role.

> For example during Ramadan we celebrate *Kuiran Bairam*,[9] nobody has this, only here. All children and parents come, they bring their donations, they help, they . . . come here, it is like one family. (History teacher from Tatar gymnásia)

The reference to family is to a metaphorical unity: one family, one school, one community, one people—the Tatar people. It is a family that shares pain and happiness. It is the belief in the family unit in its traditional sense, a group of people with the same ancestors, people who live in the same place, who share the same language, who cook the same food and sing the same songs; a family that experiences the same suffering; a conception that consolidates their notion of uniqueness and communality.

> The members of an ethnic community must be made to feel, not only that they form a single "super family," but that their historic community is unique, that they possess what Max Weber called "irreplaceable cultural values" that their heritage must be preserved against inner corruption and external control, and that the community has a sacred duty to extend its culture values to outsiders.[10]

The Tatar language is a real objective to be claimed, like property or a possession that they are not prepared to renounce again. Strong emotions are invested in how people live and experience their language and culture.

> I have a friend and he is Tatar, but his family do not speak any Tatar whatsoever. They consider themselves to be Tatars, but they don't know the Tatar language, and the same with Tatar culture, and this is like degradation. This is why it is necessary to study the Tatar language, to preserve our culture. (Male pupil)

For pupils in Tatar gymnásias, the Tatar language is a symbol and a characteristic of their group and their understanding of the notion of Tatarhood; and study of the Tatar language is not comparable to the study of English, French, or other languages that they may come across at school.

Inside Tatar gymnásias discontent centres on the long-established experience of subordination, and the marginal and minority status of the Tatar language. There is dissatisfaction with the history and development of Russian linguistic and cultural domination, and the current low level of interest shown by the Russian population in relation to the Tatar language and Tatar culture. In that sense, for some sectors of the Tatar population the Tatar language revival is a symbol of new relations and new rules of interaction, and hence new opportunities for Tatar people. In the two Tatar gymnásias the Tatar language was presented as a primordial characteristic that defines the Tatar people.

> I wish, they [pupils and parents] will know their mother tongue very well. [...] Our roots are here, we have to know our history, our culture, I think it is impossible without it. [...] I speak with parents in the vernacular—in Tatar language. They speak with me in Russian, but anyway I reply and ask them questions in Tatar, because they can understand everything, but I would like them to begin to speak. And many have already started. (Russian language and literature teacher from Tatar gymnásia)

This teacher wants pupils and parents to speak Tatar because of the symbolic meaning that surrounds the notion of the vernacular. Edwards has observed that language is still commonly taken to be the central pillar of ethnic identity.[11]

> Many analysts have claimed that language is a prime determinant of nationalist identity: those speaking the same language are liable to claim a sense of national bond. [...] The creation of a national hegemony often involves hegemony of language. It could not be difficult to construct a model of nationalism around the importance of speaking the same or different languages.[12]

Dichotomous Way of Thinking: Constructing the "Others"

Recently, considerable attention has been devoted in sociology, anthropology, political science, geography, and the social sciences in general to the notion of "otherness" and the "other," concepts of inclusion and exclusion, the outsider and insider. At the present time it is almost axiomatic that research into ethnicity, migration, racial conflicts, class antagonism, gender distinction and national policies cannot be adequately addressed without considering the notion of the other; understanding that the construction of the self is inseparable and non-detachable from the image of the "other."

The plural "others," as Riggins[13] stresses, is perhaps a more appropriate category than the singular "other". He notes that "several authors prefer the plural form, Others, because it conveys the notion that the Self in its discourses of identity is continually negotiating several identities simultaneously."[14] Multitudes of "others" perform and consolidate our social lives. Any notions of identity are an amalgam of "others," whether anonymous and undefined or well defined and presented. The representations of "others" are related to classificatory systems, categorizations and demarcations. Because "to institute, to give a social definition, an identity, is also to impose boundaries."[15] To identify what is included and what is excluded from the notion or category that we are referring to,

> [t]he transactions during which ethnicity is produced and reproduced have two complementary characters. First, there is internal definition: actors, whether as individuals or in groups, define their own identity. Second, there is external definition, the definition of the identity of other people.[16]

The construction of "others" is an integral part of the family and the school environment, producing collective images, stereotypes and simple myths about other groups that are perceived as particularly different. Rhetoric of the "other" begins to be incorporated into discourse at a very early age, from the moment we start to understand the words that apply to our day-to-day interaction.

In Tatar gymnásias, the "others" are not abstract or generic, but rather known and named "others"; Russian girls and Russian boys, Russian women and Russian men who are presented as the outsiders, the historical enemy. Through the different interviews it was possible to see that pupils in Tatar gymnásias had a strong mental division between Tatar and non-Tatar, and more precisely Tatar/Russian. They revealed a *dichotomous* way of thinking that emerged in specific discussions, showing to what extent the division Tatar/Russian is embedded, learned from an early age.

The dichotomy was particularly noticeable, for example, when pupils were asked to name their favourite writer. Every Tatar gymnásia pupil responded with the following question: "Tatar or Russian?" The response does not really answer the question, since a favourite writer is a favourite writer, regardless of whether (s)he is Tatar or Russian. Since without exception all the pupils from Tatar gymnásias tried to clarify the distinction, it probably shows that this tendency to distinguish and divide is not a random or accidental reaction but rather something deeply embedded in their perception and understanding.

There was constant repetition of rhetorical clichés, like slogans or choruses: "we are different," "we are not like them" or "we are much more civilized." These are not mere words but are incorporated as meanings deliberately transmitted inside the school environment. "[T]he social world is also will and representation, and to exist socially means also to be perceived, and perceived as distinct."[17]

> On people, the team, [...] the environment,—In here it is a purely Tatar environment. And this is quite a lot, quite a lot. This is why we are trying to stay here, don't leave, we are all trying. English teachers refer with such respect to older teachers, there is not such boorishness as in Russian schools. [...] The fact that we have such an environment, purely Tatar environment,—it is like one family. (History teacher)

In this case the history teacher is not only presenting the positive elements of the school but is also strongly defending and presenting this school as a positive example of cultural segregation. Not one person expressed any doubts or uncertainty about the future impact that a mono-cultural and mono-ethnic environment might have on pupils' perceptions and opinions, or how this Tatar environment might affect them when they start university and enter a rather more diverse reality.

The marking of difference also had a different role in each institutional environment, because in the context of Tatar gymnásias a dichotomous way of thinking clearly emerged, which illustrated to what extent the strong division Tatar/Russian ("us" and "them") is not only an occasional expression but is also embedded in their representations, and constantly reproduced inside the schools and within families; confirming that "identity is always a dialectic between similarity and difference."[18] The process is both differentiation and identification, inclusion and exclusion since in McCrone's words, "the 'difference' involves the 'same.'"[19]

Marriage inside the Group: Rhetoric of Ethno-cultural Segregation

Pupils inside Tatar gymnásias do not receive the motivation, either at school or in their homes, that would encourage intercultural or inter-ethnic interaction or marriage, since for most of the pupils, marriage outside Tatar circles would represent a tragedy for their parents. It would be perceived as betrayal of Tatar culture and traditions.

> They said to me, if you have a Russian husband, consider that you don't have parents. They don't like Tatars who are with Russians, they are against crossing, mixing. They don't want me to [...] In general, it's possible to have Russian friends, I suppose, but to see a Russian boy—my mum will not allow me, and the same goes for my father. (Female pupil from Tatar gymnásia)

In general terms, Tatarstan has a significant proportion of mixed marriages between Tatars and Russians, since it was a relatively common practice especially among the urban population. However, not all Tatars welcome it, and they persuade their children to marry within their own group, as a mechanism for maintaining and consolidating Tatar unity.

Pupils from Tatar gymnásias have very few chances to interact with non-Tatar friends on a day-to-day basis. All the pupils in their school are Tatars, their teachers are Tatars, they come from Tatar families, and most of them spend their holidays in Tatar villages with their Tatar relatives. Consequently, as most of the pupils stressed, most of their friends are from their own gymnásia and as a result they are permanently enclosed in an environment that is continuously reinforcing the notion of Tatar unity and distinctiveness, in other words reproducing and supporting ethno-cultural Tatar segregation. Quite frequently it is not only a question of who they are going to marry but also a more general phenomenon of the division and segregation that permeates their lives (i.e. who they are not going to marry). Throughout all the conversations the same justification was repeated time and again. Without exception, religion and tradition were presented as the reason why they wanted to marry a person from the same peer group. The recurring theme was: "while you are young it is fine, but when you get older you will need your religion and your traditions."

Mixed marriages and parents from different religions appear to represent evilness and badness in pupils' eyes—something above all to be rejected. It amounts to a moral duty that all Tatars should have to their people, their language and their traditions. There are many Tatars who attribute the current degradation of the Tatar language and Tatar culture to the practice of marriage between Tatars and Russians in the past; a pattern of behaviour that nationalist organizations now strongly reject.

Endogamy and closure within the group are values transmitted by the families of pupils from Tatar gymnásias because marriages outside the group are heavily stigmatized and the danger of mixed marriages is overemphasized in pupils' eyes. Marriage within the group contributes strongly to the differentiation and non-communication between different groups.

> Well, I suppose, to preserve [...] Nowadays there are many mixed marriages,—Tatar women and Russian men, I don't know, it is, to some extent it is an obstacle to our *natsional'nost*, because if you imagine when a husband and wife are getting older, because when they were young they can not follow all the religious practices, but when they are getting older, they are closer to it, so when they are older, they may have different conflicts because of their *natsiia*, and then religion. (Female pupil from Tatar gymnásia)

There is general social agreement that endogamy in religious terms (which is to marry within the same religious grouping) is likely to lead to greater agreements on child-bearing practices and family rituals, frequently presented as the only means capable of keeping religion and traditions alive. Such agreement may be based on people's experiences, or perhaps only mere speculative thoughts, which were strongly encouraged through the generations. The sense of exclusiveness does not necessarily

59

achieve the claimed purpose since cultural and religious traditions need other mechanisms to be operating at the same time.

Time after time mixed marriages were represented in negative terms. Not one person talked about possible enrichment through mixed marriages, the opportunity of learning new traditions and new habits, the experience of sharing and trying to make compatible two different points of view or separate religions, as well as learning new concepts and perceptions.

According to Enloe,[20] one of the indicators that illustrates how far religion sustains ethnic boundaries is intermarriage, which she considers to be the bottom line of ethnicity. However, she also stresses that the rate of intermarriage is not determined exclusively by religious rules. For example, in the Soviet Union intermarriages were promoted as an important element of Soviet national policy. However, as she clearly shows, Muslims are less likely to marry non-Muslims; something confirmed in the research where everyone indicated that they would prefer to marry a Tatar person rather than a non-Tatar person, religion being presented as one of the main reasons.

Religiosity: A Dimension to Reinforce

But if religion is such an important issue, how do the Tatars live and experience religion in the course of daily life? Are they practising members or is it a question of tradition? To what extent is religion incorporated in their day-to-day life after 70 years of communism? Have the new Tatar generations become more religious since the communist disintegration or is religion just another dimension of what they consider to be Tatarness?

There is no consensus on what unites an ethnic group. For different groups certain dimensions such as language, religion, images of common history, or shared traditions, to mention just a few, are more relevant than others. But in this research it was possible to observe how most of the pupils and teachers constantly associated what they considered "to be Tatar" with "being Muslim" ("we are Muslims, of course; we are Tatars"). Nonetheless their perception and understanding of Islam was circumstantial and depended on situational contingencies. "The statement that for the Tatars, Islam and nation are inseparable, was made without ambiguity by the Mufti during a reception of the Presidium in 1989."[21]

The category of being Muslim is a noticeable component in their rhetoric, but it is equally apparent that observance is more a question of personal choice, and not always in accordance with Islamic canons or laws. However, regardless of the level of transgression in teachers' and pupils' observance, from the institutional perspective—in gymnásia No. 2 to be precise—Islamic rules and attitudes are strongly encouraged and promoted. There is a definite institutional strategy based on the study of Arabic, but also through the celebration of religious festivities inside the school which does not always correspond with how people experience religion in their everyday life.

Vertovec suggests that "many young Muslims in Britain are currently adopting a strong Muslim identity, although, this often does not necessarily entail an enhanced knowledge of Islam nor an increased participation in religious activities."[22] He sees it often as a cultural Muslim identity that emerges as a form of resistance to anti-Muslim sentiment and racist attitudes. The same hypothesis might be applied to the ethno-cultural Tatar renaissance, which is understandable as an anti-Russian attitude, a reaction and resistance to Russian domination and imperialist policies, expressed through the exaltation and hyper-adoration of everything that is included in the category of being Tatar. Yet it is a category that possesses more flexible capacities than its promoters would expect, leaving enough room for a certain amount of transgression, manifested in concrete practices and attitudes.

> To be honest with you, I think, I am learning; it is interesting to learn about religions, to learn what is new in religion. I think that so far neither Islam, nor Christianity, or any of the other religions yet [...] there is not the best one among them. In each of them there is some deficiency, and Tatars are close to Islam, it is like national, it is accepted. But I know Tatar people, who [...] are Christians, they are converted Tatars. And I know some who are members of a sect. But anyway, I would like my children to learn Islam. I think ... this is one of the best religions. (Male pupil)

According to Cesari,[23] there is a tendency among Western scholars to assume that Muslims are required to conform to Islamic Law because they are Muslims. This neglects the transformations in Islamic identities among the new generations that have been born in Europe and who are experiencing a process of secularization which means that Islam is becoming increasingly a part of their private life. Also confirming what Vertovec[24] describes as cultural Muslim identity, Cesari considers that:

> for these young people (second or third generation of migrants in France) to define themselves as Arab or Muslim would represent a symbolic assertion which is not always connected with their everyday life, [...] To define themselves in France as Arab or Muslim does not mean that they are homesick but refers to their situation in France. In fact it is a reaction against discrimination.[25]

The identification does not entail, as the author stresses, that they live as Muslims, since it is "more symbolic allegiance,"[26] closely related to cultural values. According to Cesari:

> Islam is an ethic, a source of moral values giving significance to their life but without implication for their practice. [...] In this case, the collective dimension of Islamic membership is moderated by an individual logic. But this individualisation of Islam is constrained by two things: circumcision and the prohibition on intermarriage. [...] Their opposition (to intermarriage) is not justified by religious arguments but by cultural ones; they reason that there would be a cultural incompatibility between husband and wife and the risk of domination of one by the "other."[27]

61

There is a remarkable correspondence between these ideas and what was observed concerning endogamous practices. Nevertheless, alongside the parallels and common-alities, there is a considerable difference between the Tatar case and the French second and third generation of migrants. First, for most of the Tatar pupils their parents were in a quite similar situation to them in relation to religion, because they had never experienced an orthodox Islamic way of life. In the case of the French that Cesari describes, the life of parents of the new generations of Muslims who live in France was strongly governed by Islamic Law. Consequently, there is a generational conflict regarding religious perception and understanding. In the case of Tatar pupils, however, most of their parents had very little previous experience of religion since all of them were educated in a Soviet society. Present circumstances are rather different, but inter-estingly the current dynamics in both cases are somewhat similar though for different reasons: over-religiosity in one case, and the absence of religiosity in the other.

There are some parallels between the Tatar people's situation and that of second and third generation of migrants in France. Russian culture, like French culture, is dominant and Tatar people, like French Muslim immigrants, stress their Muslim belonging not as a religious belief system but as a cultural claim, a response to cultural marginalization and discrimination. The major difference is that Tatars did not migrate to the current Republic of Tatarstan, but Russians colonized them. The peripheral status applies to the Tatar people not as a numeric minority but as a symbolic one. They are a minority because their language and culture were relegated to the margins rather than to the centre. This status affects their self-representations, and consequently their belief and belonging.

> [...] a person should be developed in many directions. And also—religion—because it is our own religion, national, it has to be shown, shown and developed, and a person needs to know his own religion [...] (Female pupil)

As one history teacher noted, she believes in her God, but she does not observe Ramadan and nor has she ever done so. But she defines herself as Muslim, as Tatar, she likes her language, she respects her culture, her traditions, but she does not go to the mosque, and she believes in her own God. Nevertheless, she considers herself as truly Muslim, without the Ramadan, without the prayers, without the mosque; she has her individual interpretation. Her family celebrate religious festivities because it is something that is part of people's everyday life, even if they are not religious.

The notion of national religion is one that should be considered the leitmotiv of the present establishment and development of Islam in the gymnásias' environment. Musina[28] uses the term religious nationalism to describe the process that is taking place in Tatarstan: "when I am talking about religious nationalism, I am referring to national emotions revived through religious forms; but religion is just a form." The religious growth that started during the 1980s, the process of re-Islamization,[29] is not so much a religious re-emergence as it is the expression of national identities

62

under the specific form of religious nationalism, since according to her the young generation in particular do not know the bases of Islam.

Islam has acquired legitimacy as an ideological pillar of Tatar nationalism. Islamic rebirth in the Republic's ideology is perceived by nationalist movements and organizations as a possibility for the revitalization of the Tatar people and their culture. According to Musina,[30] in Tatarstan it is possible to observe not only political Islamization but also Islamic politicization.

"Our Rodina": Another Pillar inside Tatar Gymnásias

There can be no doubt that without exception the *amor patriae* has been, historically, one of the most recurrent imagined forms of attachment, from the North to the South, and from the East to the West of the globe; from the remembered past to the most contemporary present, *amor patriae* has been a cause to die for. In very different forms and through different mechanisms and with different intensity, most societies, at some point in their existence, have claimed a commitment to the so-called homeland, native land, territory, or what in Russia is called *rodina*. Patriotism (unconditional support) was and still is part of the youngest generations' rhetoric, who define themselves as patriots.

The notion of patriotism stood as another pillar in the way that Tatarhood was represented inside Tatar gymnásias. The Tatar gymnásia pupils', teachers' and parents' *rodina* was well defined. There was no room for misunderstanding what they meant by their *rodina* and what it was not. It combined constant dissatisfaction with the Russian government, with the wish and hope that if Tatarstan were to become an independent republic (in real terms, not only on paper) things would be much better for Tatars. It is a hope and an illusion, perhaps even a myth, which does not necessarily correspond with real conditions and circumstances but it does have a secure place in people's imaginary representations.

> We are so different from them, even if we speak Russian, we are different in spirit. I am not going to betray myself and call myself Russian. (Female pupil)

Tatar gymnásias do not only symbolize the possibility of overcoming the neglect of language, improving the Tatar language, or creating a place where pupils can learn Tatar history and traditions. For many people, Tatar gymnásias are able to consolidate and reinforce Tatar *natsiia*, especially by stressing the difference from Russian *natsiia*.

> It is good that there are such schools as this, because somehow they keep the *natsiia* together. But the Tatar *natsiia* is completely dissolved in Russia, and it's as if it was all one, and in some way I would like to have some kind of *natsiia*, to keep it; I wouldn't like to feel myself Russian. (Female pupil from Tatar gymnasia)

Tatar gymnásias are spaces where patriotism for Tatarstan is accentuated, an environment where new narratives of Tatar people are in a state of effervescence

63

and where a primordial understanding of Tatarhood is in an advanced stage of gestation.

> I think if Tatarstan separates from Russia, everything will be different. Because we have such a strong dependency on Russia, on its politics [...] But perhaps one day, somehow we will be a separate state and everyone will acknowledge us as Tatarstan, not as part of the Russian Federation, but straightaway as Tatarstan. And Tatar language will be the most important language, and all Russians will be able to speak in Tatar [...] (Female pupil from Tatar gymnásia)

From the times of ancient Russia (Rus) to the current Russian Federation, a permanent and constant sacrifice has been demanded in the name of patriotism from the people that reside in these lands; to support despotic tsars, to build a better world, to campaign for communism around the world, to struggle against the fascists, or to establish a capitalist economy. As Anderson has stressed: "it is useful to remind ourselves that nations inspire love, and often profoundly self-sacrificing love."[31] The notion of *rodina* is not static but is always liable to change as a result of political and social changes. People create specific mechanisms to adapt to these modifications, which operate with their own definitions and representations.

Transgression in Everyday Life

Language, religion and patriotism constantly emerged in pupils' and teachers' representations, and they are strongly reinforced in Tatar gymnásias as the main support and characteristic of a particular interpretation and representation of Tatar identity. The institutional praxis manifested in both Tatar gymnásias creates and encourages static notions of an ethno-Tatar universe that pupils adopt and reproduce; praxis that not always contains inclusive aims. In that sense, Tatar gymnásias appear as a powerful medium for identities transmission and (re)formulation, with the ability to enunciate and diffuse what they consider as needed. Although a certain flexibility and transgression is also visible as a consequence of people's adaptation to ideological and socio-political modifications, uni-directionality is permanently emerging from the institutional discourse, a discourse that people and teachers did not aim to hide or dissimulate. Time after time the same enunciative strategies and mechanisms of marking difference appeared through the conversations, a static representation of Tatar identity that Tatar gymnásias are encouraging and pupils and teachers are easily reproducing and accepting, and only on some occasions questioning and transgressing. The dynamic of transgression shows a certain tension between the institutional discourse and pupils' and teachers' everyday life.

There are opinions and attitudes that cannot easily be classified or organized into categories or notions of Russians, Tatars or Soviets. There are attitudes, ways of thinking and behaving that go beyond any fixed notion of what it is to be Tatar, Russian or Soviet; confirming Maffesoli's view that "our daily existence is fragmentary and polysemic."[32] People's everyday lives do not always correspond precisely with the dominant political paradigm or ideology.

However, there is a dialogue-tension between what should be according to the discursive level and what they are actually used to or what they like (as a result of many years of practical experience). Paradoxically, and without much hesitation, pupils would define themselves as Tatars and consequently in their terms as Muslims, and yet portray the New Year as their favourite festivity. This was perfectly accepted by the pupils, but not equally welcomed by the institutions. It was a point of conflict and disagreement between institutional enunciation and pupils' practices; a fissure that very well symbolized the level of transgression incorporated in their everyday life; a space where what the institutions defend or proclaim is refused.

It is often assumed that for someone who defines herself as Tatar and Muslim New Year is a strange festivity to celebrate. However, this was a transgression that was observed in almost all pupils, since almost all said that their favourite festivity was New Year. Moreover, some of them openly stated that one of their favourite festivities is 8 March, International Women's Day—one of the Soviet bastions. An adequate understanding and evaluation of the complex dynamics of everyday life does not necessarily involve rationality or intentionality; very often their dynamics can escape the direct cause–effect relationship.

What can strike the outsider as something perhaps unique or unusual is absolutely normal for Tatar pupils, the new generation that are ideologically alien to the communist time, perfectly bilingual and more familiar with Tatar culture than their parents or even their grandparents. They define themselves as religious and Muslim, but they prefer New Year to other festivities.

Conclusion

The purpose of this paper was to illustrate how Tatar national gymnásias create and reinforce static notions of ethno-Tatar identity (ethno-national representations), and at the same time to show how this process of identities construction involves and is part of a complex dialogue between political discourse, institutional praxis and everyday life. A complex dialectic emerges between three different areas: political discourse, institutional praxis and everyday life. The first defends the idea of integration (*Tatarstantsy*), the second promotes the practice of segregation (inside Tatar gymnásias), while the third manifests transgression between the apparently rigid and divisible lines of identities and accentuates their fractured and fragmented character.

It is difficult to predict what will happen in the near future in the republic, as what happens in Tatarstan is strongly related to and dependent on what happens in Moscow. If there is political or economic instability in Moscow there is bound to be some effect in the republic. The relationship between the different ethno-cultural groups inside the republic, the relation of the republic to the centre, and the political stance that the Russian Federation will adopt in the future are some of the key dimensions that will influence the situation in the republic. At the present time there is still a high level of uncertainty and unpredictability, and parents and teachers from Tatar gymnásias know that things can easily change again; they are accustomed to the instability and they have learned to live with this attitude.

According to Sagitova[33] and Kondrashov[34] there is a noticeable inferiority complex amongst the Tatar population as a result of the socio-political asymmetrical relations and class distribution between Tatars and Russians. Only now has the 'sleeping beauty' started to polish and tune its voice. Now Tatars have to show that they are not 'inferior' and that they can even be 'superior'. It is not a question of choosing one language and renouncing the "other," because they are aware that they need to know Russian for practical reasons. The process of urbanization or the passage from rural to urban[35] or the trauma of urbanization[36] and communist rule, were accompanied by the Tatar population's acceptance of its 'inferior' or 'secondary' position. The relationship between the Tatar sense of inferiority and the Russian aim of superiority is directly affecting the current tendency for national revival.

Pupils from Tatar gymnásias live in Kazan, where about half of the population is Russian. But they are maintained artificially in isolation, avoiding inter-communication with the people with whom they live. This new generation of pupils has spent its childhood in Kazan, with parents originally from rural areas, but this generation has full exposure to Russian speech, to Russian television programmes and to Russian DJs; Russian culture is not alien to them. Nevertheless, family and school discourse fosters a strong sense of exclusion; *ipso facto* rejecting any chances of cultural diversity and intercultural fusion or interaction.

In order to avoid any tendency towards reinforcing segregation, it is not only necessary to incorporate Tatar language into the curriculum and to promote policies to revive Tatar culture. These measures are only a first step. In order to build a plural society, and respect for diversity, pupils should be educated in mixed environments, where differences are accepted, along with different languages and cultures, habits and traditions. Only under such circumstances can the old phantoms be banished and new relations of respect and tolerance be established.

Inside Tatar gymnásias there is an attempt to restore what they consider to have been neglected, stolen or annihilated over many centuries; nevertheless, in the future Tatar gymnásias will have to decide which path or direction they will promote: whether to strive to return to the past they claim to have lost, or to adapt to the new circumstances and demands. It will be a question of finding a balance between what they consider to be the recovery of Tatar traditions and the dynamics of the present situation.

Tatarstan sovereignty represents different things to the Russian and the Tatar populations, and the two groups have different motives and interpretations. Russians see the value of sovereignty in economic terms and economic prosperity; therefore, the parameter is economic development. For Tatars, on the other hand, it involves economic development plus ethno-cultural Tatar renaissance, the cultural-national parameter. As long as both parameters exist together then consensus is achieved, but problems may emerge when one of the parameters becomes stronger than the other, or one starts to decline.

NOTES

1. This paper is the result of my Ph.D. thesis "Representing Identities in Tatarstan: A Cartography of Post-Soviet Discourse, Schooling and Everyday Life," School of Social Sciences, University of Wales, Bangor, 2002.
2. From the experience of this research, I believe it is essential to dispense with the notion of "identity" and to operate in terms of "identities" as one of the first axioms. Any possible approximation to the "identity" approach is a simplification that will fail to include and represent all the different dimensions that are involved in the process. In this particular research the notion of "identity" is not adequate because the research aims to illustrate the multidimensional character, the ongoing process, the diversity, situational and circumstantial idiosyncrasy, movement, different discourses, social actors, different social worlds, enunciative strategies, the past, the present and the future; and in that sense "identity," in the singular, would be deficient in representing these dynamic processes and movements.
3. For discussion in English about language policies in Tatarstan, see Davis et al., "Media, Language Policy and Cultural Change in Tatarstan."
4. Kharisov, "O Iazykovoi situatsii v byvshem SSSR," 56.
5. Calhoun, *Critical Social Theory*.
6. Drobizheva, "Natsionalizmy v respublikakh Rossiiskoi Federatsii."
7. Kharisov, *Vserossiiskoe soveshchanie rabotnikov obrazovaniia*, 66.
8. About Tatar language attitudes inside Tatar gymnásias, see Álvarez Veinguer and Davis.
9. *Kuiran Bairam* is the most significant Muslim holiday. It is a holiday of sacrifice in memory of the Prophet Ibrahim's willingness to sacrifice his son for the sake of Allah. Each Muslim has to bring a sacrifice, preferably an animal with hooves, and invite someone to eat this animal's meat.
10. Smith, *The Nationalities Question in the Soviet Union*, 189.
11. Edwards, in Billig, *Banal Nationalism*, 14.
12. Billig, *Banal Nationalism*, 29.
13. Riggins, *The Language and Politics of Exclusion*.
14. Ibid., 4.
15. Bourdieu, *Language and Symbolic Power*, 120.
16. Jenkins, *Rethinking Ethnicity*, 80.
17. Bourdieu, *Language and Symbolic Power*, 224.
18. Jenkins, *Rethinking Ethnicity*, 165.
19. McCrone, *The Sociology of Nationalism*, 36.
20. Enloe, "Religion and Ethnicity," 199.
21. Bennigsen, "Volga Tatars," 287.
22. Vertovec, "Young Muslims in Keighley, West Yorkshire," 101.
23. Cesari (1998).
24. Vertovec, "Young Muslims in Keighley, West Yorkshire."
25. Cesari (1998, 29).
26. Ibid., 30.

A. ÁLVAREZ VEINGUER

27. Ibid., 31.
28. Musina Rozalinda Nurievna, Candidate of History, Head of the Department of Ethnology of the Institute of History of TAS. Interview, 5 March 1998.
29. Musina, "Reislamizatsiia Tatar kak forma 'religioznogo natsionaliszma.'"
30. Musina, "Islam i musul'mane v sovremennom Tatarstane."
31. Anderson, *Imagined Communities*, 141.
32. Maffesoli, *Ordinary Knowledge*, 141.
33. Interview, March 1998.
34. Kondrashov (2000, 35).
35. Schöpflin, *Nations, Identity, Power*, 21.
36. Ibid., 154.

REFERENCES

Álvarez Veinguer, A. "Representing Identities in Tatarstan: A Cartography of Post-Soviet Discourses, Schooling and Everyday Life." Unpublished Ph.D. diss., University of Wales, 2002.
Álvarez Veinguer, A. and H. Davis. "Building a Tartar Elite: Language and Schooling in Kazan." *Ethnicities* 7, no. 2 (2007): 186–207.
Anderson, B. *Imagined Communities: Reflections on the Origin and Spread of Nationalism.* London: Verso, 1991.
Bennigsen, M. "Volga Tatars." In *The Nationalities Question in the Soviet Union*, edited by G. Smith. London: Longman, 1990.
Billig, M. *Banal Nationalism.* London: Sage, 1997.
Bourdieu, P. *Language and Symbolic Power.* Cambridge: Polity Press, 1991.
Calhoun, C. *Critical Social Theory: Culture, History, and the Challenge of Difference.* Oxford: Blackwell, 1995.
Cesari, J. "Islam in France: Social Challenge or Challenge of Secularism?" In *European Muslim Youth, Reproducing Religion, Ethnicity and Culture*, edited by S. Vertovec and A. Rogers. London: Ashgate, 1998.
Davis, H., P. Hammond, and L. Nizamova. "Media, Language Policy and Cultural Change in Tatarstan: Historic vs. Pragmatic Claims to Nationhood." *Nations and Nationalism* 6, no. 2 (2000): 203–26.
Drobizheva, L. "Natsionalizmy v respublikakh Rossiiskoi Federatsii: ideologiia elity i massovoe soznanie." *Panorama-Forum*, no. 1 (1997): 64–77.
Enloe, C. "Religion and Ethnicity." In *Ethnicity*, edited by J. Hutchinson and A. Smith. Oxford: Oxford University Press, 1996.
Jenkins, R. *Rethinking Ethnicity: Arguments and Explorations.* London: Sage, 1997.
Kharisov, F. "O Iazykovoi situatsii v byvshem SSSR." *Nauchnyi Tatarstan* 3 (1998): 54–57.
——. *Vserossiiskoe soveshchanie rabotnikov obrazovaniia.* Moscow: Ministerstvo Obrazovaniia Rossiiskoi Federatsii, 2000.
Kondrashov, S. *Nationalism and the Drive for Sovereignty in Tatarstan, 1988–92. Origins and Development.* London: Macmillan Press, 2000.
Maffesoli, M. *Ordinary Knowledge: An Introduction to Interpretative Sociology.* Cambridge: Polity Press, 1996.
McCrone, D. *The Sociology of Nationalism: Tomorrow's Ancestors.* London: Routledge, 1998.
Musina, R. "Islam i musul'mane v sovremennom Tatarstane". In *Islam v Tatarskom mire: Istoriia i sovremennost* edited by S. Diuduanbon, D. Iskhakov and R. Mukhametshin. Kazan': *Panorama-forum*, 1997.

——. "Reislamizatsiia Tatar kak forma 'religioznogo natsionaliszma.'" In *Religiia v sovremennom obshchestve: istoriia, problemy, tendentsii*, edited by R. Nabiev, R. Khakimov, V. Bukharaev, Iu. Mikhailov, and V. Nikiforov. Kazan': Zaman, 1998.

Riggins, S., ed. *The Language and Politics of Exclusion: Others in Discourse*. London: Sage, 1997.

Schöpflin, G. *Nations, Identity, Power: The New Politics of Europe*. London: Hurst, 2000.

Smith, G., ed. *The Nationalities Question in the Soviet Union*. London: Longman, 1990.

Vertovec, S. "Young Muslims in Keighley, West Yorkshire: Cultural Identity, Context and 'Community.'" In *Muslim European Youth: Reproducing Ethnicity, Religion, Culture*, edited by S. Vertovec and A. Rogers. Aldershot: Ashgate, 1998.

Crystallizing and Emancipating Identities in Post-Communist Estonia

Triin Vihalemm

This article concerns collective identities in the context of EU enlargement and the post-Soviet transition of Estonian society, particularly of the two main ethno-linguistic groups: ethnic Estonians and the Russian-speaking population in Estonia. The empirical basis of the study is formed by factor structures of self-identification. The data were obtained from nationally representative surveys carried out in 2002, before Estonia joined the EU, and in 2005. The thinking patterns behind the structures of self-categorization are discussed mainly on the basis of theoretical concepts of individualization and transition culture. For background information, comparative data collected in Latvia (2006) and in Sweden (2003) are used. The survey results reveal that in the post-communist transformation, EU integration and spread of global mass culture have homogenized the mental patterns of the Estonians and the Russians. It is characteristic of post-communist Estonia that both minority and majority groups have utilized trans-national and civic identity and individualistic patterns of self-identification in terms of (sub)culture and social and material achievement, extracted from social norms and existing structures. Surveys confirm that for political actors in both Estonia and Russia it is hardly possible any more to create a common umbrella identity for the Russians in Estonia—the self-designation patterns of the Estonian Russians have been emancipated during the transition period.

The purpose of this study is to open the universalities and peculiarities of the formation of collective identities in post-communist Estonia, with special attention to the dynamics of the collective identities of the Russian minority. The cultural and political allegiances of the Russians between Russian, Western and local frames of reference have been the subject of extensive discussion. Despite the fact that during the first decade of the transition the Russian-speaking population used mainly individual adaptation strategies, researchers have proposed that social deprivation may lead to the formation of collective group consciousness and mobilization of the Russian-speaking community.[2] When discussing this issue, not only should the relations between the majority and minorities be taken into account but also the broader cultural context. The novelty of the present approach is that the formation of geopolitical allegiances is analysed in relation to other forms of social belonging and a focus on the structures of self-categorization, with an ambition to elucidate the meta-level (general) thinking patterns behind people's identities. To that end, Estonia is compared with Latvia, which has similar geopolitical macro-conditions and ethnic composition, and with the stable welfare society of Sweden. Thus, the analysis will shed some light on the transitional culture in comparison with Western societies that have undergone a gradual process of cultural self-transformation. Recently published conceptualizations of post-communist transition culture[3] point out the importance of cultural inertia, which makes possible the parallel existence and interaction of the "new" and the "old" culture in transitional societies despite quick changes at the level of social structure and ideology. Therefore, in the second decade of the transition period, it is appropriate to analyse how the transition processes form the peoples' thinking patterns. Unfortunately, there are no analogous empirical studies from the end of the Soviet era and for that reason in this article the survey data are used to create a certain framework for discussion, rather than report on empirical measurement.

The first section discusses the theory of individualization and specifically of the transition culture and ethnic relations in Estonia. The second and third sections give an overview of the methodology and data of the study. The fourth section presents the main findings regarding the structures among Estonians and the Estonian Russians, the changes in identity structures in 2002–2005, and the comparison of the Estonian data with the relevant data from Latvia and Sweden.

Empirical and Theoretical Background of the Study

The focus of the current article is the dynamics of collective identities in post-communist Estonia. Collective identities in Estonia and other post-Soviet successor states have been analysed in the political science and sociological academic works mainly in two contexts. The first of these are discussions about the rise of nationalism among titular nations and the challenges it poses to EU policies and common values. The second concerns the strategies of the Russian minority in the former republics of the Soviet Union compared to the strategies of large minority diasporas in host countries in general.[4] Much of scholarly attention has emphasized the question of political and cultural allegiances of the Russian minority in the context of Estonian nation building. I will give a short overview of the situation.

One-third of the Estonian population comprises Russians, Ukrainians, Byelorussians and other ethnicities whose mother tongue or everyday language is predominantly Russian. Settled in Estonia in the Soviet period largely as a result of coerced immigration by the Soviet authorities, they had an extraterritorial status and the right to use their own language, and they had Russian-language institutions (e.g. schools) throughout the country.[5] After the dissolution of the Soviet Union, the earlier Soviet citizenship lost legitimacy; in order to apply for citizenship in the Republic of Estonia, one has to pass language and citizenship examinations. Thus, the Russians and other ethnicities faced a double challenge of self-determination—in terms of both transition and the new Estonian nation-state. Despite the fact that during the first decade of transition the Russian-speaking population used mainly individual adaptation strategies, researchers have proposed that social deprivation may have led to the formation of collective group consciousness and the mobilization of the Russian-speaking community.[6] This was caused by the Soviet legacy of social atomization, radical political and economic restructuring (former structures, which could have mobilized people, disappeared) as well as by the lack of a common communication space. Legislative (citizenship and language acts) and socio-cultural (attitudes of the Estonians, the media space) environments favour a situation where language becomes a basis for the collective self-awareness and possible mobilization of the Russian-speaking population.[7] For Russian-speaking Estonians, the language requirement, intertwined with the individualistic-liberal pathos dominant in the Estonian public sphere, raises the dilemma of choosing between collective and individual adaptation strategies.[8] Research indicates that so-called "ethnization" is dominating in the collective self-determination of the Russian-speaking population, the orientation of localization is also significant, and the diasporic orientation (orientation to Russia) is less evident.[9] Although Russian television dominates the media consumption of the Russian-speaking population, it is forming a culturally distinctive local hybrid identity rather than a diasporic orientation.[10]

This article continues the discussion about the development of the identity of the Russian minority, focusing the analysis on general thinking patterns and identity structures of the majority and the minority groups and presuming that Estonia's rapid inclusion in the EU and the general global technological and cultural space have created a specific environment of symbols and values peculiar to a transition society and have formed the basis for new collective identities.

The advance of English-based mass culture has been explosive rather than gradual in Estonia since the re-establishment of independence. Having been quite isolated from outside influences during the Soviet era, Estonia has moved rapidly into global communication networks and open media spheres. For example, 60% of Estonia's population, including almost every 10–24 year old, uses the Internet and 39% of households have home access to the Internet.[11] Satellite TV is also widespread. Estonian transitional culture is characterized by the rapid penetration of consumer culture[12] and its values, with consumption opportunities becoming more important in constructing identity and social success.[13] Self-positioning in the above-mentioned hierarchy of "winners and losers" of transition is highly correlated with evaluation of one's consumption possibilities.[14]

Thus, Estonia represents an example of transition characterized by rapid and radical political and economic restructuring, and the domination of liberal ideology reinforced by consumerism and a belief in new technology. Considering this context, I compare and interpret the dynamics of identifications of the minority and majority groups on the basis of theoretical concepts of individualization and transition culture.

To interpret what has happened during the post-communist transition, theories of individualization and reflexive modernity should be considered. Although expressed differently by different authors, the main thesis of the theory claims that in a complex global society it is impossible to define "collective sources of problems," meaning that the group consciousness and collective mobilization of large groups— a class, a gender, a nationality—"do not justify themselves"[15] Theoreticians of reflective modernity[16] argue also that technological development and dissemination of knowledge have made individuals doubt the ability of state and other institutions to regulate social developments and have emancipated them.[17] A solution is thought to be the emergence of critical feedback mechanisms, and the changing of the relationships between the state and individuals from normative to (more) reflective. Scholars expect completely new situation-based collective identities to emerge, shaped by protest against the levelling influence of the market economy, anxiety caused by environmental risks, preferences, and so on.

Like many other East European countries, Estonia has quickly adopted "Western" patterns—a privatized economy based on a neo-liberal ideology and advances in information technology. The political and economic pathfinders (and later winners) of transition quickly utilized economic rationality and liberal ideas as the legitimizing ideology. The neo-liberal reforms carried out in Estonia at the beginning of the 1990s acquired social legitimization also partly as a result of the accumulated wish for human emancipation from authoritarian state dependency and predictability, which had severely restricted personal choice. We may call the process that started in the post-communist Estonia in the early 1990s "enforced" individualization. Estonia represents a case of transition characterized by rapid and radical political and economic restructuring, domination of liberal ideology reinforced by consumerism and a belief in new technology. The post-Soviet period in Estonia has been characterized by high social turbulence in which peoples' social positions were subject to rapid change. The well-known description of the risk society seems to fit the description of the social conditions in post-Soviet Estonia: risks and contradictions continue to be socially produced but the duty and the need to cope with them is individualized.[18] Poor adoption of the new culture was presented in public texts as a shortage of individual skills (especially in the case of older people) or ideological resistance (especially in the case of the Russian community). While the social environment in democratic Estonia has become complex, characteristic of a risk and knowledge society, and demands individualized solutions, regulation of social development has remained normative and minimally reflexive—characteristic of early modernity. Partly as a consequence of normative politics and partly as a prerequisite for its continuation, individuals have disentangled themselves from established social structures. Thus, in parallel with rapid economic growth—partly as a prerequisite, partly as a consequence—the disintegration of society is deepening. This process is character-ized, *inter alia*, by low voter turnout, underdeveloped civil society structures and prac-tices, weak party institutionalization and low interpersonal trust.[19] The findings of research dealing with political participation, third-sector policy-making practices[20] indicate that Estonian society has low potential for the creation of reflectivity through either top-down or bottom-up strategies. Thus, on the basis of theories, further atomization and disintegration of society can be expected. At the same time, theories developed in Western societies, in which cultural self-transformation is gradual, cannot be fully applied to a transition society subject to forced individualiza-tion. A well-known analyst of post-Soviet transition, Piotr Sztompka, stresses that pol-itical and institutional changes can be made relatively quickly but culture is in essence inert. "Old" and "new" are mixed, forming a specific transitional context, in which values, identities and other "collectively shared symbolic mental resources used for filtering and interpreting the facts of change" are shaped.[21] Other authors who have written about the cultural prerequisites and consequences of transition also stress cul-tural inertia.[22] Therefore it is possible that although in Estonian society there is see-mingly a clear shift towards individualistic-liberal strategies accepting "new culture" at both the institutional and individual level, culture does not transform in one direction only. The main concern of this article is whether the overall fragmenta-tion will continue or whether people's thinking patterns will favour looking for a way out of the social complexity on a collective basis by believing in "common solutions to the troubles." Will the present atomized, minimally reflexive type of society establish itself or will a hybrid culture of social inclusion, where old identification and partici-pation forms are mixed with the forms of new sociality, form in Estonia, situated as it is in the global space? Among other social forces that may initiate the cultural trans-formation, ethnic questions may also be considered. Considering the ethnic aspect of transition, referred to above, this analysis is interested primarily in how the members of the majority and minority groups understand ethnic and civic identities in the context of other forms of social belonging. Based on the argument that culture remains inert during major social changes, we may presume that, during the second decade of transition, changes in culture will be more visible, and on the basis of the data collected now about people's values and identities it is possible to give meaning to what has happened and make prognoses of future scenarios.

Methodological Considerations

This analysis is based on the presumption that at the individual level one's social iden-tities form an organic structure. Geopolitical allegiances are formed in interrelation-ship with other social identities, and therefore it is not practicable to be analysed as such. Therefore, the analysis focuses on different social identities. I understand social identity in general as a process of systematic establishment and signification between individuals and/or collectives, distinguishing them in their social relations with other individuals and/or collectives.[23] The process of identification involves the publicly offered *external* definition, known as *social categorization*, and the *internal* process of the (partial) acquisition or rejection of identities, known as *internalization*.[24] I have operationalized the concept of identity by relying on the definition proposed by social psychologist Henri Tajfel: identity is part of an individual's self-conception which derives from knowledge about one's belonging in social groups, together with the value and emotional meaning ascribed to the groups.[25] In addition to this research, this definition has fed several empirical studies on the political and cultural identity of minority groups.

In the comparative surveys, identity was measured by the question: "Which groups do you feel a certain belonging to, so that you could say 'we' about them and yourself?" The multi-variable question included different categories, from which a respondent could choose as many as he or she wanted: friends; family; relatives/kin; Estonians/ Estonian Russians/Russians;[26] colleagues/workmates; school-, class-,and course-mates; people with similar taste, preferences; people with similar lifestyle; people with similar world-view; people with whom I share common memories or experiences of certain events and activities; people of the same generation; Europeans; people of Northern countries; humankind; all people living in Estonia; people of the same citizenship; neighbours/people living in the same street, district; co-inhabitants of the town, county; wealthy people; successful people; people who have no luck in life; poor/ people in economic difficulties; ordinary working people.

I do not assume that the list is complete so I am fully aware of the limits of the self-categorization approach in exploring identity—a complex phenomenon. But I am quite convinced that the technique is suitable for a comparative analysis of answering patterns within the framework of the given variables.

Collective identities are discussed mainly on the basis of frequency analysis.[27] Less attention has been paid to structural analysis.[28] This article focuses on the structures of self-identification, assuming that these help to understand the construction of identities as a process, bringing out the patterns of thinking, interpretation and rationalization of transitional changes at grassroots level.

In order to reduce more than 20 categories of self-identification to generalized mental structures consisting of items with similar meanings, factor analysis (the principal components method with Varimax rotation) was used. To be able to analyse and compare different factor solutions according to their natural internal structure I used the criterion of eigenvalues over one, not any fixed number of factors, in extracting the factors.

To discover the possible shifts in people's thinking patterns, I compared the factor structures of the 2002 and 2005 surveys. To bring out any possible peculiarities of a transitional society, a stable welfare society was used for comparison. There was a possibility to use data collected in Sweden, more precisely in the Södertörn area (the southern part of Stockholm), where the share of immigrants is large,[29] in order to compare the identity structures of Russians in Estonia and Latvia with the mental structures of the representatives of ethnic minorities in a welfare society, namely Sweden. The differences between Estonia and Sweden are discussed in Kalmus and Vihalemm.[30]

The identification patterns of the population of Estonia were compared with those of the population of a society as similar as possible, namely Latvia. Both Estonia and Latvia are transitional ex-communist societies that have much in common—a relatively rapid and sharp political and economic turn to the West and a liberal individualistic ideology, a relatively large Russian-speaking population that settled in these countries during the Soviet period, and their descendants. Both have used the logic of restoration in their new nation-building processes. In the new integration programmes acculturation, especially the importance of language, is stressed.[31]

However, in Latvia we may speak about ethnically divided political parties,[32] whereas in Estonia the Russian parties have not succeeded in gaining a voice in the parliamentary elections. Political theorists have hypothesized that the possibility of participating in the local elections in Estonia gave the local Russian elite an opportunity for local self-realization and, moreover, motivated many political parties to target political marketing on the Russian-speaking electorate. For example, the Central Party, under the leadership of Edgar Savisaar, has succeeded in gathering a major part of the Russian-speaking electorate in all elections since 1991.

Data Source

Our analysis is based on the data from a panel questionnaire survey entitled "Me. The World. The Media" that covered the Estonian population aged 15–74. The first stage took place from December 2002 to January 2003. A proportional model of the general population (by areas and urban/rural division) and multi-stage probability random sampling was used with a total sample size of 1,470 respondents. A self-administered questionnaire, together with a follow-up interview, was used.

The second stage was carried out in November 2005. The sampling points (geographical areas) were the same as those used in 2002. Interviewers applied the method of starting address for sampling the households and the "rule of the youngest male" for sampling the respondents in households. The achieved sample was 1,475.

To conduct the factor analysis the national samples were divided into ethnic subsamples of ethnic Estonians and Russians, formed on the basis of the respondents' self-reported ethnic group.

As background data, survey results from Latvia and Sweden were used in the analysis. The Latvian data were derived from a survey entitled "Social Identity: Latvia," organized by the Baltic Institute of Social Sciences. This survey consisted of 1,005 face-to-face interviews conducted in spring 2006 with Latvian inhabitants aged between 15 and 75. The sampling method used was similar to that described in the case of Estonia. The Latvian data were also analysed in two sub-samples—ethnic Latvians and Russians, based on the respondents' self-determination.

In Sweden, the survey covered the Södertörn region, the southern area of Stockholm. Self-administered questionnaires were distributed and collected by mail in the period from November 2002 to February 2003. The net sample was 2,422 individuals and the response rate was 52.6% (1,272 individuals). The material, however, showed a fairly high correspondence with the official distribution of people from the eight municipalities involved. The representation of immigrants in the sample was fairly good.[33]

Results

The Identification Structures of Ethnic Groups in Estonia in 2005

The factor structures of self-identification in 2005 are presented in Table 1, which shows that the groups of identification are structured into similar factors in the ethnic Estonian and Russian sub-samples.

The common label for the categories in the first factor could be *subcultural identity*. This factor is based on the acknowledgement of "we-ness" with people with similar taste preferences, world-views, lifestyle and memories of certain events. Among Estonians, this also includes identification with peers. Thus, the Estonians mark subcultural differences and similarities with belonging to a certain generation.

The second factor in the Estonian sub-sample and the third factor in the Russian sub-sample could be labelled *network identity*, which includes the categories family, friends, workmates, schoolmates, relatives/kin, and own ethnic group ("Estonians" and "Russians" or "Estonian Russians," respectively).[34]

While the Russian sub-sample belongs to the network identity factor, which includes the categories of close relationship (relatives, kin), in the Estonian sub-sample these categories have almost equal factor loads in both the network identity and the local identity factors. Thus, when constructing the identities of neighbourhood and community, for Estonians family relations are important, especially in rural areas and small towns. The share of rural population is very small among Russians compared with Estonians.

On the other hand, among Estonians the factor load of the ethnic group category is very weak compared with the load of other components forming the factor structure. In the Russian sub-sample the ethnic group component has a significantly stronger load. Thus, among ethnic Estonians, the ties between personal networks and ethnic group identity are looser. This is confirmed by the fact that ethnic belonging has separated from network identity and forms the independent factor in the answering structure in the sub-sample of young, i.e. 15–29-year-old, Estonians.[35] Moreover, qualitative studies have shown that Estonian youngsters cannot easily make

TABLE 1 The structures of self-identification among ethnic Estonians ($N = 1,033$) and Russians in Estonia ($N = 442$) in 2005 (results of factor analysis)

Ethnic Estonians		Russians in Estonia	
F1 Subcultural identity		F1 Subcultural identity	
People with similar taste, preferences	0.741	People with similar taste, preferences	0.801
People with similar world-view	0.717	People with similar world-view	0.773
People with whom I share common memories or experiences of certain events and activities	0.717	People with similar interests	0.675
People with similar interests	0.653	People with whom I share common memories or experiences of certain events and activities	0.622
People of the same generation	0.439		
F2 Trans-national and civic identity		F2 Trans-national and civic identity	
Europeans	0.802	People of Northern countries	0.729
Humankind	0.740	Humankind	0.651
People of Northern countries	0.699	All people living in Estonia	0.626
All people living in Estonia	0.459	Humankind	0.602
People of the same citizenship	0.382	People of the same citizenship	0.412
		People of the same generation	0.360
F3 Network identity		F3 Network identity	
Friends	0.688	Family	0.658
Family	0.674	Friends	0.628
School-, class-, and course-mates	0.608	School-, class-, and course-mates	0.611
Colleagues, workmates	0.600	Relatives, kin	0.565
Relatives, kin[a]	*0.472*	Own ethnic group (Russians, Estonian Russians)	0.559
Own ethnic group (Estonians)	0.247	Workmates	0.486

(Table continued)

TABLE 1   Continued

Ethnic Estonians		Russians in Estonia	
F4 Local community identity		F4 Local community identity	
Neighbours	0.777	Neighbours	0.709
Co-inhabitants of the town, county	0.643	Ordinary working people	0.677
Relatives, kin	0.487	Co-inhabitants of the town, county	0.562
F5 Identification with high social position		F5 Identification with high social position	
Wealthy people	0.799	Wealthy people	0.817
Successful people	0.748	Successful people	0.762
F6 Identification with low social position		F6 Identification with low social position	
People who have no luck in life	0.802	People who have no luck in life	0.789
Poor, people in economic difficulties	0.792	Poor, people in economic difficulties	0.787
Ordinary working people	0.611		

spontaneous associations and describe their feelings in relation to ethnic belonging. The interpretation of ethnic identity tended to be somewhat primordial—"I was born an Estonian, nothing else" was a typical answer in focus groups.[36] Qualitative studies indicate that for Russians ethnic belonging and self-determination as a Russian or an Estonian Russian is justified first of all by personal relations, friends and family. A typical answer to the question as to why the respondent feels that he/she is a Russian was: "From an early age I have been surrounded by the Russians at home, at school, among friends, and spoken Russian. I follow Russian traditions and customs, my community is Russian." Self-determination as an Estonian Russian was explained the same way: "Some of my friends are the Estonians, from an early age I communicate with both the Estonians and the Russians and in both the Estonian and the Russian language, although I use Russian more."[37]

The third factor in the Estonian sub-sample and the second factor in the Russian sub-sample could be labelled *trans-national and civic identity*. The trans-national categories such as Europeans, humankind, people of Northern countries, but also the civic categories such as all people living in Estonia, people having the same citizenship/co-citizens, belong in this factor. Thus the new civic solidarity, either in its narrower (citizenship) or wider form (all people living in Estonia), is strongly connected among both Estonians and Russians with mental belonging to the Western socio-cultural space and with a certain universalist orientation (solidarity with the whole of humankind). "Return to Europe" is a metaphor used widely in Estonian public discourse[38] and joining the EU has obviously strengthened it. The universalist orientation has probably been reinforced by the mass media. In the qualitative survey it was pointed out that discussing global environmental problems, disasters and wars on TV strengthens the feeling that the human race has common problems that in the context of globalization also concern Estonia.[39]

In the sub-sample of Russians in Estonia the category "same generation" belongs also to the trans-national and civic identity structure. The fact that generational identification belongs to this structure indicates that in the Russian community different orientations and the values of different generations are expressed most vividly in the dimension of geopolitical openness. Other surveys have confirmed the global orientation of young Russians.[40]

The fourth factor can be labelled *local community identity*. This structure indicates the feeling of "we-ness" with the people living in the neighbourhood, and in the same town or county. However, it has some variations in the Estonian and Russian sub-samples. Among Estonians the factor also includes the category relatives, kin. This phenomenon has already been explained above. In the sub-sample of Russians, the category "ordinary working people" forms a common structure with local community identity categories. We have to bear in mind that Russians reside mainly in districts comprising blocks of flats in industrial cities, and thousands of them are employed in large enterprises, such as the electronics manufacturing company Elcoteq in Tallinn and the oil shale company Eesti Põlevkivi in north-eastern Estonia. The main local employer, especially in north-eastern Estonia, hugely influences the quality and range of social services and also arranges activities for its employees. Thus, knowledge of their common employer is an important source in the creation of community identity among the Russians.

The fifth factor in both ethnic sub-samples includes the categories which mark material and social advancement (wealthy people, successful people). We labelled this factor *identification with high social position*. The sixth factor in both sub-samples comprises the opposite categories: "poor people" and "people who have no luck in life," and therefore we labelled the factor *identification with low social position*. It is significant that among Estonians the category "working people" also belongs to this factor, clearly having a connotation of the lack of success for one group of the Estonian people. This type of identification may be related to the metaphor of winners and losers, which is used widely in the public sphere in the sense of material prosperity resulting from opportunistic coping with changed situations versus a decline in living standards and social position after the collapse of the Soviet system.

The fifth and the sixth factors form opposite poles on the dimension of social and material success. They are structurally clearly separated, and thus different people accepted or rejected these categories for self-designation. For example, in the thinking patterns of the Swedish people these categories are not mutually exclusive and there is also a group which identified itself with both categories.[41] This may be explained by the more developed post-material value culture in Sweden, or as Beck and Beck-Gernsheim have described this shift: "The struggle over the distribution of material goods, which still monopolizes the public attention, has been undermined by a struggle over the distribution of rest, leisure, self-determined commitments, adventure, and interchanges with others."[42]

Changes in the Patterns of Self-Identification in Estonia in 2002–2005

The same type of measurement carried out at the end of 2002 enables us to observe changes in the thinking patterns. Although not long in terms of time, this represents a period of significant changes in Estonian society—joining the EU, increased economic growth, a clearer distinction between left- and right-wing politics and diversification of public discourse. People's involvement in the global culture via new media is also increasing year by year.

Table 2 presents the self-identification structures of ethnic Estonians and Russians in Estonia in 2002 and 2005. To give a better overview, I have presented the structures schematically without the numeric values of factor loads. Identification categories of almost equal numeric values in different factors are presented in *italic* in each relevant factor. Category labels are presented in a short, one-word form: for example, the category "people with whom I share common memories" is presented as simply "memories."

The factor *subcultural identity* is based on the acknowledgement of "we-ness" with people with similar taste preferences, world-views, interests and memories of certain events formed both in 2002 and 2005. However, in the Estonian sub-sample in 2002 Factor 1 did not include the component of generation (see Table 2). Thus, generation as an indicator of subcultural differences and similarities is more pronounced among Estonians, marking also an increasing cultural gap between generations. In the identity structure of the sub-sample of Russians in Estonia in 2002 cultural identity also included the category "successful people," which indicates that self-identification based on interests and world-view was considered somewhat elitist, related to being successful in society. However, in 2005 no socio-demographic variable determining subcultural belonging can be distinguished. Thus, the meaning space of subcultural self-identification in thinking patterns of Estonian Russians has become more "democratic" and independent from the existing social hierarchies. The formation of the "independent" pattern of subcultural identification can partly be explained by the fact that Estonian Russians are avid TV watchers: they spend more than four hours a day watching TV.[43]

The factor labelled *network identity* formed in 2002 as the second factor in the Estonian sub-sample and as the first factor in the sub-sample of the Russians in Estonia. In 2005, it forms the third factor in both ethnic sub-samples. By the "core," the factors have identical structure. When comparing the structures in 2002 and 2005 we can see that the factor load of ethnicity in the factor of Identity has weakened significantly. Thus, among ethnic Estonians, the ties between personal networks and

TABLE 2 The structures of self-identification in 2002 and 2005 in sub-samples of Estonians and Russians in Estonia (results of factor analysis)

2002		2005	
Ethnic Estonians N = 940	Russians in Estonia N = 509	Russians in Estonia N = 442	Ethnic Estonians N = 1,033
F1	F1	F1	F1
Taste	Family	Taste	Taste
World-view	Friends	World-view	World-view
Interests	Relatives, kin	Interests	Interests
Memories	Schoolmates	Memories	Memories
	(Estonian)		Generation
	Russians		
	Workmates		
	Neighbours		
F2	F2	F2	F2
Family	Unsuccessful	Northern people	Northern people
Friends	Poor	Humankind	Humankind
Schoolmates	Working people	All in Estonia	All in Estonia
Workmates	All in Estonia	Europeans	Europeans
Relatives, kin	Citizenship	Citizenship	Citizenship
Estonians$^{score\ 0.553}$	Generation	Generation	
F3	F3	F3	F3
Neighbours	Taste	Family	Family
Inh. of city/county	World-view	Friends	Friends
All in Estonia	Interests	Relatives, kin	Schoolmates
Generation	Memories	Schoolmates	Workmates
Working people	Successful	Workmates	Relatives, kin$^{also\ Factor\ 4}$
		(Estonian) Russians	Estonians$^{score\ 0.247}$
F4	F4	F4	F4
Successful	Europeans	Neighbours	Neighbours
Wealthy	Northern	Inh. of city/county	Inh. of city/county
	Humankind	Working people	Relatives, kin$^{also\ Factor\ 3}$
	Inh. of city/		
	county		
F5	F5	F5	F5
European	Wealthy	Successful	Successful
Northern		Wealthy	Wealthy
Humankind			
Citizenship			
F6		F6	F6
Unsuccessful		Unsuccessful	Unsuccessful
Poor		Poor	Poor
			Working people

83

ethnic group identity are loosening. Elsewhere[44] I have discussed the fact that in the course of history Estonians have practised the so-called resistant, defensive minority identity construction pattern.[45] Although this was constructed through public manifestations, such as Song Fests,[46] identity was re-created mainly through everyday communication. Estonians, for example, in their communication with Russians, have long used the strategy of linguistic convergence,[47] switching over to Russian in order to retain symbolic divergence with regard to Estonian—not letting "others" speak "our" language.[48]

Thus the meaning of ethnic belonging had a somewhat tribal connotation—with close links to personal communication networks. As a result of the restoration of Estonian statehood and Estonians becoming the nation-state the patterns of construction of ethnic identity will probably face the challenge of further change. Qualitative studies indicate that in the perception of ethnic belonging contacts with the outside world (working/studying aboard, Estonia's achievements in the international arena) and other factors have become more important than everyday communication partners.[49]

Research has shown that after the dissolution of the Soviet Union, Russians in Estonia have started to understand the symbolic value of language—its symbolic content as an indicator of belonging to a group or of a social role is reproduced on a daily basis in mutual interaction both with Estonians and other Russian speakers.[50] This may explain why among the Russians a close connection persists between ethnic belonging and personal communication networks.

Significant changes have occurred in regional and civil identity categories compared with 2002. In 2002 an independent structure of *Self-Designation on the Basis of Shared Social Space and Position* was formed in the sub-samples both of Estonians (Factor 3) and Russians in Estonia (Factor 2).

In the sub-sample of Estonians the mental pattern (Factor 3 in 2002), which included local identity and wider civic solidarity, generational and class consciousness (working people), has been restructured: independent categories of local identity (Factor 4 in 2005) and low social position (Factor 6 in 2005) were formed. Generational belonging has shifted to the subcultural field of meaning (Factor 1 in 2005).

In the sub-sample of Russians in Estonia, a separate mental structure (Factor 2) was formed, joining low socio-economic self-positioning (poor people who have no luck in life), class (working people), and civic and generational identities. This shows that the Russians associated civic identity with low status—being a "loser." A model of the generations of "winners" and "losers" originally proposed by social researches[51] was in the beginning of the transition actively used by the mass media, where the critical message of researchers has often been transformed into simplified images: the Soviet Union collapsed and the young coped with it better than the older generations. In 2005, this pattern was restructured. Thus, the geopolitical opening of Estonia has created a new positive field of meaning to construct civic identity.

In general, in the period 2002–2005—including the year of Estonia's joining the EU—the mental patterns related to civic identity changed remarkably. Compared with 2002, the groups of regional and civic identity categories formed in 2005 have a clearer basis—instead of one large heterogeneous group of components a structure combining civil and trans-national categories and a structure describing local cohesion in both ethnic sub-samples can be distinguished. The local and global dimensions have begun to distinguish more clearly in the structure of identities. Estonia's geopolitical opening up has created a new positive field of meaning for both Russians and Estonians to construct civic identity.

Low and high social positioning as a basis for creating an identity each form an independent structure (Factor 5 and Factor 6 in 2005). This shows that low and high socio-economic positions in Estonian society have become independent bases for creating identity and are not related to other social structures in people's mental patterns.

In general, in 2002–2005 the mental patterns of self-identification of both the Estonians and the Russians became more similar to each other and we can talk about a certain "crystallization" in the post-communist transitional culture in Estonia.

Identity Structures in Estonia, Latvia and Sweden

To shed some light on the question as to how universal or unique the above-described self-identification patterns are, we can use analogous data collected in Latvia in 2006 and in Sweden (the southern part of Stockholm) in 2002–2003.

Table 3 presents the self-identification structures of ethnic Estonians, Russians in Estonia, ethnic Latvians, Russians in Latvia, Swedes, and other ethnicities living in Sweden.[52]

For the purpose of better understanding, the structures are presented schematically, without the numeric values of factor loads, and category labels are presented in a short, one-word form similar to the labelling system adopted in Table 2. In my commentaries I refer to the Latvian and Swedish results as background data for the more profound interpretation of the findings of the Estonian surveys, without discussing the peculiarities of those countries.

Factor 1 in all sub-samples joins all categories of *subcultural identity*. The "core" of the structure is formed from the categories "common taste," "memories," "interests" and "world-view." However, this structure has significant variations across different countries. The Latvian and Swedish structures are similar—in both cases the shared subculture also includes other factors of belonging determined by the existing social structures.

In the thinking patterns of the Swedish people, self-identification on the basis of social position and habitation is connected with perceived similarities in lifestyle (taste, memories) and opinions (interests, world-view). In the case of immigrants, sub-cultural belonging is also connected with national belonging.

In the sub-sample of the Latvians, subcultural belonging is related to social success in addition to civic identity. This means that similar to the thinking patterns of

TABLE 3 The structures of self-identification in the sub-samples of Estonians, Russians in Estonia, Latvians, Russians in Latvia, Swedes and other ethnicities in Sweden (results of factor analysis)

Ethnic Latvians N = 652	Russians in Latvia N = 262	Russians in Estonia N = 442	Ethnic Estonians N = 1,033	Swedes N = 1,002	Other ethnicities in Sweden N = 254
F1	F1	F1	F1	F1	F1
Taste	Memories	Taste	Taste	Interests	Taste
World-view	Interests	World-view	World-view	Taste	Memories
Interests	Taste	Interests	Interests	World-view	World-view
Memories	World-view	Memories	Memories	Memories	Generation
Citizenship	Generation		Generation	Generation	Town
Generation	Schoolmates[3]			Working people	Swedes
Successful[3,4]				Inh. of town	Citizenship
				Citizenship	
				Neighbours	
F2	F2	F2	F2	F2	F2
Relatives, kin	Europeans	Northern	Northern	Successful	All in Sweden
Family	Humankind	Humankind	Humankind	Unlucky	Europeans
Fiends	Baltic	All in Estonia	All in Estonia	Wealthy	Humankind
Workmates	Successful	Europeans	Europeans	Poor	Neighbours
Schoolmates	Wealthy	Citizenship	Citizenship		Schoolmates
		Generation			Workmates[3]
F3	F3	F3	F3	F3	F3
Latvians	Family	Family	Family	Europeans	Family

Humankind
Europeans
Baltic people
All in Latvia
Successful[1,4]
F4
Unlucky
Poor

Working people
Wealthy
Successful[1,3]
F5
Neighbours
Inh. of town/county

Relatives, kin
Fiends
Russians
Schoolmates[1]
Workmates[6]
F4
Neighbours
Citizenship

F5
All in Latvia
Inh. of town/county

F6
Unlucky
Poor
Working people
Workmates[3]

Friends
Relatives, kin
Schoolmates
Workmates
Russians
F4
Neighbours
Working people

Inh. of city/county

F5
Successful
Wealthy

F6
Unsuccessful
Poor

Friends
Schoolmates
Workmates
Relatives[4]
Estonians[0.247]
F4
Neighbours
Inh.of city/county
Relatives[3]

F5
Successful
Wealthy

F6
Unsuccessful
Poor
Working people

All in Sweden
Humankind
Northern people
Schoolmates
Swedes[4]
F4
Family
Relatives, kin

Friends

Workmates
Swedes[3]

Relatives
Friends
Workmates[2]
F4
Unlucky
Poor

F5
Successful
Wealthy

Working people

87

Russians in Estonia in 2002, on the one hand, subcultural self-identification is considered by Latvians as socially elitist and, on the other, subculture is also a basis of civil identity. Thus, the structural coherence of *social distinction* in Bourdieu's meaning of the term became more evident in the identity structures of the Latvians and the Swedish people.[53]

In the identification patterns of the Estonian people, social, spatial and mental solidarities are separated. It is characteristic of the thinking patterns of both ethnic groups in Estonia that belonging to a subculture is defined as something "abstract," accessible through individual choice and not much shaped by norms proceeding from the individual's positioning in the social structure. The interpretation of the (new) civic and territorial identities is somewhat "formal," outwardly defined, and not connected with the acknowledgement of shared ideas and cultural symbols (memory, worldview, interests). This can be partly explained by the somewhat earlier and radical shift in the political and economic spheres in the early 1990s and the perhaps more dominating Individualistic Ideology in the public sphere. The quite similar "emancipatory" thinking pattern seems to form among Russians in Latvia as well.

Network identity is also evident in all sub-samples, forming Factor 2 in the sub-sample of ethnic Latvians, Factor 3 in the sub-samples of ethnic Estonians, Russians in Estonia and Latvia, and other ethnicities in Sweden. In the sub-sample of Swedes it forms Factor 4.

It is common to Russians in both Latvia and Estonia that ethnic belonging is linked closely to personal networks of communication. The same identification patterns are expressed more weakly in the case of ethnic Estonians. As discussed above, because of the linguistic division of the ethnic majority and minorities both in Estonia and Latvia, the sense of group belonging is reproduced on a daily basis in mutual interaction between the majority and minority group members. Thus, among the Russians the close connection between ethnic belonging and personal communication networks is strong and probably adds a "tribal" connotation to the construction of the ethnic minority identity both in Estonia and Latvia.

The trans-national and civic identity pattern can be recognized also in all sub-samples, forming Factor 2 in the sub-samples of ethnic Estonians, Russians in Estonia and Latvia, and other ethnicities in Sweden, and Factor 3 in the sub-sample of ethnic Latvians and Swedes. However, this structure shows significant variations across different countries.

In Sweden, civic solidarity is structurally connected with trans-national solidarity. It is interesting that in Sweden this factor also comprises the category of "schoolmates." Among other ethnicities this factor also includes the category of "workmates." A long tradition of multicultural civic education programmes and increasing mobility in the sphere of education (some education is acquired abroad) and the labour market may have shaped this pattern of identification.

In the sub-sample of ethnic Latvians the trans-national identity has an elitist connotation (successful people) and also includes ethnic belonging. Thus, the ethno-national identity of Latvians is intertwined with supranational categories, and accession to the EU has created a basis for positive distinction as an ethnic group. Among the Russians in Latvia, the trans-national identity connotes social success and economic prosperity, but this does not create a basis for a new, positive civic identity. Unlike the identification pattern of Estonian Russians, civic identity categories are missing from the trans-national identity pattern of Latvian Russians. Russians in Latvia have shown quite a strong Euroscepticism.[54] As Zepa reports from a qualitative study, Russians in Latvia do not embrace a European identity, referring at first to the higher standard of living in Western Europe as opposed to Latvia, and second to the fact that democracy has not yet fully developed in Latvia. She quotes from a focus-group: "To me, a European is someone who is normal and rich ... well, not quite rich, but a normal person who makes a good living. There aren't many such people in Latvia. It's just in geographic terms that I say 'yes.'"[55] Although in Estonia, too, young Russians used similar arguments in a qualitative study, it seems that compared with Russians in Latvia they are more eager and ready for positive self-determination in trans-national and civic terms. The reason for such a difference may lie also in the Western versus Eastern (Russian) orientation. The Western orientation might be more desirable for Estonian Russians. The qualitative study revealed that although Latvian Russians are critical about the poor social and economic situation in Russia, they feel that they are connected with Russia through relatives and friends and also through Russian television. Russian television is watched extensively in Estonia too[56] but links with friends and family in Russia are somewhat weaker than in the case of Russians in Latvia.[57]

The local community identity pattern comes out in Estonia and Latvia (Factor 4 in the sub-samples of Russians in Estonia and ethnic Estonians, Factor 5 in the sub-sample of ethnic Latvians and Factor 4 and Factor 5 in the sub-sample of Russians in Latvia). While Russians in Estonia create a new civic identity in relation to the trans-national frame of reference, Russians in Latvia seem to construct the new civic identity on the basis of local community belonging. In Swedish sub-samples no independent structure of local community belonging was formed; local community belonging is combined with subcultural identity. It seems that "pure" local identity is specific to transitional societies—self-identification on the basis of lifestyle similarities (taste, memories) and opinions (interests, world-view) is not intertwined with social identities on the basis of habitation. As discussed above, this response pattern brings out a certain *social distinction*, in Bourdieu's sense, in the identification patterns of the people in Sweden.

The pattern of *high and low self-positioning* also comes out in different ways across all sub-samples. In the sub-samples of ethnic Estonians, Russians in Estonia and Latvia and among other ethnicities in Sweden, self-identification on the basis of supply and lack of economic and social resources is clearly divided into different structures of identification on the basis of high and low socio-economic position. Among Latvian Russians, high social position and material prosperity is linked with trans-national, Western orientation. It is interesting to compare the identification structure of ethnic Estonians and other ethnicities in Sweden. In neo-liberal Estonia, the category "working people" is placed in the structure of low socio-economic positioning (see Factor 6 of the sub-sample of ethnic Estonians) but in the thinking patterns of the minority group members living in social-democratic Sweden the category "working people" connotes wealth and social success. It might also be explained by the fact that unemployment is high among immigrants in Sweden. Unemployment rates in Estonia are low—the unemployment rate for people of working age is 2.3%.[58]

In the thinking patterns of ethnic Latvians and Swedes these categories are not mutually exclusive. The strong symbolism of social and material success seems to be a specific feature of Estonian transitional culture, which is common both to the majority and minority groups. However, in Latvia and Sweden the dichotomy in the way of thinking is characteristic of the ethnic minority groups. Such a mental structure was probably created by the strong political turbulence in Estonian society in the early 1990s. To a certain extent it shows that Estonian society is democratic—high or low social status is not embedded into the existing cultural, regional, political, generational, etc. hierarchies. On the other hand, the division of the members of society on the basis of material and social achievement represents a "modern" thinking pattern which forms a common post-traumatic "frame of reference" for the interpretation of post-communist transformation and EU integration.

Conclusions

In general, the thinking patterns shaping collective identities have crystallized during the second decade of post-communist transition in Estonian society. Different factors—joining the EU; fast economic growth, which legalizes the prevalence of individualistic-liberal ideology in the public sphere; a significant increase in the usage of the Internet and other communication technologies, which reinforces the spread of global mass and consumer culture—have shaped the formation of a specific transition culture in Estonia. In this cultural context the self-identification patterns of the ethnic minority and majority have homogenized. The structures of Estonians and Russians in Estonia are significantly more similar than the structures of Latvians and Russians in Latvia and those of the Swedes and other ethnicities of Sweden. Thus, we may say that the transitional culture that emerged in Estonia after the dissolution of the Soviet Union has had a homogenizing impact on the latent mental patterns of people, which has been more important than the differences arising from the different historical-political legacy of the two ethnic groups.

Although this study does not aim to map all possible frames of references for the creation of a collective identity, it highlights important thinking patterns that will probably shape the formation of collective identities and minority–majority relations in post-communist Estonia.

In both ethnic groups similar *subcultural identity* patterns and patterns of high and low self-positioning could be observed, which indicates that Estonian transition culture is shaped strongly by an individualistic-liberal, even opportunistic, way of thinking. In the existing social structures and hierarchies, people do not perceive any barriers or facilitators when choosing a desired lifestyle or subculture in order to achieve social success and material prosperity.

It signifies, on the one hand, the rise of emancipatory self-consciousness, extricated from the social norms and structures and, on the other, low potential for the acknowledgement of shared ideas and cultural symbols (memory, worldview, interests). In the individualization process that is taking place in post-communist Estonia the new forms of social solidarity envisaged by theoreticians of Western post-industrial societies—such as spontaneous political activism, ecological movements, self-organization, voluntary work and care for others—have rather a weak socio-cultural basis.

It is likely that the emancipatory pattern of thinking is also determining the further formation of geopolitical and ethno-cultural allegiances. It seems that there is a strong potential in Estonia for the creation of a new, common civic identity according to the trans-national and civic pattern. However, this pattern can also turn into pragmatic resistance of the minority group members in the majority-dominated nation-state. Research on language attitudes has shown that young Russians feel that the European space is extending to Estonia and they can benefit from it; for example, English is becoming a new form of capital, offering an alternative to the Estonian-directed acculturation.[59] Like the *subcultural identity* pattern, the transnational pattern is shaped by the international rather than by national agenda. On the other hand, the construction patterns of *ethno-cultural identity* are quite responsive to the patterns of inter-group communication—if interethnic communication becomes more active and mutual linguistic tolerance increases (e.g. accepting English as a third local language) in the course of generation replacement the ethnic identity of Estonian Russians may become more hybrid, more open to different cultures. If the current, rather separated, Estonian and Russian language communication spaces remain, the defensive minority identity construction pattern will probably dominate. As the pattern of ethnic identity construction inherited from the Soviet period seems to begin to change among ethnic Estonians, there are preconditions for the creation of a hybrid local ethno-cultural identity among Russians in Estonia.

In general, the findings of this study confirm the conclusions of other studies that were carried out using different methodologies: for political actors in both Estonia and Russia it is no longer possible to create a common umbrella identity for Russians in Estonia. The self-designation patterns of both Estonians and Estonian Russians have evolved during the transition period and are now divided into mental structures, choosing between different identifying narratives which circulate in the public space.

NOTES

1. The author wishes to acknowledge the fact that the research for this article was funded by the Estonian Science Foundation (ETF), project grant no. 5845.
2. See, for example, Melvin, *Russians beyond Russia*; Aasland, "Russians outside Russia"; Linz and Stepan, *Problems of Democratic Transition and Consolidation*; Laitin, *Identity in Formation*; Smith, "Russia, Estonia and Ethno-politics"; Kolstø, *Political Construction Sites*.
3. Sztompka, 2000; idem, "The Trauma of Social Change"; Vogt, *Between Utopia and Disillusionment*.
4. Linz and Stepan, *Problems of Democratic Transition and Consolidation*; Chinn and Kaiser, *Russians as the New Minority*; Aasland, "Russians outside Russia"; Melvin, *Russians beyond Russia*; Pilkington, *Migration, Displacement and Identity in Post-Soviet Russia*; Kolstø, 2000; idem, *Political Construction Sites*; Lebedeva, 1998; Brady, "Categorically Wrong?"; Poppe and Hagendoorn, "Types of Identification among Russians in the 'Near Abroad.'"
5. Goble, "Three Faces of Nationalism in the Former Soviet Union," 125.
6. See, for example, Melvin, *Russians beyond Russia*; Aasland, "Russians outside Russia"; Linz and Stepan, *Problems of Democratic Transition and Consolidation*; Laitin, *Identity in Formation*; Smith, "Russia, Estonia and Ethno-politics"; Kolstø, *Political Construction Sites*.
7. Vihalemm, "Formation of Collective Identity among the Russophone Population of Estonia"; idem, "Usage of Language as a Source of Societal Trust."
8. Laitin, *Identity in Formation*.
9. Vihalemm and Masso, "(Re)Construction of Collective Identities after the Dissolution of the Soviet Union."
10. Vihalemm, "Identity Formation in the Open Media Space."
11. E-monitoring, TNS Emor.
12. Slater, *Consumer Culture and Modernity*.
13. Keller and Vihalemm, "Coping with Consumer Culture."
14. Lauristin, "Eesti ühiskonna kihistumine."
15. Bauman, *The Individualized Society*; Beck and Beck-Gernsheim, *Individualization*; Castells, *The Information Age*; Appadurai, *Modernity at Large*; Lash and Friedman, *Modernity and Identity*.
16. Beck and Beck-Gernsheim, *Individualization*; Stehr, *Knowledge Societies*; Delanty, *Modernity and Postmodernity*; Touraine, *Can We Live Together?*
17. Examples of positive emancipation are the third sector and the development of Western civil society; the seamier sides are, for example, the concentration of wealth, violence, and so on.
18. Beck and Beck-Gernsheim, *Individualization*.
19. *Estonian Human Development Report*; Vihalemm and Masso, "The Nation-Building and Perspectives of Formation of Civic Identity in Post-Soviet Estonia."
20. See Siiner, "Planning Language Practice"; Kiisel, "Keskkonnateadvuse kujunemine Eestis 1980ndatest 2005ni"; Lagerspetz et al., "The Structure and Resources of NGOs in Estonia."
21. Sztompka, "The Trauma of Social Change," 176.
22. Vogt, *Between Utopia and Disillusionment*; Kennedy, *Cultural Formations of Post-Communism*.
23. Jenkins, *Social Identity*.
24. Ibid.; Jenkins, "Categorization."

25. Tajfel, *Human Groups and Social Categories*.
26. For Russian respondents, the list of identifying categories in 2005 included both versions: "the Russians" and "the Estonian Russians." As identification with these overlapped 90%, I added them up to make the results of factor analyses more comparable and created a new variable "own ethnic group."
27. Poppe and Hagendoorn, "Types of Identification among Russians in the 'Near abroad'"; Kolsto, *Political Construction Sites*.
28. Danilova and Yadov, "Social Identification in Post-Soviet Russia."
29. Bolin and Notini, "Character of Sample and Responses."
30. Kalmus and Vihalemm, "Distinct Mental Structures in Transitional Culture."
31. "Integration in Estonian Society 2000–2007" Programme.
32. See, for example, Karklins and Zepa, "Political Participation in Latvia 1987–2001."
33. Bolin and Notini, "Character of Sample and Responses."
34. Ibid., 26.
35. Vihalemm, "Changes in Identification Patterns of Estonian Youth."
36. Identity Research Network.
37. Ibid.
38. See also Feldman, "Shifting the Perspective on Identity Discourse in Estonia."
39. Identity Research Network.
40. Vihalemm, "Changes in Identification Patterns of Estonian Youth"; Kalmus, "Changes in the Value Consciousness of Estonian Youth."
41. Kalmus and Vihalemm, "Distinct Mental Structures in Transitional Culture."
42. Beck and Beck-Gernsheim, *Individualization*, 161–62.
43. P. Vihalemm, *Meediasüsteem ja meediakasutus Eestis 1965–2004*, 442.
44. Vihalemm, "Formation of Collective Identity among the Russophone Population of Estonia"; Vihalemm and Masso, "(Re)Construction of Collective Identities after the Dissolution of the Soviet Union."
45. Castells, *The Information Age*, 6–7.
46. Lauristin and Vihalemm, "Recent Historical Developments in Estonia."
47. Giles, *Language, Ethnicity and Intergroup Relations*.
48. In fact, it is the same strategy that the Baltic Germans used against the Estonians in the nineteenth century—the Baltic barons spoke broken Estonian in order not to let the lower classes speak broken German (see Plank, "The Assimilation and Non-Assimilation of European Linguistic Minorities").
49. Identity Research Network.
50. Vihalemm, "Formation of Collective Identity among the Russophone Population of Estonia."
51. See Tallo, "Erinevad generatsioonid üleminekuperioodi Eestis"; Titma, *Kolmekümneaastaste põlvkonna sotsiaalne portree*.
52. The Södertörn area in Stockholm, where the study was conducted, is special in having a large proportion of immigrants (Bolin and Notini, "Character of Sample and Responses").
53. See Kalmus and Vihalemm ("Distinct Mental Structures in Transitional Culture") for more detailed analysis.
54. Zepa, "The Changing Discourse of Minority Identities."
55. Ibid.
56. Vihalemm, "Identity Formation in the Open Media Space."
57. Masso, "The Personal Spatialities in Estonia and Sweden."
58. Statistical Office of Estonia.
59. Vihalemm, "Usage of Language as a Source of Societal Trust"; idem, "Changes in Identification Patterns of Estonian Youth."

REFERENCES

Aasland, Agne. "Russians outside Russia: The New Russian Diaspora." In *The Nationalities Question in the Post-Soviet States*, edited by Graham Smith. London and New York: Longman, 1996.

Appadurai, Arjun. *Modernity at Large*. Minneapolis: University of Minnesota Press, 1996.

Bauman, Zygmunt. *The Individualized Society*. Cambridge: Polity Press, 2001.

Beck, Ulrich, and Elizabeth Beck-Gernsheim. *Individualization*. London: Sage, 2002.

Bolin, Göran, and Agnes Notini. "Character of Sample and Responses." In *The Media Landscape of Södertörn 2002*, edited by G. Bolin. Huddinge: Department of Media and Communication, Södertörn University College, 2005.

Bourdieu, Pierre. *Distinction: A Social Critique of the Judgement of Taste*. Translated by R. Nice. Reprint. London: Routledge, 2000.

Brady, Henry. E. "Categorically Wrong? Nominal versus Graded Measures of Ethnic Identity." *Studies in Comparative International Development* no. 3 (2000): 1–36.

Castells, Manuel. *The Information Age: Economy, Society, and Culture. The Power of Identity*. Oxford: Blackwell, 1997.

Chinn, Jeff, and Robert Kaiser. *Russians as the New Minority: Ethnicity and Nationalism in the Soviet Successor States*. Boulder: Westview, 1996.

Danilova, Elena, and Vladimir Yadov. "Social Identification in Post-Soviet Russia: Empirical Evidence and Theoretical Explanation." *International Review of Sociology* no. 2 (1997): 319–35.

Delanty, Gerard. *Modernity and Postmodernity*. London: Sage, 2000.

E-Monitoring, TNS Emor, 2006, <http://www.emor.ee/eng/arhiiv.html?id=1553> (accessed 29 August 2006).

Estonian Human Development Report. Chap. 4: "Civil Society, Culture and Identity: Will Estonia Survive?" Tallinn: TPÜ RASI, 2001, <www.iiss.ee/nhdr/2001/en/4.1.html> (accessed 29 August 2006).

Feldman, Gregory. "Shifting the Perspective on Identity Discourse in Estonia." *Journal of Baltic Studies* 31, no. 4 (2000): 406–28.

Giles, Howard, ed. *Language, Ethnicity and Intergroup Relations*. London: Academic Press, 1978.

Goble, Paul. "Three Faces of Nationalism in the Former Soviet Union." In *Nationalism and Nationalities in the New Europe*, edited by C. A. Kupchan. Ithaca, NY: Cornell University Press, 1995.

Identity Research Network. "The Political Activity and Usage of Free Time among Youth in Tallinn. Results of a Qualitative Study Presented at the Meeting of Inter-Universities." Identity Research Network, Tallinn University, 2006.

"Integration in Estonian Society 2000–2007" Programme, <www.rahvastikuminister.ee/en/home/plans/integrationprogram.html> (accessed 13 June 2006).

Jakobson, Valeria. "Role of Estonian Russian-Language Media in Integration of Russian Minority into Estonian Society and Forming its Collective Identities." Ph.D. diss., University of Tampere, 2002. *Acta Universitatis Tamperensis 858*.

Jenkins, Richard. *Social Identity*. London: Routledge, 1996.

Jenkins, Richard. "Categorization: Identity, Social Process and Epistemology". *Current Sociology* 48 (2000): 7–25.

Kalmus, Veronika. "Changes in the Value Consciousness of Estonian Youth: An Attempt of Meso-Level Analysis of Transitional Culture." Paper presented at the 5th International Conference "Young People at the Crossroads," Petrozavodsk, Russia, 2006.

94

Kalmus, Veronika, and Triin Vihalemm. "Distinct Mental Structures in Transitional Culture: An Empirical Analysis of Values and Identities in Estonia." *Journal of Baltic Studies* 36, no. 1 (2006): 94–123.

Karklins, Rasma, and Brigita Zepa. "Political Participation in Latvia 1987–2001." *Journal of Baltic Studies* 32, no. 4 (2001): 334–46.

Keller, Margit, and Triin Vihalemm. "Coping with Consumer Culture: Elderly Urban Consumers in Post-Soviet Estonia." *Trames* 9, no. 1 (2005): 69–91.

Kennedy, Michael. *Cultural Formations of Post-Communism: Emancipation, Transition, Nation, and War*. Minneapolis and London: University of Minnesota Press, 2002.

Kiisel, Maie. "Keskkonnateadvuse kujunemine Eestis 1980ndatest 2005ni" [Formation of Environmental Consciousness in Estonia from the End of the 1980s to 2005]. MA diss., University of Tartu, 2005, <www.jrnl.ut.ee/maie/akadeemiline/magistritoo.pdf> (accessed 29 August 2006).

Kolstø, Pål. *Political Construction Sites: Nation Building in Russia and the Post-Soviet States*. Boulder: Westview, 2000.

Kosmarskaya, Natalya. "Russkiye Diaspory: polititcheskiye mifologii i realii massovogo soznaniya – Russian Diasporas: political mythology and realities of mass consciousness," Diasporas - *Diaspori* 4, no. 2 (2002): 110–154.

Lagerspetz, Mikko, Erle Rikmann, and Rein Ruutsoo. "The Structure and Resources of NGOs in Estonia." *Voluntas: International Journal of Voluntary and Nonprofit Organizations* 13, no. 1 (2002): 73–87.

Laitin, David, D. *Identity in Formation: The Russian-Speaking Populations in the Near Abroad*. Ithaca, NY: Cornell University Press, 1998.

Laitin, David, D. "Three Models of Integration and the Estonian/Russian Reality." *Journal of Baltic Studies* 34, no. 2 (2003): 197–222.

Lash, Scott, and Jonathan Friedman. *Modernity and Identity*. Oxford and Cambridge, MA: Blackwell, 1992.

Lauristin, Marju. "Eesti ühiskonna kihistumine" [Stratification of Estonian Society]. In *Eesti elavik 21. sajandi algul: uurimuse "Mina. Maailm. Meedia" aruanne* [Estonian Life-World in the Beginning of the 21st Century: Report of the "Me. The World. The Media" Survey], edited by V. Kalmus, M. Lauristin, and P. Pruulmann-Vengerfeldt. Tartu: Tartu University Press, 2004.

Lauristin, Marju, and Peeter Vihalemm. "Recent Historical Developments in Estonia: Three Stages of Transition (1987–1997)." In *Return to the Western World*, edited by M. Lauristin, P. Vihalemm, K.-E. Rosengren, and L. Weibull. Tartu: Tartu University Press, 1997.

Lebedeva, Natalia. "Russkijye v stranah blizhnego zarubezha." *Vestnik RAN* no. 4 (1998): 296–305.

Linz, Juan, L., and Alfred Stepan. *Problems of Democratic Transition and Consolidation: Southern Europe, South America, and Post-Communist Europe*. Baltimore and London: Johns Hopkins University Press, 1996.

Masso, Anu. "The Personal Spatialities in Estonia and Sweden." *Journal of Baltic Studies*, forthcoming.

Melvin, Neil. *Russians beyond Russia: The Politics of National Identity*. London: Royal Institute of International Affairs, 1995.

Pilkington, Hilary. *Migration, Displacement and Identity in Post-Soviet Russia*. London and New York: Routledge, 1998.

Plank, Pieter Van der. "The Assimilation and Non-assimilation of European Linguistic Minorities." In *Advances in the Study of Societal Multilingualism*, edited by J. A. Fishmann. The Hague: Mouton, 1978.

95

Poppe, Edwin, and Louk Hagendoorn. "Types of Identification among Russians in the 'Near Abroad.'" *Europe-Asia Studies* 53, no. 1 (2001): 57–71.

Siiner, Maarja. "Planning Language Practice: A Sociolinguistic Analysis of Language Policy in Post-Communist Estonia." *Language Policy* 5, no. 2 (2006): 161–86.

Slater, Don. *Consumer Culture and Modernity*. London: Routledge, 1997.

Smith, David. "Russia, Estonia and Ethno-politics." *Journal of Baltic Studies* 29, no. 1 (1998): 3–18.

Statistical Office of Estonia. "Employment is the Largest in the Last Twelve Years," 2006, <http://www.stat.ee/179860> (accessed 23 August 2006).

Stehr, Nico. *Knowledge Societies*. London: Sage, 1992.

Sztompka, Piotr. "Cultural Trauma. The Other Face of Social Change." *European Journal of Social Theory* 3, no. 4 (2000): 449–466.

Sztompka, Piotr. "The Trauma of Social Change: A Case of Postcommunist Societies." In *Cultural Trauma and Collective Identity*, edited by Jeffrey Alexander, Ron Eyerman, Bernhard Giesen, Neil J. Smelser, and Piotr Sztompka. Berkeley: University of California Press, 2004.

Tajfel, Henry. *Human Groups and Social Categories*. Cambridge: Cambridge University Press, 1981.

Tallo, Annika. "Erinevad generatsioonid üleminekuperioodi Eestis" [Different Generations in Transitional Estonia]. In *Estonian Human Development Report*, 1998, <www.undp.ee/nhdr98/et/1.2.html> (accessed 23 August 2006).

Titma, Mikk. *Kolmekümneaastaste põlvkonna sotsiaalne portree* [Social Portrait of the Generation of 30-Year-Olds]. Tallinn: Academy of Sciences Press, 1999.

Touraine, Alain. *Can We Live Together? Equality and Difference*. Cambridge: Polity Press, 2000.

Vihalemm, Peeter. *Meediasüsteem ja meediakasutus Eestis 1965–2004* [The Media System and Media Usage in Estonia 1965–2004]. Tartu: Tartu University Press, 2004.

Vihalemm, Triin. "Formation of Collective Identity among the Russophone Population of Estonia." In *Dissertationes de mediis et communicationibus Universitattis Tartuensis*. Tartu: Tartu University Press, 1999.

Vihalemm, Triin. "Usage of Language as a Source of Societal Trust." In *The Challenge of the Russian Minority*, edited by M. Lauristin and M. Heidmets. Tartu: Tartu University Press, 2002a.

Vihalemm, Triin. "Identity Formation in the Open Media Space." In *The Challenge of the Russian Minority*, edited by M. Lauristin and M. Heidmets. Tartu: Tartu University Press, 2002b.

Vihalemm, Triin. "Changes in Identification Patterns of Estonian Youth: Attempt of Meso-Level Analysis of Transitional Culture." Paper presented at the 5th International Conference "Young People at the Crossroads," Petrozavodsk, Russia, 2006.

Vihalemm, Triin, and Anu Masso. "The Nation-Building and Perspectives of Formation of Civic Identity in Post-Soviet Estonia." In *A Collection of Papers on the History and Today's Situation of the Russian-Speaking Population in Estonia and Latvia*, edited by N. Hashimoto, K. Obata, S. Mizobata, and H. Komori. Hiroshima: Proceedings of Hiroshima University, 2005.

Vihalemm, Triin, and Anu Masso. "(Re)Construction of Collective Identities after the Dissolution of the Soviet Union: The Case of Estonia." *Nationalities Papers* 35, no. 1 (2007): 71–91.

Vogt, Henri. *Between Utopia and Disillusionment: A Narrative of the Political Transformation in Eastern Europe*. New York and Oxford: Berghahn Books, 2005.

Zepa, Brigita. "The Changing Discourse of Minority Identities: Latvia," 2006, <http://www.biss.soc.lv/?category=publikacijas&lang=en> (accessed 23 August 2006).

Europeanization and Euroscepticism: Experiences from Poland and the Czech Republic

Søren Riishøj

On National and European Identity

National identity was already the object of scholarly studies by the 1950s and 1960s, e.g. by analysts such as Karl Deutsch and Ernest Hass, to a great extent inspired by the start of European integration and German and French reconciliation. One of the crucial questions has been (and still is) to what extent national identity constitutes a barrier to Europeanization and integration, and to what extent overlapping multiple identities can co-exist.

After some years of post-communism "Euro-optimism" was dampened and neo-realism and rational choice took over. Sometimes identity was used as an explanation "of the last resort"[1] and as "a negative residual category,"[2] included when rational explanations had to retreat. Europeanization was studied in rationalist ways taking as the point of departure the transfer of EU laws and rules (*"acquis communautaire"*) into national laws and administrative practice. Later, in the 1980s and 1990s, with the wars in the Balkans, the end of the Cold War and transition to unipolarity, more emphasis was placed on national identity using social constructivist approaches.[3] As stated by Benedict Anderson,[4] a nation (and "Europe") has to be "imagined" in order to be a reality. The Central East European Countries (CEECs') "return to Europe" and prospects of EU membership soon became additional factors. Distinctions like "we-ness" versus "otherness," "them space" versus "we space" and "inclusion" versus "exclusion" became normal practice. In particular, *interpretation* of history and historic events tends to separate national identity from other types of collective identity as each nation follows its own "myths" and "narratives," folklore, geography, language and national symbols. Thus, in a social constructivist perspective, the term national identity may be defined as "a set of self-perceptions, shared memories and experiences (history), traditions, and the geographical and cultural predisposition of a nation"[5] and in Lesaar's formulation as "people's sense of being equal with each other or of belonging to a community";[6] and finally, according to Kiss, as "a synthesis of values, sentiments of attachments, and social representations that are associated with cognitive factors structuring the identification process."[7]

In a rational institutional perspective, studies of *Europeanization* have paid attention to the extent of the changes in each member country in the case of implementation of EU decisions and to what extent the prevailing structures (and norms and rules) have come under pressure by developments at the European level. Changes may take place before ("anticipatory adaptation") as well as after membership in the EU. Neo-functionalists see those changes of behaviour as "inevitable" and "automatic," reinforced by "spillover effects" and the "upgrading of common interests." When speaking about Europeanization, historical institutionalists like to talk about the significance of former decisions and institutional practices and a path "dependence." Liberal institutionalists such as Andrew Moravcik emphasize the "negotiation games" and the shaping of national preferences, inspired by game theories. In that perspective Europeanization involves mutual adaptation of national and subnational governance systems to one European centre and the common European norms and rules, as "An incremental process re-orientating the direction and shape of politics to the degree that EC political and economic dynamics become part of the organizational logic of national politics and policy making,"[8] and when including both institutional aspects and identity as "processes of (a) construction (b) diffusion and (c) institutionalization of formal and informal rules, procedures, policy paradigms. Styles, 'ways of doing things' are shared beliefs and norms which are first defined and consolidated in the making of EU decisions and then incorporated in the logic of domestic discourse, identities, political structures and public policies."[9]

Thus, most observers agree that "Europe" and Europeanization make a difference, that they "do matter" and have become an integral part of domestic politics, i.e. have been "domesticated."[10] Today, institutional and political processes, earlier discussed at a national state level (e.g. political parties and local politics), are studied mostly in a European and perhaps even global perspective. To a still greater extent European institutions and EU rules are taken for granted more than previously, thus making an impact on national players and inevitably raising questions concerning the future of the national states. Nonetheless, it may be difficult to make clear to what extent institutional and organizational changes take place through Europeanization, or whether explanations can be found elsewhere, just as it can be difficult precisely to measure the exact impact from Europeanization. Sometimes national institutions are so robust and deep-rooted in society that they survive in spite of Europeanization and globalization. Great countries like France have even strived to shape international institutions according to their national model[11] and sometimes successfully.

For the *new* EU member countries it might be difficult to separate the changes and the convergence towards a market economy and democracy caused by internal and external factors, respectively. As regards the external factors, it may be difficult to determine to what extent institutional changes result from demands from the EU or, alternatively, from other institutions such as the IMF and the World Bank. After all, most observers share the opinion that the foundation of the EU rests more on *formal* institutionalization than on common attitudes and identities. Thus, Europeanization has been signified by "overinstitutionalization" and weaknesses on the "support side," i.e. concerning the socio-cultural foundation and normative integration.[12] The common identity that makes institutions *legitimate* tends to lag behind *formal* institutional crafting.

Adaptation to EU rules and norms in the new EU member countries will also be examined in the context of the previous years of triple transitions. After the breakthrough in 1988–1989 the CEECs passed from one-party systems and planned economies to market economies and democracy, and national identities had to be changed; some, such as the Baltic States, were "reborn" after decades under Soviet rule. Besides the triple transitions, a "fourth" transition had to be included, namely the unexpectedly complex and long-term adaptation to EU norms and rules (the *acquis*).

For the citizens in the CEECs concepts like "Europe" and "return to Europe" had different meanings. The vision of the future Europe was mostly vague, as most resources were absorbed by accession negotiations. For many the notion of Europeanization was connected with a return to the "normal order" after 40 years under communism, with high expectations for modernization and catching up with Western Europe. The experience with state socialism and the high costs of transition gave rise to an almost "anti-utopian spirit" with a built-in mistrust of almost all long-term idealistic plans for the future and a preference for the "secure" and already tested.[13] Opinion polls show that many East Europeans see themselves both as "nationals" and "Europeans." Less than 40% declare themselves primarily "nationals," e.g. being a Hungarian or a Pole before being a European (see Figure 1). In the liberal variant, "Europe" has been connected to individualism, liberalism, the rule of law, constitutionalism, a free market economy, openness and secularization.

The new EU countries had their own specific "model countries." Some admired certain West European countries or systems, others the US, and some did not separate Europe and the US, expressing themselves in "Euro-Atlantic" ways. To speed up all-European values and identities, Europe needs its own positive narratives and myths; unfortunately on that point we face many problems. Often, identities are multiple, multilayered and cross-cutting and only rarely clear-cut and mutually consistent. After the Cold War and the demise of state socialism it is no longer sufficient to have a common enemy (an "otherness").

Many small states, and states which for decades have been under foreign rule and overlay, experience the so-called "integration dilemma,": either the state gives up a substantial part of its sovereignty with the danger of being "entrapped" in the integration system i.e. being so constrained that it loses its freedom of action, or the state insists on its independence with the danger of being "abandoned", i.e. not included in the integration process with the disadvantages which might ensue (p. 154).[14] National and European identities may be in harmony, but at times they can also be in conflict.

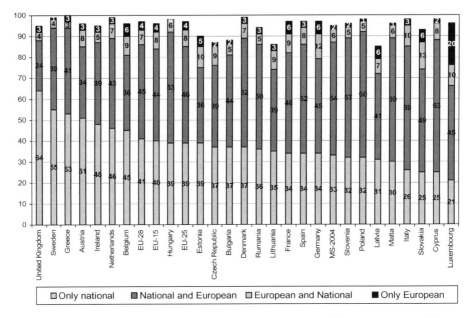

FIGURE 1 The various identities in Poland (distribution in percentages). *Source*: Eurobarometer EB59-CC-EB, 2003:2, "Comparative Highlights," July 2003

Despite many barriers, in official declarations there has been much talk about the formation of a common European identity, not least as a means for strengthening cooperation in the security and foreign policy field, which has been predominantly intergovernmental. The question is, however, whether a common European identity can be realized at all, and to what extent the greater diversity and new medieval and imperial characteristics after the enlargement may blur the differences between the EU "insiders" and "outsiders," and eliminate all dreams and plans about establishing a common European "superstate" signified by closed frontiers and high cultural homogeneity.[15]

Euroscepticism

The absence of strong European institutions and a common European identity and a high resistance, or rather apathy, to the EU at the referenda in the CEECs on EU treaties has increased the interest in "Euroscepticism" and enhanced efforts to limit the democratic deficit in the EU system by introducing a new treaty constitution and a new vision for the EU, "*la finalité*." However, evidence seems to suggest that common European attitudes that should back up the Europeanization process do no exist and, if they do, then only in embryonic forms. The issue of EU accession has played a modest role in national election campaigns and appears to have had no significant impact on party choice of the electorate. Euroscepticism also tends to manifest itself differently in the "new" and the "old" Europe and in small and large states. According to a worst-case scenario, after EU accession the new EU members from the East become the "others" for the "old" Europe, i.e. the "EU-15."

The years immediately following the "breakthrough" in 1989 were marked by considerable "Euro-enthusiasm" or "uninformed enthusiasm," and the then widespread Euro-optimism was not backed up by much concrete experience and knowledge about the EU system. Among the political parties the question of future EU membership became a "valens issue," i.e. an issue about which a high degree of consensus was predominant, at least as far as the goal (EU membership) was concerned. Disagreements concerned different ways to reach the common goal. Unfortunately, Euro-enthusiasm was accompanied by a too modest debate about the EU and European affairs in the public domain, and thus the unanimity in EU questions tended to be signified by "consensus without discussion."[16] Nonetheless, the debates on "la finalité" of Europe in the CEECs reflected the status of countries that had recently regained their sovereignty. For that reason, before long the issue of national versus European identity, i.e. the integration dilemma, became a "hot issue."

As EU membership came closer and became a realistic option, EU enthusiasm waned. Inevitably the costs of future EU membership became an important subject for discussion. After the opening of negotiations the populations and the political leaders gained a more realistic picture concerning what "the EU really is about." Thus, coming closer to "paradise" many changed their attitudes from being "Euro-naives" to become "Euro-realists," perhaps soft or hard "Eurosceptics."

Even before membership in the EU became a reality in May 2004, disagreement arose on some crucial questions, e.g. about the war in Iraq and the new treaty constitution for the EU. On the horizon difficult negotiations about the future budget of the EU were lurking which could re-activate the Eurosceptic attitudes. The war in Iraq divided the "new" and the "old" Europe, but the disagreements also centred on the question of the future shape of the European project. As Henrik Richard Lesaar puts it,[17] it turned out to be easier to expand the Union than to overcome the old division of Europe. The lack of confidence between the "new" and "old" Europe inevitably reinforced Atlanticism in the many new EU member states, especially in Poland and the Baltic States, thereby undermining popular support for European integration in those countries.

As argued above, in most cases "Euroscepticism," as well as "Europeanization," has been vaguely defined. In working papers and discussion papers published in connection with the "Opposing Europe" cross-country research project started in 2000 under the auspices of the University of Sussex, Aleks Szczerbiak and Paul Taggart strove to overcome that problem by better defining the most relevant concepts and putting forward more robust classifications of Euroscepticism. Nevertheless, we are still facing the danger of conceptual stretching, e.g. by including almost all EU-critical proclamations and articulation of normal interest under the notion "scepticism."

Here I want to take just one example: should Poland's defence of the decisions taken at the 2000 Nice EU summit and Poland's support of Britain's and the US' policy in Iraq be regarded as "normal defence of national interests," also found in the EU-15, or should we consider Polish intergovernmentalism and Atlanticism as soft or even hard Euroscepticism, i.e. as reservations in relation to the EU and the European project in general?

Aleks Szczerbiak and Paul Taggart[18] argue that Euroscepticism "expresses the idea of contingent or qualified opposition, as well as incorporating outright and unqualified opposition to the process of European integration." The separation of "hard" from "soft" is crucial, but also difficult to put into practice empirically. Szczerbiak and Taggart[19] strove to find a more sustainable conceptualization, arguing that hard Euroscepticism implies "outright rejection of the entire project of European and economic integration and opposition to their country joining or remaining members of the EU." i.e. a principled opposition to the project of European integration as embodied in the EU.[20] By contrast, soft Euroscepticism involves contingent or qualified opposition to EU integration.[21] In other words, soft Euroscepticism has been expressed in the shape of a "Yes, but ..."

Classifications of Euroscepticism

Different classifications have been put forward:

- *Identity*-based Euroscepticism is closely linked to the above-mentioned integration dilemma involving a contradiction between national identity and European identity and including a fear of being "absorbed" by a supranational institution like the EU, thereby loosing national sovereignty.
- *Cleavage*-based Euroscepticism is linked to the main divisions in society, e.g. town–country, work–capital, religion–secularism, etc. People living in the country tend to be more Eurosceptic. Socio-economic cleavages include the distinction between transformation "winners" and transformation "losers."
- *Policy*-based scepticism, or "functional Euro-realism," is based on some resistance against concrete policies and single issues, e.g. the CAP, the common currency, the euro and/or demands from the EU for transition periods for the movement of labour. In some cases we are dealing with "single-issue scepticism," i.e. sceptical attitudes to the EU on one main issue, e.g. agriculture, the buying of land, the environment, moral questions, etc.
- *Institutionally* based scepticism is based on the legitimacy of national versus EU institutions. Low confidence in national institutions may increase support for EU institutions and for the EU as a whole.
- *National interest*-based scepticism includes a contradiction between common European goals and national goals, e.g. in the case of negotiations about the EU "*la finalité*." In case of national interest-based Euroscepticism, the main goal is

to defend vital national interests in spite of a weakening of the common European project.

- *Experience*-based scepticism is the feeling that the negotiations concerning membership of the EU have been unfair and asymmetric, and the final result of the negotiations, for that reason, has been imposed.
- *Party*-based Euroscepticism is formed in a top-down manner from political parties and charismatic political leaders using neo-liberal ("Thatcherite"), anti-modern traditionalist or left-populist argumentation.
- *Atlantic*-based scepticism is the feeling of a contradiction or dilemma between pro-Americanism and pro-Europeanism, e.g. in the case of the establishment of a common European foreign and security policy.
- And, finally, there is what I call a *practice*-based Euroscepticism. Here we find no principled resistance to the EU and Europeanization, but Europeanism is defined in a "national" way and different from that of Brussels and demanded by the EU according to the "mainstream" interpretation of the Copenhagen criteria. Few resources have been directed towards implementing the EU *"acquis communautaire"* and speeding up market economic and social reforms. This type of Euroscepticism was exhibited by "reluctant democracies" such as Slovakia under Meciar and Ukraine under Kuchma.[22]

Political Parties and Euroscepticism

Studies of Euroscepticism have often focused on the attitudes and strategies of political parties. Politics just after 1989 was signified by weak parties and "non-party systems." Many new politicians tended to be "moral politicians" and politics was marked by identity politics. Most political parties were established almost overnight and without any close links to the most important groups in society. Anti-politics and the fight against the old system were still striking. The numerous broad anti-communist movement parties, e.g. the popular fronts in the Baltic States, Solidarity in Poland and the Civic Forum in the Czech Republic all referred to patriotism, national values and anti-communism.

Under these circumstances "future-directed" policies played a minor role. The slogan "Back to Europe" became an integrated part of the new anti-communist discourse. Thus, in most countries the first free elections were won by using primarily anti-communist symbolic slogans, as the first free elections mostly were referenda for or against the old systems and not elections between parties. Later, national elections became more retrospective and politics in general more "ordinary" and interest based.

After a while voters tended to place more emphasis on good governance and the ability to communicate when making their party choices at elections. As stated above, concurrently with the transition to more "ordinary" politics, elections

103

became more retrospective and less symbolic and abstract. The most "Euro-enthusiastic" seemed to be the reformed communists. Gradually Euro-realism, Euro-apathy and even Euroscepticism became more striking. Thus, throughout Europe, and especially in Eastern Europe, the elections to the European Parliament in June 2004 failed to arouse any enthusiasm or passion.

Roughly speaking, three types of party-based Euroscepticism emerged, namely neo-liberal, traditionalistic conservative and left populist (see Figure 2). As will be seen in the following, ODS in the Czech Republic has expressed soft Euroscepticism and even Euro-realism, the League of Polish Families (LPR) conservative traditionalism, and the Czech Communist Party (KSCM) has been Eurosceptic in the more left popular variant. To a large extent the upcoming party-based Euroscepticism was policy- and experience based and, moving closer to EU accession, also became more national interest based.

In other words, the attitudes to the EU gradually became more practice- and policy related and less symbolic and abstract. Under the negotiations concerning the EU's new constitution, the small EU countries emphasized keeping their own EU commissioner and giving the Commission more power at the expense of the Council of Ministers, which is seen by the small countries as the large countries' "battlefield." In the accession countries themselves, policy questions related to the EU never became decisive at national elections. Thus, social frustrations made an impact mostly on national elections and domestic politics, and thus rarely were reflected in the popular attitudes to the EU as such.

Also in the EU-15 countries, EU questions played no crucial role at national elections, as seen in the cases of Great Britain and the countries of Scandinavia. As noted above, in the new member countries EU questions became "valens issues," in which all relevant parties agree on the common goal, i.e. EU membership. In most cases, discussions and disagreements concerned the extent to which the governments had done their "homework," e.g. sufficiently defended national interests in negotiations with the EU. Only a few parties declared themselves hard Eurosceptics,

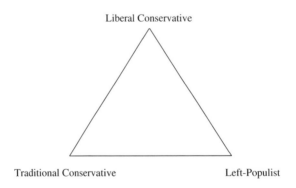

FIGURE 2 The three party-based dimensions of Euroscepticism.

i.e. against membership of the EU as such. More problematic was the lack of interest and apathy concerning the EU. Thus, in the referenda on membership, the political elite feared the non-voters more than the no-votes.

Szczerbiak and Taggart[23] have taken as their point of departure some working hypotheses that they want to test without knowing the final conclusions, as there have been no scientifically verified answers. The most important include the following:

- that a party's position on the left–right scale is not decisive when determining whether or not a party should be considered Eurosceptic;
- that the party's place in the party system plays a crucial role. Normally outsider parties express hard or soft Euroscepticism;
- that Euroscepticism at the party level does not necessarily follow the extent of Euroscepticism in the population; in other words, Euroscepticism can be expressed differently at the elite and the popular level;
- that Euroscepticism tends to be strongest in states that are close to gaining EU membership;
- that hard Euroscepticism is less widespread than soft;
- that resistance to the EU among parties is strongest in states that are new nation-states;
- that variations in the form and strength of Euroscepticism work differently from country to country.

Some of the classifications and working hypotheses mentioned above will be included in the following sections.

"Outsider" parties have been defined differently, and among these parties resistance against the EU has not been decisive, as outsider parties do not necessarily constitute "protest parties." In the case of "protest parties," such as "Smer" in Slovakia, "Respublica" in Estonia, and "New Era" in Latvia, we are dealing with protest parties for the most part criticizing the bad governance of the parties in government, but these parties are relevant in that they feel able to take over government responsi-bilities, maybe constituting national interest-based Euro-realists, but nonetheless supporting future EU membership. The Hungarian extreme right-wing party MIEP, however, has followed a clearly "hard" Eurosceptic line, but its strong Euroscepticism has been only one of several forms of xenophobia that have characterized the party's policy. More important for MIEP than the EU have been questions connected to the Hungarian minorities in the neighbouring states, in particular Slovakia and Romania.

The Slovak party "Slovak Movement for a Democratic Slovakia" (HZDS) is one of the parties that in their official statements speak about Europeanization, but in their behaviour express "anti-Europeanism" for internal political reasons, e.g. in questions about the rights of minorities. Thus, the Euroscepticism of HZDS tends to be "practice related." In the programme declarations and election manifestos of the party there has been much talk about a unified Europe, which guarantees freedom, peace and security, promotes economic growth and social justice and, at the same time, guarantees the invulnerability of existing frontiers and territorial status quo. Thus, the picture of Europe is "coloured" because of national values and national interests. HZDS can hardly be placed on a left–right scale of the type visible in West European countries, despite the fact that here also the right–left divide has become blurred. The Christian-Democratic KDH has used the more common argumentation about national sovereignty and defence of moral issues, e.g. in the case of debates about the proposed new EU constitutional treaty agreed upon at the EU summit in June 2004.

In Slovakia, Euroscepticism did not increase the closer membership in the EU became. The main problem has been a general lack of public debate and widespread apathy towards the EU. Not even in the case of protest parties such as "Smer" have EU questions played a crucial role. The polarization of the political scene has been caused mostly by the many conflicts and a general lack of loyalty and coherence among the political elites and by the use of social and economic issues for mainly political purposes. In other words, the hypothesis that right–left does not have any real impact on the policy choices and strategies of political parties in relation to the EU can be confirmed in the case of Slovakia.

Also in the case of the Hungarian party FIDESZ it has been no easy task to separate "Euro-realism" from "soft" Euroscepticism. FIDESZ was the ruling party between 1998 and 2002 and constitutes the strongest opposition party in the Hungarian parliament today. Before the 2002 election, and later in opposition to the socialist-liberal government after the 2002 election, FIDESZ leader Viktor Orban repeatedly put forward views that some observers considered "Eurosceptic."

Before the Hungarian referendum on EU membership, he declared that Hungary in principle could remain outside the EU. That declaration was strongly criticized by both socialists and liberals. After the 2002 election Orban repeatedly became a spokesman for a Europe of nation-states, defending intergovernmentalism and raising the question of whether the EU needed a new treaty. He also raised the questions of the Benes decrees and, when in government, proposed the controversial "status laws" involving special rights in Hungary for the Hungarian diaspora. As in the case of HZDS in Slovakia, with FIDESZ we can also observe practice-related Euroscepticism determined by the domestic political agenda, thereby neglecting or even contradicting "Europe-ness." When speaking in West European countries, Viktor Orban behaved more like a standard "good European."

The more refined delimitation of the concept "Europeanization" decides to what extent acts and declarations should be interpreted as interest-based Euroscepticism, or only as a normal defence of national interests and as a part of the "political game" without any great impact. The limit is unclear, but not impossible to draw. Real reservations against the EU as a project have not been striking in the case of FIDESZ. Somewhat soft Eurosceptic declarations have been part of the electoral game. In the case of FIDESZ, we are in reality really dealing with a normal defence of national interests. In Hungary, EU questions have in general been valens issues, for, if we disregard MIEP, the questions have not been related to EU member-ship as such, only the handling of EU questions by the government, i.e. its ability to negotiate successfully with the EU and defend national interests. The soft Euroscepti-cism that has been seen has emanated mostly from right-wing parties (MIEP and FIDESZ). Thus, unlike Slovakia, Euroscepticism can be said to follow a right–left divide.

National Identity, Europeanization and Euroscepticism in the Region as a Whole

Party-based Euroscepticism is closely linked to the dominant attitudes and discourses in society as a whole and is clearly connected to the ideological uses of history. Successive generations have been moulded to see the past in certain ways. To a large extent the relationship between Germany and France has been linked to mem-ories of wars between the two countries. In the new EU member countries from the East, the "We versus Them" dimension has been closely connected to the communist and pre-communist past, the Soviet Union and neighbouring states, and, in the case of Hungary, especially to Slovakia and Romania (see Figure 3). The Serbs proudly spoke about their resistance to the Turks when defending their policies in Kosovo, the Romanians talked about their Dacian past and Latin alphabet. The Bulgarian Revival in the nineteenth century (until 1878) and the uprising in 1876 present a source of coveted symbolic capital for the building of Bulgarian self-identity and the anchoring of the collective "we."[24] For most Slovenians the Yugoslav past, not Europe, constitutes the negative "Other." During Slovenia's negotiations with the EU, some problems arose concerning its relations with Italy, which for a time blocked negotiations between the EU and the applicant countries from the East. The problems were due to the unresolved restitution questions connected to the questions about the buying of land by foreigners in Slovenia. In the conflict between Slovenia and Italy, the EU Commission became the mediator.

In countries such as Slovakia and the Baltic States national identity was formed by the circumstances leading to independence and the need to fill the discursive vacuum caused by the collapse of the old state socialist systems. The integration dilemma has not played any crucial role in the case of Slovakia, but rather a fear of being kept

"We versus Them":	the official system versus opposition, low consensus in society
"I":	short-term individual strategies are dominant
"Ourselves":	identities are formed within social groups, collective feelings predominant
"I–We":	one's own identity confronted with group identity
"I myself–the others":	"national egoistic" short-term thinking

FIGURE 3 Post-communist identities

"outside" the European integration process as a whole. Territorial integrity and inviolability of frontiers have gained a high priority because of widespread fear of Hungarian revisionism. In practice these issues are more important than EU-related subjects, but these subjects can hardly be integrated into a common European identity. As regards attitudes to European problems, differences between political elites and civil societies have not been important. The main problem has been a high level of apathy and a low level of interest in EU-related subjects. The hypothesis that newly independent states are characterized by a relatively high Euroscepticism cannot be confirmed in the case of Slovakia. Slovakia became independent in 1993, but persistently strove to catch up with the other applicant states after having been "frozen out" of Europe under Meciar's rule.

Some post-communist states have based their new post-communist identity on memories and myths going back to pre-communist times. Patriotic feelings, the defence of the rights of Hungarian diasporas, and respect for national symbols have all been regarded as important for calling oneself a "true Hungarian."[25] Hungary, it has been argued, has always been part of the West and a bulwark against penetrating "outsiders"—e.g. the Turks—and only for a short time was it forcibly separated from the West. However, for Hungary it has not been easy to accept the present territorial frontiers, decided at the Trianon peace conference just after World War I. Thus, former Prime Minister Jozef Antall frankly declared that he saw himself as the spiritual leader of all Hungarians, i.e. also of those Hungarians living abroad. Some observers saw entering the EU as a solution to the "Trianon problem" due to the breaking down of existing territorial and mental frontiers and the free movement of people.

More on National Identity, Europeanization and Euroscepticism in Poland

Poland is the largest and most complicated due to its specific "activism" in foreign and security policy, of the new EU member countries. In many ways Poland is similar to some of the old EU countries, in that the Poles are considered to be stubborn like the Spaniards, arrogant like the French and Eurosceptic like the British. Also for the Poles, the old bulwark thesis, referring to the argument that in the history of Europe, the Poles several times defended Christianity against penetration by outsiders, especially from the East, has played a crucial role, not least at a symbolic level. This perception has forged a spiritual community and aroused a feeling of belonging, clearly manifested during the negotiations on the new EU constitutional treaty by the Polish demand for the inclusion of Christian values in the preamble of the new treaty constitution.

Poland is different from the other new EU member countries not only in size but also in its attitude to Europe and Europeanization in general, and not least in the *way* to negotiate. Instinctively most Poles tended to behave like intergovernmentalists—i.e. favouring state-to-state cooperation, like Gaullists in France, and British Conservatives—serving as spokesmen for interstate cooperation and a Europe of homelands without federal structures and including a certain amount of Atlanticism and close bonds to the US. Thus, Polish soft Euroscepticism has to a large extent been Atlantic based.

Since 1980 national identity has been influenced by the Solidarity movement or the Solidarity myth. From the outset Solidarity constituted not only a trade union in the normal sense but also more a patriotic movement fighting for the liberation of Poland from communist rule. After 1989 Solidarity took over governmental responsibilities and became the ruling party, thereby deciding the speed and form of transition. Ideologically Solidarity repeatedly spoke in favour of returning to Europe; however, several times the national appeals and the economic and social policy of the movement deviated from the demands from Brussels. Unlike the case of the Slovak Movement for a Democratic Slovakia (HZDS), Solidarity never came under heavy fire from the EU, maybe because of political "self-limitation" and pragmatism and, not to forget, the fact that Solidarity was regarded as the leading force in the fight for the liberation of Poland from communism.

From the outset, the formulation about a solidary EU (i.e. money from the EU) and an intergovernmentalist and transatlantic-oriented EU with a continuous American military presence in Europe had a strong appeal in Poland. After a time most politicians and negotiators gained a more realistic picture of what the EU really is about, and that one condition of electoral success is to give the voters at least the impression that vital Polish interests are strongly defended.

Support for EU membership had a clear *institutional* aspect. For many voters strong European institutions might compensate for low support for domestic political institutions, e.g. national parliament and political parties. As shown in Figure 4, a great majority of the Poles support EU institutions much more strongly than national institutions. Only the presidential institution obtained high popular support. As regards support for national versus EU institutions, the Polish population is closer to "Italianization" than "Scandinavianization," for in Italy also a low level of support for national institutions has been "compensated" by higher support for European institutions. For many East European citizens common European institutions are considered better able to secure a "catching up" in welfare and modernization than national institutions. To a large extent Polish Euroscepticism seems to have been identity based (to a smaller extent institutional), connected as it is to the integration dilemma and with an almost "instinctive" support for intergovernmental principles. Polish Euroscepticism has also to some extent been policy based and been the result of popular demands for better safeguarding of national interests in negotiations with the EU in relation to EU accession. Cleavage-based Euroscepticism has mostly been expressed by the relatively strong resistance of the rural population to EU membership.

Before the EU referendum there was fear that the question about EU membership would develop into a referendum for or against the transformation of Poland itself, in which case the transformation losers would transfer their social frustrations to

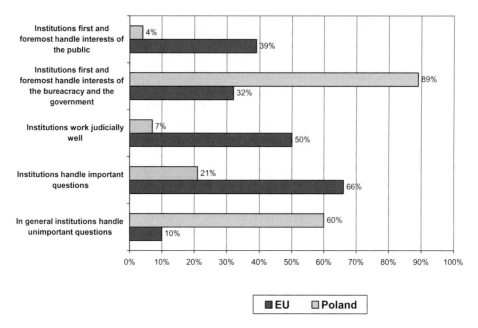

FIGURE 4 Degree of trust and distrust in national and EU institutions in Poland. *Source*: the Polish newspaper *Gazeta Wyborcza*, 4 August 2003, in cooperation with the opinion polling institute CBOS

the EU, thereby setting up barriers for Polish EU membership. However, in the end EU membership was supported by a large majority of those going to the ballot boxes. Even among Polish farmers, there was a majority for EU membership, but not a great one. Opinion polls, conducted since the Copenhagen summit in December 2002, have not changed that, though the majority of Poles also share the opinion that Poland is not sufficiently prepared for membership of the EU.

As we know, Poland caused some trouble during the Copenhagen summit, and, one year later, during the EU summit in Rome, Poland together with Spain vetoed the proposal about a new treaty constitution and new voting principles, which on Germany's instigation would have changed the voting rules in the Council of Ministers decided upon in Nice, thus adhering to the famous "Nice or die" slogan formulated by Jan Rokita and the Civic Platform (PO) in the Polish parliament.

The topic of Poland and the new Europe has been eagerly discussed, but mostly among intellectuals. Bronislaw Gemerek, former foreign minister and member of the think tank on Europe, established by former prime minister of Belgium Guy Verhofstadt to prepare the EU Convention, argued that after 40 years of state socialism, EU membership had simply become a "must" for Poland. However, many Poles still have the feeling that the EU-15 do not want Poland as a member, which means that some of the EU apathy and scepticism tend to be experience based. In other words, the "old Europe" must show more understanding for the situation in the future EU member countries. Gemerek also referred to the negative experiences resulting from the accession negotiations, and said:

> I don't think that one can exclude from politics the social psychology as a factor. It wouldn't be good to accept candidate countries after, I would say a depressive process of negotiation which will leave the public of these countries feeling humiliated ... Continuing passivity within the European Union, the passivity of its citizens towards European politics would have a disastrous effect.[26]

In the parliament elected in 2001 the Eurosceptic parties gained quite strong parliamentary representation. Thus, the then new Catholic Eurosceptic party, the League of Polish Families (LPR), and populist agrarian movement "Self-Defence" (Samoobrona) led by Andrzej Lepper, came out with strong Eurosceptic statements and such criticism has not abated after the election. Self-Defence has put forward an extreme policy-based Euroscepticism, while the League's criticism has been stronger and much more identity based. Thus, in the case of Poland, Euroscepticism has been expressed mostly by the "outsider parties." As already mentioned, the resistance to the EU on the part of LPR has been strong and identity based, with Self-Defence supporting Polish EU membership in principle, but not accepting the conditions imposed by the EU-15.

Also, the third among the new parties, the Right and Justice Party (PiS), supports membership of the EU in principle, at the same time arguing against the EU Convention's proposal of a new Union treaty, demanding a referendum on the new treaty and speaking strongly in favour of a "Europe of nation states." First, the party recommended a "no" vote in the EU referendum, but changed its position to a "yes" shortly before the referendum. At the 2004 election to the European Parliament, PiS obtained 16.42% of the votes and 10 seats in parliament. The liberal Civic Platform (PO) tends to behave more "European," but has spoken in favour of better defence of Polish national interest and launched the famous slogan "Nice or dead" when debating the new EU constitutional treaty proposal. At the 2004 election to the European Parliament, PO came out as the largest party, obtaining 23.48% of the votes and 15 seats.

The Peasants Party (PSL) has been split on the question of EU membership and especially on the conditions of membership. The scepticism that has been shown has been mostly in relation to the question of the sale of land to foreigners and financial support to Polish farmers from the EU. At the 2004 election to the European Parliament, PSL obtained 6.88% of the votes and four seats. In other words, the Euroscepticism has been soft and policy related. Inside the then ruling parties, the SLD and the Labour Union (UP), no distinct hard and soft Eurosceptic factions have been found, but because of the government's weak position in parliament and according to the opinion polls, the two parties were exposed to "blackmailing" from the more Eurosceptic parties such as PO, PiS and "Self-Defence" (Samoobrona). However, Euroscepticism has been more striking among social democratic voters than among the party leaders. The weak position of the left was confirmed at the election to the European Parliament in June 2004, where SLD-UP obtained only 9.11% of the votes and five seats in the European Parliament. The new social democratic "defector party," Poland's Social Democratic Party (SDPL), obtained 5.07% of the votes and three seats. Participation in the Polish election was modest: only 20%.

At the end of the negotiations the blackmailing potential and the strength of opposition became stronger. The different attitudes of the political elite and demands for the strong defence of Polish national interests were reflected in the population as a whole. In other words, the political parties aimed to bring their EU policies in line with the attitudes of the electorate and the most important social groups. As already noted, most people shared the opinion that the government should better defend vital Polish national interests and that Poland was not sufficiently prepared for membership. Furthermore, the many "trade wars" between Poland and the EU and the criticism from the EU of insufficient progress in relation to the implementation of the *acquis communautaire* in Poland inevitably reinforced Eurosceptic attitudes among the population. The extent of Euroscepticism has been fluctuating over time and even increased in 1999, but decreased towards the end of accession negotiations.

Since the end of the 1990s Catholic Church leaders have supported Polish EU membership, thereby aiming to eradicate the impression held by many believers that ethical values and Polish patriotism that emphasizes national suffering and the bulwark thesis cannot be upheld in the event of EU membership. Thus, before the EU referendum the Church encouraged the Polish population to say "yes" to EU membership. However, the leadership of the Church had to fight against strong anti-Semitic and anti-German feelings based on the strong national democratic tradition ("*Endecja*"), including fundamentalist and xenophobic messages, in most cases originating from the "bottom" within the Catholic Church and brought to people from, for example, the fundamentalist "Radio Mariya."

As we know, Poland's behaviour during accession negotiations and negotiations on the constitutional treaty has been the object of much domestic and internal debate. Some reactions have been sharp as well as confrontational, but the conclusions have normally been inconclusive. From Germany and France there was talk about enhanced cooperation among the "old" EU countries, while the British reactions have been more accommodating. Also the comments in the European press have varied. The German *Süddeutsche Zeitung* did not hide its frustrations and declared openly that Poland's insistence on keeping the voting rules decided in Nice showed that the Polish government does not understand that the principle about leaving some sovereignty to the EU is the secret behind the success of the EU and the European project as a whole, and subsequently warned that the end result might be the establishment of a "core Europe" with Germany and France as the core. Others, such as *Frankfurter Allgemeine*, criticized Poland's behaviour more moderately and declared that the breakdown in Rome showed us that an EU with 25 countries and more will simply make a further deepening of integration impossible. And the

French *Liberation* argued that the French–German motor had lost its original strength, and that Euroscepticism seems to be growing stronger.[27]

In Poland itself only few questioned the government's "tough" negotiating line. Most important was to "keep the flag high." In the general foreign policy debate in the Polish parliament in January 2004, Foreign Minister Wlodzimierz Cimoszewicz declared that Poland "today stands stronger than ever before." The most crucial tasks, he argued, had been to enhance national sovereignty, normalize the relationship to neighbouring countries, enhance regional cooperation and promote security and social welfare by entering NATO and the EU. These goals, he said, had all been achieved.[28]

For geostrategic reasons it has been important for Poland to impact the EU's new neighbourhood policy and bring an EU membership perspective to Ukraine, thereby avoiding being the EU's new "frontline state" in the East. These national interest-based policies do not necessarily correspond to the prevailing priorities in the EU Commission and among the EU-15 countries, where national sovereignty and further EU expansion to the East are not especially high on the political agenda.

Only the two populist parties in the Polish parliament, Self-Defence (Samoobrona) and the League of Polish Families (LPR), criticized the outlines put forward by the government, demanding an even harder line in the negotiations with the EU. LPR requested legal proceeding against the then prime minister, Marek Belka, because of the Polish government's support for the compromise on the European constitutional treaty at the EU summit in Ireland in the summer of 2004. Also, the Peasants Party (PSL) and the party chairman, Janusz Wojciechowski, rejected the compromise, calling the government's foreign policy "weak" and out of touch with the mood in the parliament and the population, but did not support the demand for legal proceedings against the prime minister.

The national interest-based policy line was basically supported by the two "responsible" opposition parties, Civic Platform (PO) and the Rights and Justice Party (PiS). There is nothing to suggest that the negotiation tactics will become "softer" under a centre-right government. PO and PiS support Polish EU membership, but have demanded a hard line in the negotiations on a new EU constitutional treaty and have spoken in favour of Polish foreign policy activism and stricter defence of national interests, yet without being placed in the group of hard and soft Eurosceptic parties. The "hard" negotiating line with the EU was supported not only by the two opposition parties (PO and PiS) but also by intellectuals such as Adam Michnik, chief editor of *Gazeta Wyborcza*, Poland's largest daily newspaper, who has directed his attention mainly to the alleged "arrogance" of France towards Poland, and in general has been pro-British and pro-Atlantic.

The two main opposition parties, the Civic Platform (PO) and the Right and Justice Party (PiS), have underlined the hard line also in the case of the appointment of Danuta Hübner, Minister of European Affairs in Leszek Miller's government, as the first Polish EU commissioner, arguing that Hübner had been too "soft" in negotiations

113

with the EU system, serving more the interests of France and Germany than those of Poland. Some argue that when former EU President Romano Prodi talked about the need for more women in the EU Commission, he was thinking about Danuta Hübner.[29] The alternative was to appoint a "hardliner" like Jacek Saryusz-Wolski, member of the Civic Platform (PO).

Atlantic-based Euroscepticism has been striking. The participation in the war in Iraq, the choice of US F-16 fighters in the "arms deal of the century" and the veto at the EU summit in Rome fostered considerable self-confidence inside the foreign policy establishment. As mentioned above, on the one hand it cannot be called Eurosceptic, but on the other it does not promote European integration and the formation of a separate European foreign policy profile. France and Germany's sympathy for Russia's demands concerning the status of Kaliningrad after EU enlargement raised indignation in Warsaw and Vilnius and gave an impetus for more policy-based Euroscepticism. Neither did the agreement between the EU Commission and Russia in April 2004 go down well in Poland and the Baltic States. In examining Polish policy towards the EU, one must take into consideration the deterioration of relations between Poland and the US, resulting from the terms of equipment sales to the new Iraqi army and the US refusal to liberalize its visa policy towards Poland, despite Poland's status as a "friendly" country that participated in the occupation of Iraq. Furthermore, Poland has called for more financial support and better equipment for the Polish military forces. In addition, the loss of several Polish citizens' lives in Iraq has not heightened support for staying in Iraq. More parties have now openly requested Poland's withdrawal from the country.

A move to improve its relationship with the more war-sceptical "old Europe," primarily Germany and France, may take place. Thus, in the coming years Poland may move some way towards the "old Europe," but close relations with the US and the continued US military presence in Europe will remain important for Poland as a guarantee for hard security, better opportunities for influence in Ukraine and as a limitation on French and German (and Russian) domination of the European scene.

The above-mentioned Polish foreign policy activism has activated the so-called "integration dilemma"—on the one hand a fear of being "excluded," on the other a fear of being "absorbed." Repeatedly the fear has been expressed not only of French–German dominance in Europe but maybe also an even greater fear of a Berlin-based triangle, an "intergovernmental directoire" consisting of the three largest EU countries—France, Germany and Poland's ally in the Iraq war, Great Britain—which might include security and foreign policy questions and undermine Poland's close relations with Britain, as well as the British "understanding" of Polish requests concerning the future shape of the European project.[30] The passing of a resolution in the Sejm in September 2004 demanding more economic compensation from Germany because of the German occupation in World War II once again underlined the cooling of German–Polish relations shortly after Poland's accession to the EU and NATO.

At a conference at the presidential palace in February 2004 there was discussion of how Poland may avoid the integration dilemma and the "deadlock" in its relations with the EU. New elements to the debate were not brought to light, but former Prime Minister Tadeusz Mazowiecki spoke in favour of a "defence of Nice," but not to "die for Nice" as proclaimed by Jan Rokita and PO, as close cooperation was crucial for Poland. There was a risk of being isolated and marginalized. Therefore a new political slogan was proclaimed: "For a strong Poland in a strong EU."

In general, the official "semi-sceptical" and activist line has been criticized, e.g. in the open letter from October 2003 subscribed to by 2000 citizens, mainly intellectuals supporting the Convention draft of a new constitutional treaty. Open criticism of the official Polish position has also been put forward by two former foreign ministers, Andrzej Olechowski and Dariusz Rosati (now MEPs), expressing a fear of Polish isolation and marginalization in the EU and expressing resistance against the fragile alliance with Spain on the constitutional draft, arguing in favour of stronger Polish support for the Weimar Triangle and for cooperation with the Visegrad group. The keywords of Polish EU policy should have been dialogue and compromise. EU membership has been considered an act of justice, a moral issue and compensation for 40 years of suffering under communist rule.[31] In contrast, the EU does not raise moral issues and regards the communist past as something that will not be repeated—and nothing else. Before the European Parliament election in June 2004, Bronislaw Gemerek, former foreign minister (like Dariusz Rosati elected to the European Parliament in 2004), argued that future Polish Euro deputies should spare no effort in averting the threat of a multi-speed Europe, for "A two-speed Europe would mean that new members of the EU, Poland among them, will stay in a room watching through the windows of what is happening in this European Union, in the centre of European integration, this best speed of the EU."[32]

Mateusz Stachura pointed out the contradiction between, on the one hand, refusing to offer the large countries in the EU better voting rights and, on the other, demanding more money from the larger EU member states, pointing out a contradiction between the aim of a more "solidaric" EU spending more money on poor countries and working against further deepening of integration.[33] Poland appears, perhaps not intentionally, like a cool, calculating "money thinking" and Eurosceptic country. It will be a major task to change that picture of Poland within the EU-15.

According to Marek Ostrowski, the "Nice or die" slogan and the negative comments on the constitutional draft have not set in motion any constructive debate about the future of Europe, but rather brought old stereotypes, historic wounds and national phobias to the surface. The consequence, argues Slawomir Sierakowski, chief editor of *Krytyka Polityczna*, may be a further marginalization of Poland, and the appearance of a multi-speed Europe led by France, Germany and maybe Great Britain.[34] As noted above, the Polish government may accept those arguments, at least to some extent.

President Alexander Kwasniewski attempted to achieve a balance between Euroscepticism, a national interest-based foreign policy and the inevitable national

115

self-limitation in relationship to the EU's largest countries. Commenting on the breakdown of the Rome EU summit in December 2003, he openly and honestly declared that Poland kept to the Nice agreement primarily because of a fear of dominance by the strongest EU members (i.e. Germany, France and Great Britain). Germany, he continued, aimed to change the decisions from Nice because in the longer run it may not be able to count on support from Great Britain, Poland and maybe even France. In short, *distrust* seems to constitute the main problem for Europe.[35] Europe, Kwasniewski continued, not only fears competition from the US but also fears *itself*. After the change of government in Spain in March 2004, Poland lost its most important ally in the issue of the war in Iraq and the negotiations on the constitutional treaty. However, the change of government in Spain paved the way for the compromise at the EU summit in Ireland in June 2004. After the 2005 national election and the PiS take over of government the policy line became more "hard national" or "soft eurosceptical" with great emphasis on defence of national interest, use of the veto-power, underlining the EU neighbourhood policy (ENP), energy policy and the principle of EU solidarity.

Euroscepticism in the Czech Republic

After 1989, after 40 years of communism, the Czechs quickly changed their attitudes to democracy, religion and history, and almost all topics could be questioned and were constantly changing. Until then, self-criticism had been rare, and it has not been moral victories and heroic uprisings but rather the ability to *survive* the 300 years under Habsburg rule, six years of Nazi occupation and 43 years under Stalinism and post-Stalinism that has left its marks on national identity. Many Czechs feel that national identity has been "given" from outside, forced upon them by foreign great powers. Thus, the claim that Euroscepticism is greatest in new nation-building states cannot be confirmed in the case of the Czech Republic, for the Czech Republic is not a country "without history" like Slovakia. Neither could the hypothesis be confirmed that Euroscepticism would grow as membership of the EU drew closer, at least not to the full extent. Almost all participants in the Czech "Future of Europe debate" agreed on the fact that there was practically no alternative to the country's entry to the EU.

Compared to the debates in other candidate countries, the Czech debate seemed a more intense one and involved all key players in the political arena. As in the case of Poland, the resistance to EU membership was the greatest in the late 1990s and decreased during the membership negotiations and up to the EU referendum in the summer of 2003. Evidence from opinion polls shows us that Czechs are not "Eurosceptics," even though many Czechs still had certain fears in relation to the EU a year after the country became a member. When STEM asked citizens to define their stand on the EU, only a quarter said they were "Euro-optimists," 54.5% said they were "Eurorealists" and 20.5% said they were "Eurosceptics." However, according to STEM, less than 20% of the voters would participate in a referendum on the EU constitutional treaty if it was held in spring 2005.[36] There has been much talk of Czech "littleness" and the "small Czech man" ("*malý ceský clovek*"), both described movingly in the history of the Good Soldier Svejk. In addition, and more problematically, many find an inclination to cooperate silently or openly with occupation powers, to prefer the easiest solutions to complex problems, believe in "nothing," move to internal exile, and act in opportunistic ways when seeking the easiest and best ways in relation to social and national survival. These negative characteristics seem to be more striking than heroism, national uprisings and active resistance, such as has been the case in Poland and Hungary and has enhanced national pride in those two countries. In a more positive way, Czech intellectuals regard their country as democratic, civilized and cultural, situated at the crossroads between East and West Europe, and belonging to the West as the "normal order." The deviation from that order has been explained as the "un-normal," as the "negative otherness."

Unlike the Czechs, the Slovaks have been seen as a people "without a history" and historic consciousness. There have been references to the Moravian kingdom in the ninth century and the missionaries St. Cyril and St. Metodius, the introduction of Christianity and national awakening in the nineteenth century, but these references are few. Thus, for the Slovaks we are dealing mostly with "going to Europe," not "returning to Europe" as in the case of the Czech Republic, which can refer proudly to the great Bohemian kingdom in the Middle Ages and the democracy under Tomas G. Masaryk in the mid-war years. For 1,000 years the Slovaks were under strict Magyar rule and perhaps for that reason they do not have the same heroes and no great uprisings such as those of Poland and Hungary.

Soon after the "velvet revolution" in 1989, the Czech Republic experienced a dramatic stage in the steady search for a new political identity and the best possible construction of the federation.[37] Furthermore, the Czechs and the Slovaks interpreted the "breakthrough" in 1989 and the velvet revolution differently, as in the case of the Prague Spring and the "normalization" years. Intellectuals, in particular, supported the quickest possible "return to Europe," transition to a free-market economy and the establishment of a new functional Czech–Slovak federation in accordance with civic principles.

These aims, and especially the positive attitudes to a free-market economy, were not shared by very many Slovaks, who supported a more confederative construction and, in addition, did not share the Czechs' "enthusiasm" for a free-market economy. After the division of Czechoslovakia, the Czechs moved closer to the West. Not only did the Czech Republic not share common borders with the former Soviet Union but also the direct geographical link to the Danube area was gone. Thus, also literally, the Czech Republic became part of Western Europe, to which it, according to the official discourse, has always belonged.

Anti-communism was explained differently by the two "strong men" in Czech politics, former president Václav Havel and former ODS party leader and president of the country since 2002, Václav Klaus. In addition, their model countries were different.

117

Havel gave high marks to the Scandinavian social-liberal welfare model, while Klaus was more "Anglo-Saxon" and neo-liberal minded and therefore critical of the "Scandinavian model," which he had come to know as a visiting professor at Aarhus University in Denmark in the late 1980s.[38] Also, questions about the federation and the future of Europe and the way "back to Europe" were given different meanings.

In short, three different "tracks" in Czech foreign policy can be observed:

- the *pan-European*, characterized by an undivided Europe without military pacts and with the Organization for Security and Co-operation in Europe (OSCE) as a pivotal point;
- the *federal*, characterized by belief in a strong EU with functional institutions and backed up by a common European identity;
- the *liberal Eurosceptic* (and Euro-realist), characterized by an EU with an internal market and "nothing else."

Kaj-Olaf Lang points out a "national realpolitik" focusing on protecting Czech national interests and keeping national independence, much in line with the above-mentioned liberal Eurosceptic track. The second line he calls the "value-based moral policy line," referring to the "non-political politics" and the visions for Europe presented by former president Václav Havel. This line is close to the "federal" one. And, finally, he outlines a "European activist line," based on flexibility, pragmatism and constructive cooperation and engagement when constructing the "new Europe."

At the beginning Havel spoke about a pan-European system without military pacts and about a confederal Europe with OSCE as the pivotal point inspired by former President Tomas G. Masaryk's ideas about a Europe with "unity in differences." Like then Foreign Minister Jiri Dienstbier, he flirted with a utopian vision of dismantling all existing European institutions and replacing them with a loose confederal structure.[39] A revitalization of the old plans for a Polish–Czech confederation was also raised. Havel became an energetic spokesman for "Euro-optimism" and "transatlanticism," speaking in favour of a federal type of construction for Europe on the same lines as the German Foreign Minister Joschka Fisher calling for a second chamber of the European Parliament whose members would not be elected by direct ballot, but rather by the parliaments of the member states from among their ranks. Havel spoke in favour of Czech membership in NATO and the reinforcement of transatlantic connections. As regards the wars against Serbia and Iraq, he argued along US and British lines.

At the end of the 1990s Havel expressed his concern that the Czech Republic might be left out in the competition to be an EU member in the first EU enlargement to the East. Therefore he opposed the pacifism as well as Euroscepticism that were gaining strength as a result of the air strikes against Serbia and the negotiations with the EU Commission on EU membership, which were expressed not only by communists (KSCM) but also by the Civic Democratic Party (ODS). Criticism was not absent in speeches made by the president himself. Several times Havel addressed questions relating to a common European identity. Thus, in a speech in the European Parliament in 1994, he said that for many Europeans the EU looks like a bureaucratic institution with mainly economic goals. Only few see the Union as a community of *values*. Therefore, he continued, "That is why to me the perhaps most important task facing the European Union today is coming up with a new and genuinely clear reflection on what might be called European identity ..." and about the Maastricht treaty "simply reading the Maastricht Treaty, despite its historical importance, will hardly win enthusiasm for the European Union. Nor will it win patriots ..."[40]

According to Václav Havel, the Maastricht Treaty seemed to be too "technical" and thus unpopular. Therefore, he spoke in favour of adopting a charter for the Union that would emphasize common European ideas and values and be a lever in encouraging popular support. In other words, the common European institutions and the technocracy should, to a greater extent than hitherto, adhere to democratic, moral and ethical values, thereby also lowering the democratic deficit. Furthermore, Havel warned repeatedly against a new division of Europe after the first enlargement to the East. There needed to be *one* Europe despite the inevitable greater diversity.

In the Czech Republic the visions for Europe put forward by the former president had some impact on the debate on the future of Europe and the role to be played by the Czech Republic despite the limited power of the president as set by the constitutional rules. The Czech *finalité* debate tended either towards *federal* settlements or in the direction of *intergovernmentalism*, while former President Václav Havel's supranationalist views seemed to show some *post-Westphalian* characteristics. As we shall see, federalist concepts have been those to which ruling social democrats and parties of the former Quad-Coalition (4K) have subscribed. The Civic Democratic Party has been the strongest proponent of intergovernmental cooperation and, according to ODS, it is in the internal market that national groups and enterprises have to compete.

The Czech negotiating line with the EU has not been signified by the same activism as that in Poland. In general, European policy and attitudes to closer cooperation among the Visegrad countries have varied over time. The nation-state line has dominated under the rule of Václav Klaus, while "flexibility" and "dynamism" have been key words under the social democrat-led governments. The social democrat-led government was not enthusiastic about the draft for a new constitutional treaty put forward by the European convention and, for that reason, called for a meeting in Prague of smaller EU countries with the aim of strengthening the position of small countries in the "endgame" of the negotiations. During the EU summit in Rome in December 2003, the Czech Republic accepted the proposal for a new distribution of votes in the Council of Ministers; although not deploring the breakdown in Rome, the Czechs argued that the decisions had been taken too quickly, without the necessary consultations. The statements from the government side, however, were not clearcut. Some were "Eurosceptic" and some expressed the well-known fear expressed by the smaller EU countries of a multi-speed or core Europe consisting of the "old" EU countries, primarily Germany, France and the Benelux.

As noted above, *party-based* Euroscepticism has until now mostly been connected with the communist party (KSCM) and to some extent the liberal Civic Democratic Party (ODS) and the former chairman and present president Václav Klaus. The xenophobic populist Republican Party (RS-RSC) of Miroslav Sladek lost parliamentary representation at the 1998 election. The Czech Social Democratic Party (CSSD) did not gain seats in parliament at the first free election in 1990 and only a modest representation at the 1992 election. However, from the mid-1990s the situation changed, and at the 1998 election CSSD became the largest single party. From the outset, CSSD spoke about Europe in almost enthusiastic ways. Thus, the chairman, Milos Zeman, declared that the future lies in federalism, but Europe, he argued, must be "strong, flexible and diversified."[41] The EU has to be more than just a market. It is in need of a common foreign and security policy and a common social and economic policy, including a common tax system. Furthermore, Europe needs an active industrial policy, a social dimension, and increased cooperation in relation to foreign and security policy. And during his hearing in the European Parliament the nominated Czech Euro commissioner, former CSSD premier Vladimir Spidla, claimed that the European social model will be part of Europe's competitive advantage and that it is possible to create an effective balance between employment, the economy and the social sphere, or between solidarity and productivity.[42]

Foreign minister until the 2002 election, Jan Kavan quoted former president Tomas G. Masaryk's formulation, that Europe will become a "big union of great and small nations," claiming that peace in Europe will rest on close cooperation between former enemies like Great Britain, France, Italy and Germany. Europe will be cooperative and "solidaric" based on respect for national identities and a stronger role for the European Commission as initiator and engine for EU integration. Kavan became a proponent of the community method with retention of intergovernmental decision making at some levels and in some areas.[43] Later, in spring 2005, he became a spokesman for leaving the "soft" pro-US foreign policy line, e.g. on the war in Iraq, instead joining the French–German line.

Parts of the policy of the then social democratic government did not correspond with the "spirit" of the EU's demands for free competition and a functional internal market, such as the revitalization programme giving support to debt-ridden state enterprises, as well as statements from Prime Minister Milos Zeman about the Benes decrees, the expulsion of Czechoslovakia's then 2.5 million-strong ethnic German population, and relations with Germany and Austria being regarded as "Eurosceptic." In 1999, the EU progress report was critical of the Czech Republic for its slow and insufficient implementation of EU laws and rules (the *acquis communautaire*), thereby fostering more Euroscepticism.

From the outset, the Communist Party (KSCM) followed an almost hard Eurosceptic line, but gradually that line became more "blurred" and even "softer." At the same time the resistance to Czech membership was sharpened as a result of the NATO bombing of Serbia in 1999 and the war in Iraq from 2003. The proposals adopted at the 1999 party congress revealed the dilemma. On the one hand the form of EU integration was rejected, on the other it was argued that the Czech Republic should maximize its influence in the EU. Miroslav Ransdorf even spoke about a future "socialist Europe," a vision that was rejected by the majority of delegates. In general, party members seemed to be more Eurosceptic than the party leaders. The criticism was directed mostly against the EU in its *present shape*, that is overly dominated by Germany and too liberal and bourgeois. In principle the party was not against EU integration, and there was also talk about further democratization of the EU's institutions and more power to the European Parliament. Due to its past, KSCM remained an "outsider party," but no longer distinctly anti-European, thereby moving closer to the Slovak sister party (KSS), which behaved more "pro-European," but at the same time was strongly against Slovak membership in NATO. Prior to the 2003 EU referendum, KSCM declared that it would respect the decision of the voters, knowing that the likely result would be a "yes" and about a quarter of KSCM voters would vote in favour of Czech membership of the Union.

Thus, after the Czech referendum a qualitatively new situation emerged. On the one hand, KSCM insisted that the Czech Republic was not sufficiently prepared for EU membership and that the Czech government had yielded too much to the demands from Brussels. On the other hand, the party would intensify endeavours to reform the EU from "within." In addition, a more accommodating line might contribute to breaking the political isolation. Yet persistent resistance to EU membership might be tempting, as resistance against the EU might increase in the first "hard years" after membership. In the first years the Czech Republic might even be a net contributor to the EU budget. In other words, the EU strategy contained tactical and strategic dimensions. Miroslav Ransdorf, known for his "soft" EU line, became the EU frontrunner and head of the party campaign in the European Parliament election in June 2004 and argued in favour of establishing a common European Left Party.

As already noted, much focus has been directed towards the policy of the main liberal party, the Civic Democratic Party (ODS), the "Eurosceptic" political entrepreneur and party chairman until late 2002 and the present president, Václav Klaus. The statements from the party were relatively EU positive in the first years, as the slogan about the "return to Europe" was quite persuasive. The main argument was that the Czech Republic was the "frontrunner" among the Central European countries, referring to the fact that the Czech Republic was the first full member of the OECD.

For that reason ODS was sceptical about closer cooperation among the Visegrad countries, especially with the more "foot-dragging" ones. At the same time the belief in an almost crisis-free transition from plan to market gained strength and was one of the reasons for the more Euro-critical, high-profile "Thatcherite" line in the second half of the 1990s. According to Klaus, the EU's desire for supranationalism, manifested in the new treaties, indicated "left-collectivism," exaggerated

121

bureaucratization and a false belief in a future for the social democratic welfare state. ODS also opposed the development of a European defence capacity as unnecessary, impractical and undermining NATO. In short, ODS Euroscepticism was mainly ideo- logically based. Nonetheless, in many cases ODS used economic arguments. Euro- scepticism was only to a small extent cleavage-based, as most ODS voters voted in favour of EU membership without the same reservations as Klaus.

Thus, by the end of the 1990s, the national "self-confidence" of ODS manifested itself in still sharper criticism of the federal visions for Europe, a firm belief in the nation-state and an "Anglo-Saxon" neo-liberal-inspired opposition to the introduction of a common currency. Mistrust of German influence in the EU also came up. As regards the common currency, the Temelin nuclear power station and EU sanctions against Austria as a result of Haider's Freedom Party's participation in the government, ODS refused to follow the common EU line, which was regarded as interference in a sovereign state's internal affairs.

The Euro-realist or Eurosceptic line may be most clearly manifested in the "Czech Euro-realist Manifesto," formulated at the third "idea conference" in 2001, in which scenarios for Czech non-membership of the EU were contemplated according to the Norwegian or Swiss model. The Manifesto argued strongly against further extension of qualified majority voting (QMV), asking instead for existing national veto rights to be maintained as a tool for safeguarding national sovereignty. In the Manifesto, which was authored largely by the foreign affairs spokesman Jan Zahradil, the EU in its present shape was signified by "lobbyism" and "corporatism." Therefore, intergovernmentalism was the preferred construction. The Euro-realist line of the Manifesto also featured prominently in the 2002 election programme.

Later, during a visit to France in July 2003—i.e. after assuming the post of President and the introduction of the common currency in the EU—Klaus maintained his criticism of EMU and the common currency, which, according to him, was not necessary and deprived the countries of the possibility of choosing their own monetary policy and decisions about the most appropriate exchange rates. In general, the convergence criteria were not suitable for countries that had lived 40 years under planned economies. In fact, the common currency was the main explanation for Europe's economic recession and first and foremost a political project. Europe, he continued, simply lacked a common identity. Europe was in possession of its own currency but no common policy to back up the project. The inflexible monetary policy of the European Central Bank (ECB) only reinforced the serious problems being experienced by the European econ- omies.[44] Later, in a speech at Passau University in Germany, Václav Klaus made clear that the common currency constitutes primarily a political project, a "Trojan Horse" for harmonizing the economies, policies and laws. The lack of financial and economic discipline, he also argued, may easily do irreparable damage to the new fragile post-communist economies. He ironically and provocatively stated that the experience of the division of Czechoslovakia was evidence that it is relatively easy and almost cost free to do away with a common currency.[45] Finally, during his official visited to Spain in September 2004, he once again claimed that the authors of the constitutional treaty had based their ideas on false preconditions, such as the idea of a non-existent European identity. In regard to the label of being a "Eurosceptic," Klaus said he preferred the terms "Euro-realist" and "Euro-naivist," adding that the second group reminded him of those naïve people under the communists—"they had the same mentality." In contrast, Euro-realists like himself believe that Europe must be freer, more democratic and more efficient when it comes to productivity.[46] He even called for a new name for the EU, something like the "Organization of European States."

In addition, the support of the EU-15 for the bombing of former Yugoslavia in 1999, which, according to Klaus, grossly violated the sovereignty of Yugoslavia, was met by sharp criticism from ODS and brought the party on a collision course not only with the EU but also the US. Thus, Sean Hanley[47] associates the relatively strong Euroscepticism of ODS from the late 1990s with the war against Serbia, which questioned the quality of supranational decision making and underlined the necessity of the right to say "no." Furthermore, he argues that the Eurosceptic line should be seen in light of the ongoing organizational problems within the party and the problems concerning the formulation of consistent and long-term strategies. Those characteristics can also be found in other weakly institutionalized new centre-right political formations in Europe, signified by populist leadership, e.g. the Austrian Freedom Party, Forza Italia and some Gaullist associations in France.

To a great extent the Eurosceptic line was concentrated among a group of individuals around the chairman, Václav Klaus. To those belonged, among others, one of the party's vice-chairmen and spokesman in defence affairs, Petr Necas, and Jan Zahradil, the shadow foreign minister and leader of the election campaign before the 2004 election to the European Parliament, and a member of the Eurosceptic anti-federal alliance of Euro-critical movements "TEAM" that consists of more than 40 cross-party political groups.[48] Zahradil has persistently argued against a transfer of more power to supranational institutions. As an example, he referred to an article in the French daily newspaper *Le Monde* that pessimistically predicted that the EU after enlargement would be transformed to a free trade zone without much supra-state regulation, a development that Zahradil considered as beneficial for a small country like the Czech Republic with an open economy that would profit from an internal market, but be "absorbed" in a supranational federation.[49] In other words, the enlargement to the East might constitute the best guarantee against the formation of a European "superstate."

Thus, ODS's scepticism has been strikingly ideological, closely connected to the "integration dilemma," the fear of being "absorbed" and with an Anglo-Saxon-type "Thatcherite" critique intending to keep the EU as an internal market and "nothing else." As noted above, the resistance against further EU integration has been much stronger among the leaders than among ODS voters, who typically have belonged to the "transformation winners" and therefore to a great extent have spoken in favour of Czech EU membership, thus confirming ODS's Euroscepticism as only to a small extent cleavage based. Some among the leaders of the party, e.g. former

Foreign Minister Josef Zieleniec, Finance Minister Ivan Kocarnik and the former dissidents Václav Benda and Jan Ruml, have taken a more pro-EU integration position.

After Václav Klaus's resignation as ODS party chairman and the takeover of the post by Mirek Topolanek, the EU policy line became somewhat "softer." Topolanek, critical of the result of the December 2002 Copenhagen summit, later also expressed some reservation about the compromise on the constitutional treaty in June 2004. At the voting in the European Parliament on the constitutional treaty in January 2005 a greater proportion of the Czech members, 15 of 24, including the nine from ODS, voted against, more votes than from any other of the 25 member states.[50] However, before the EU referendum Topolanek recommended a "yes," and on the constitutional treaty he asked for time for closer "studies," arguing that the new European constitutional treaty must not be unduly hastened and that people should be given one and a half to two years to study the constitution, indicating that the final result would be a "yes," with perhaps the final decision being taken after an ODS takeover of government responsibilities. However, ODS-sponsored polls showed a large "yes" majority among ODS voters. Therefore, ODS might lose votes in the 2006 national election because of its Eurosceptic stance. Perhaps the Dutch and French people's "no" to the treaty will "save" the ODS at the next election. In contrast to the social democrats, ODS argued in favour of cancelling the ratification procedure as a result of the French and Dutch rejection of the treaty. After the take-over of government by ODS in the beginning of 2007 the ODS and Mirek Topolanek maintained its "euro-realist" line, arguing against further "federalisation" of the EU, e.g. in case of revision of the constitutional treaty that had been rejected at the referenda in Netherlands and France.

Before the referendum, President Václav Klaus refused to recommend a "yes" or "no," and his comments on the result of the EU referendum did not indicate any shift in attitude towards EU integration. Klaus's "Eurosceptic" line led him on a course of confrontation not only with former president Václav Havel but also with the then social democratic Prime Minister Vladimir Spidla and the liberal Foreign Minister Cyril Svoboda, e.g. at the ceremony in Athens in April 2003 with the signing of the accession treaties, on which occasion the Czech government, contrary to Klaus's line, spoke in favour of developing a common foreign and security policy in the EU and a rotating EU chairmanship.[51]

It also attracted attention that Klaus refused to take part in the ceremony in the National Theatre marking the Czech accession to the EU but did attend the ceremony in Rome on the European constitution treaty. Furthermore, Klaus did not hide his satisfaction with the French and Dutch "no" votes on the constitutional treaty in May 2005, now calling himself a "Euro-optimist," speaking in favour of a new "minimalist"-type constitutional treaty.[52] The different policy of the government and the president inevitably exacerbated the conflicts between the president and the prime minister (Paroubek) in June 2005.

Final Remarks

As we have seen, questions concerning national identity and Europeanization have been the object of much and increasing attention. Until recently subjects connected to "Euroscepticism" have not been explored in any major way. However, we need not start from scratch because we have access to the cross-country research project ("Opposing Europe"), figures from Eurobarometer and several national opinion polls. The approach has shifted between rationalist, institutional, emphasizing each state's policy and institutional choices and administrative structures, and social-constructivist with a focus on identity.

National consciousness and identity matter, but do not need to be separated from rationalist and interest-based approaches. With time, along with a transition to more ordinary interest-based national policies and the adaptation to the EU, interest and institutional approaches seem to be becoming more relevant. Symbolic politics was most striking about the time of the demise of the old systems, and also in relation to questions connected to the future of Europe ("*la finalité*"). In the course of time, East European political leaders and populations have behaved in more Euro-pragmatic, more Euro-realistic ways, in some cases on the basis of national interests and soft Euroscepticism.

Several research questions and working hypotheses have been raised, and in the course of time these have also been better discussed, explored and defined. Some delimitations and definitions remain undecided, not least as regards the notion of "Euroscepticism." Thus, it remains difficult to say when we are talking about "normal safeguarding of national interests, or soft/hard euroscepticism. Just one example: "shall the slogan about "Nice and die", put forward by Civic Platform (PO) until spring 2007 be labelled "defence of national interests" or "soft euroscepticism"".

As we have seen, Euroscepticism has an institutional as well as an identity-based aspect. Institutionalist as well as social constructivist approaches have been used. The integration dilemma has a special East European aspect, for we are dealing with young states, with 40 years under communist rule and with the hope of a "return to Europe" and "catching up with the West." Most East Europeans tend instinctively to be intergovernmentalists (the fear of being "absorbed") and Atlanticists, but hard Euroscepticism has not been widespread due to the fear of being kept "outside." Accession to the EU has not solved the dilemma; to be "kept outside" became connected to second-rank membership and development of a multi-speed Europe consisting of core and non-core member states. In addition, Euroscepticism has an institutional aspect, as the mistrust of national institutions in most cases seems to be higher than mistrust of European institutions (known as "Italianization"). In those cases in which mistrust of national institutions is great, people seem to be more willing to leave some national sovereignty to the EU. Among EU institutions, the small accession countries have received most support from the EU Commission, as the EU Council of Ministers is considered the "big countries' club."

125

The question of EU membership has been a "valens issue," but nonetheless an integral part of the domestic policy game. These questions, which have split the parties and the voters, have concerned whether parties in government have defended national interests strongly enough, e.g. when negotiating with the EU. If not, soft Eurosceptic declarations have been put forward, e.g. by the then centre-right opposition parties, the Civic Democratic Party (ODS) in the Czech Republic and FIDESZ in Hungary.

Thus, among the political parties we do not find many that can be called "hard Eurosceptic." Several "soft Eurosceptic" parties have emerged, but the exact delimitation of hard and soft Euroscepticism and soft Euroscepticism and Euro-realism is no easy task. In all circumstances, a change can be observed away from identity-based Euro-enthusiasm, according to the "back to Europe" slogan, towards a clearly more interest-based relationship to the EU, often based on simple "cash thinking." Euroscepticism can be found in different forms. The cleavage-based and policy-based type of Euroscepticism has been most striking in the case of the Polish Peasant's Party (PSL) and Self-Defence (Samoobrona), and identity-based and policy-based Euroscepticism by the Civic Democratic Party (ODS) in the Czech Republic. Finally, practice-related Euroscepticism has signified the Movement for a Democratic Slovakia (HSDS) under Vladimir Meciar and to some extent FIDESZ in Hungary.

By left–right standards, self-declared Eurosceptic attitudes can be found on both sides in the Czech Republic, most strikingly in the case of ODS and KSCM. However, the exact boundary between Euro-realism and Euroscepticism is blurred. In the case of Poland and Hungary, strong Euroscepticism belongs to the traditionalist right, in Poland represented by the League of Polish Families (LPR) and in Hungary by Istvan Czurka's extreme right-wing party MIEP. However, outsider parties and protest parties do not necessarily view resistance to Brussels as their key policy issue. More likely we are dealing with a voter protest against domestic politics and bad governance by the ruling parties, such as in Slovakia through the strengthening of the position of the party "Smer," and in the Baltic States by paving the way for the two protest parties New Era (Latvia) and Respublica (Estonia).

Finally, it should be reiterated that attitudes to European politics have assumed more "ordinary" characteristics. As in domestic politics, EU politics has become more interest based and elections more retrospective. As regards EU politics, national interests have gained a high priority. EU parliamentary elections in June 2002 reflected domestic politics. National governments and political parties today are mostly evaluated according to the *quality of governance*, not to their role under communist rule. As the new EU member states have moved to more "ordinary politics," politics connected to the EU to a still larger extent reminds us of EU politics in the "old Europe" and in the "EU-15."

NOTES

1. Lapid, "Cultures Ship."
2. Schöpflin, *Nations, Identity, Power.*
3. Drulák, *National and European Identities in EU Enlargement*, 11.
4. Anderson, *Imagined Communities.*
5. Jiri Bordsky, in Drulák, *National and European Identities in EU Enlargement*, 21.
6. In Drulák, *National and European Identities in EU Enlargement.*
7. Kiss, *Hungarians about their Nation, Others, and Europe*, referring to de Rosa, "Reality Changes Faster than Research."
8. Laffan, "Managing Europe from Home."
9. Radielli, "Whither Europeanization?"
10. Gwiazda, "Europeanisation in Candidate Countries and Eastern Europe," 13.
11. Grote, "Delimiting Europeanization."
12. Kelstrup, "Small States and European Integration," in Tiikainen and Petersen, *Small States and European Integration*, 148.
13. Rupnik, "Europe Moves Eastward."
14. Kelstrup, "Small States and European Integration," in Tiikainen and Petersen, *Small States and European Integration*, 154.
15. Rupnik, "Europe Moves Eastward."
16. Gyarfasova, "From Defence against the 'Others' to the Formation of its Own Interests," in Drulák, *National and European Identities in EU Enlargement*, 55.
17. Lesaar, "Simpler Idem?," in Drulák, *National and European Identities in EU Enlargement*, 194.
18. Aleks Szczerbiak and Paul Taggart, "Theorizing Party-Based Euroscepticism," 6–7.
19. Taggart and Szczerbiak, *Parties, Positions and Europe*, 9–10.
20. Ibid.
21. Ibid., 10.
22. This classification is inspired by the classification made by Taggart and Szczerbiak, *Parties and Europe: Euroscepticism*, 10–11.
23. Szczerbiak and Taggart, "Theorising Party-Based Euroscepticism."
24. Daskalov, *The Making of a Nation in the Balkans.*
25. Kiss, *Hungarians about their Nation, Others, and Europe.*
26. "Radio Netherlands," 14 December 2001, <www.rnw.nl>.
27. *BBC News*, 15 December 2003, <www.bbc.co.uk>.
28. "Rzeczpospolita silna jak nigdy."
29. Gmyz, "Praktyczna pani, Danuta Hübner bedzie najlepszym komisarzym Unii Europ."
30. These questions are discussed in "Trójkat berlinski?"
31. Olechowski, "Oglad I poglad, Nadal sami?"
32. "European Elections Important for Poland."
33. Starucha, "Z zachodnieogo na nasze."
34. An overview of the EU debate is available in Kim (2004).
35. Kim, "Poland Continues to Muse over the EU Constitution Impasse."
36. "Czechs Still Have Certain Fears."
37. Drulák, *National and European Identities in EU Enlargement*, 26.
38. Hanley, "Czechs Seek Yet Another Model."
39. Hanley (2002).
40. Václav Havel, in Drulák, *National and European Identities in EU Enlargement*, 188–89.

41. <www.ceskenoviny.cz>, 15 March 2002, "Diversity is EU's Asset, the Future Lies in Federation."
42. <www.ceskenoviny.cz>, 28 September 2004, "Spidla Favours EU Social Model, but Also for Reforms."
43. Stated, for example, in Kavan's speech at the European Policy Center, 22 February 2002, <www.Euroskeop.cz>, 30 April 2002, "The Future Functioning of the European Union."
44. <www.ceskenoviny.cz>, 21 July 2003, "Klaus Describes Adoption of the Euro as 'unreasonable.'"
45. <www.rferl.org/newsline>, 11 February 2004.
46. <www.ceskenoviny.cz>, 28 September 2004, "Klaus Says that Iraq Shows there ..." and "Klaus Criticises European Constitution ..."
47. Hanley (2002).
48. Zahradil, "EU Enlargement will Help Prevent its Further Unification."
49. Ibid.
50. Spritzer, "Czech MEPs Lead Euroskeptic Faction."
51. "Klaus–Svoboda Meeting."
52. "Klaus na Ukrajine."

REFERENCES

Ágh, Atilla. *The Politics of Central Europe*. London: Sage, 1998.

Anderson, Benedict. *Imagined Communities: Reflections on the Origin and Spread of Nationalism*. London: Verso, 1991.

"Czechs Still Have Certain Fears of EU after One Year Membership." *Czech Happenings*, 2005, <www.ceskenoviny.cz>.

Daskalov, Roumen. *The Making of a Nation in the Balkans: Historiography of the Bulgarian Revival*. Budapest: CEU Press, 2004.

Rosa, A. S. "Reality Changes Faster than Research: National and Supranational Identity in Social Representations of European Community in the Context of Changes in International Relations. In *Changing European Identities: Advances in Social Psychology*, edited by G. Breakwell and E. Lyons. Oxford: Butterworth Heinemann, 1996.

Drulák, Petr. *National and European Identities in EU Enlargement*. Prague: Institute of International Relations, 2001.

"European Elections Important for Poland." *Insight Central Europe*, 11 June 2004, <www.incentralEurope.com>.

Gmyz, Cezary. "Praktyczna pani, Danuta Hübner bedzie najlepszym komisarzym Unii Europ." 2003/ jskiej- dla Francji i Niemiec." *Wprost*, 31 December 2003.

Grote, Jürgen R. "Delimiting Europeanization." Paper presented at the Marburg Conference Session, ECPR, Marburg, 18–21 September 2003.

Gwiazda, Anna. "Europeanisation in Candidate Countries and Eastern Europe." Paper prepared for the EPIC workshop in Florence, EUI, 19–22 September 2002.

Gyarfasova, Olga. "From Defence against the 'Others' to the Formation of its Own Interests: The Case of Slovakia." In *National and European Identities in EU Enlargement*, by Petr Drulák. Prague: Institute of International Relations, 2001.

Hanley, Sean. "Czechs Seek Yet Another Model." *Central Europe Review*, 19 April 1999.

——. "Party Institutionalisation and Centre-Right Euroscepticism in East Central Europe: The Case of the Civic Democratic Party in the Czech Republic." Paper presented at the 29th ECPR Joint Sessions of Workshops, Turin, 22–27 March 2002.

——. *The Political Context of EU Accession in the Czech Republic*. Royal Institute of International Affairs, European Programme, Briefing Paper, October 2002.

Kelstrup, Morten. "Small States and European Integration." In *Small States and European Integration: Reflections on Theory and Strategy*, edited by Teija Tiikainen and Ib Damgaard Petersen. Copenhagen: Copenhagen Political Studies Press, 1992.

——. "Danish Integration Policies: Dilemmas and Options." In *Denmark's Policy towards Europe after 1945: History, Theory and Options*, edited by Hans Branner and Morten Kelstrup. Odense: Odense University Press, 2000.

Kim, Inassa. "Poland Continues to Muse over the EU Constitution Impasse," 22 January 2005, <www.tol.cz>.

Kiss, Paszkál. *Hungarians About their Nation, Others, and Europe: Popular Views in Public*. Report (D5) prepared for the EURONAT project by the European Commission Research DG. Brussels: European Commission, 2001.

"Klaus na Ukrajine: Jsem Eurooptimista," 15 June 2005, <www.ceskenoviny.cz>.

"Klaus–Svoboda Meeting Does Not Settle their Dispute over EU," 23 April 2003, <www.ceskenoviny.cz>.

Kupchan, Charles A. *Nationalism and Nationalities in the New Europe*. Ithaca, NY and London: Cornell University Press, 1995.

Laffan, Brigid. "Managing Europe from Home: Impact of the EU on Executive Government: A Comparative Analysis." Paper prepared for the ECPR Conference, Marburg, September 2003.

Lapid, Y. "Cultures Ship: Returns and Departures in International Relations Theory." In *The Return of Culture and Identity in IR Theory*, edited by Y. Lapid and F. Kratochwil. London and Boulder: Lynne Rienner, 1996.

Lesaar, Henrik Richard. "Simper Idem? The Relationship of European and National Identities." In *National and European Identities in EU Enlargement*, by Petr Drulák. Prague: Institute of International Relations, 2001.

Neumann, Iver B. "Diskursanalyse av politikk: Forutsetninger og metodeproblemer." *Statsvetenskaplig Tidsskrift* 102, no. 2 (1999).

Olechowski, Andrzej. "Oglad I poglad, Nadal sami?" *Polityka*, 9 October 2004, 28.

Radielli, Claudio M. "Whither Europeanization? Conceptual Stretching and Substantive Change?," 2000, <http/eiop.or.at>.

Rupnik, Jacques. "Europe Moves Eastward: Concluding Reflections." *Journal of Democracy* 15, no. 1 (2004).

"Rzeczpospolita silna jak nigdy." *Gazeta Wyborcza*, 22 January 2004, 8.

Schöpflin, Georg. *Nations, Identity, Power*. London: Hurst, 2000.

Spritzer, Dinah A. "Czech MEPs Lead Euroskeptic Faction." *The Prague Post*, 19–25 January 2005.

Starucha, Ateusz. "Z zachodnieogo na nasze." *Gazeta Wyborcza*, 10 February 2004, 16.

Szczerbiak, Aleks, and Paul Taggart. *Theorising Party-Based Euroscepticism: Problems of Definition, Measurement and Causality*. SEI Working Paper no. 69. Brighton: Sussex European Institute, 2003, <www.sussex.ac.uk>.

Taggart, Paul, and Aleks Szczerbiak. *Parties, Positions and Europe: Euroscepticism in the EU Candidate States of Central and Eastern Europe*. SEI Working Paper no. 46. Brighton: Sussex European Institute, 2001, <www.sussex.ac.uk>.

"Trójkat berlinski?" *Gazeta Wyborcza*, 4 February 2004, 11.

Zahradil, Jan. "EU Enlargement Will Help Prevent its Further Unification," 11 March 2002, <www.ceskenoviny.cz>.

National Identity and National Interest in Polish Eastern Policy, 1989–2004

Krzysztof Fedorowicz

The processes of democratic social and political changes in Poland that have gained momentum since 1989 have radically altered the foundations and the goals of Polish foreign policy. In addition to re-establishing Polish interests as the basis for foreign policy, they have also started the process of establishing a new element of Polish diplomacy, namely its eastern policy. In these altered political conditions it was the right time to ask the question of how to establish new relationships in the East, how to normalize relations with the USSR and, finally, what stance should be adopted towards the increasing independence claims of individual Soviet republics. The process of establishing a democratic Poland was concurrent with the reconstruction, and later, with the fall of the USSR. In addition, the convoluted history of Polish–Ukrainian and Polish–Lithuanian relationships from the very beginning hindered the attempt of Polish diplomacy to establish new contacts with its eastern partners.

Until the middle of 1990 Polish eastern policy assumed that the USSR would exist in perpetuity. The Union's position as a superpower was clearly acknowledged and any independence movements within the empire were treated with reserve. Contacts with neighbouring republics were limited and modest, without defining specific prospects for cooperation.[1] Initially for the Polish authorities it was more beneficial to have the USSR as a neighbour, rather than to have individual sovereign republics. It was believed that the results of the potential fall of the USSR would have negative consequences for Poland.[2] Polish policy towards the USSR at that time in essential issues paralleled the policy of the US and the West European states, for which Mikhail Gorbachev was the only partner worthy of support. Therefore, Polish Foreign Minister Krzysztof Skubiszewski was often criticized at home for his extreme prudence in contacts with the USSR and the newly established republics.[3]

As late as the middle of 1990 the programme of an active Polish eastern policy in relations with the USSR and eastern neighbours was established. The programme was referred to as a "two-track" policy, based on the principles of maintaining reformed relations with the USSR and, simultaneously, establishing and developing relations with the Union republics. It was assumed that the role of individual republics within the USSR would increase. This meant for the future a readiness to acknowledge the republics' right to autonomy and self-determination, as well as a promise to establish secure diplomatic relations.[4] The implementation of the principle was not easy, since such a policy was not totally approved either in the republics or in Moscow, and in Poland opinions varied. The cause of independent republics was supported mostly by "Solidarity" MPs and senators, while the policy of the government and President Lech Wałęsa was more prudent.[5]

The "two-track" approach was in essence an answer to the independence declarations of the Baltic republics (Lithuania, Latvia, Estonia), which found themselves in open conflict with Moscow, as well as to the independence aspirations of other Soviet republics, which were becoming increasingly visible. Officially, Poland responded cautiously to such movements and independent actions, trying to avoid any unnecessary irritation of the USSR. However, most politicians already treated the republics as independent states. Therefore, after some period, the target of Polish diplomacy was to gradually establish such bilateral relations with the Union republics, which are normally binding between fully independent and sovereign countries.[6]

Intensive contacts with eastern neighbours began in the second half of 1990, after sovereignty was declared by Russia (in June 1990), as well as Ukraine and Belarus (in July 1990). The Polish authorities handed over to those republics drafts of political declarations on good-neighbourly relations that were supposed to be signed in the near future.

The first element of the "two-track" policy that was implemented and which manifested the readiness of Polish diplomacy to establish a dialogue at state level was a visit paid on 12–15 October 1990 by Polish Foreign Minister Krzysztof Skubiszewski to Kiev, Minsk and Moscow. During this visit two documents were signed—the Polish–Russian "Declaration of friendship and good-neighbourly cooperation between the Republic of Poland and the Russian Soviet Federative Socialist Republic" and the "Declaration on the principles and major directions of Polish–Ukrainian relations' development."

At that time Russia was the real driving force behind the transformations taking place in the USSR; it was the only republic in which a group of politicians could develop as an alternative to the Kremlin. It was led by Boris Yeltsin, whose popularity in Russia was greater than that of Mikhail Gorbachev. Although Boris Yeltsin did not meet with the Polish Foreign Minister, apparently the declaration was finally signed thanks to him. In the signed document both parties underlined the fact that they did not have any territorial claims against each other, nor would they have such claims in the future. The existing border was accepted as unalterable then and in the future. It was also decided to commence work to establish legal grounds for the development of bilateral business cooperation and to start diplomatic and consular relations as soon as possible.[7] During the visit to Moscow Minister Krzysztof Skubiszewski also held discussions with the government of the USSR. As a result it was agreed to commence negotiations to withdraw the Soviet army from Poland.

In the Polish–Ukrainian declaration, on the other hand, the countries declared their intention to strengthen good-neighbourly relations between them as sovereign states and to maintain and develop cooperation, which would be beneficial for both parties and also correspond to their national interests. The document stressed the inalienable right of both states to determine freely their internal and external political status.

Poland and Ukraine announced that they did not hold any territorial claims against each other, nor would they hold any such claims in the future; and they treated the border existing between them as unalterable then and in the future.[8] It was also agreed to establish consular relations and it was announced that consultations concerning the establishment of full diplomatic relations were to be arranged in the near future. The parties also made an obligation to consistently secure and respect the rights of the national minorities—the Poles in Ukraine and the Ukrainians in Poland, as well as to improve their situation. Keeping in mind the ethnic and cultural affinity, both parties decided to grant extensive support to Polish–Ukrainian contacts.

It is worth stressing that the declaration refers to history and tradition as the foundation for the renewal of Polish and Ukrainian relations and underlines the ethnic and cultural links between the Polish and Ukrainian nations. The document showed that Ukraine was not in fact exclusively Russia-oriented, but, as was the case with Poland, it identified itself with Central Europe. From the Ukrainian point of view, the signed declaration was basically the first document that legitimized Polish and Ukrainian relations at the level of two independent states of Central and Eastern Europe. The Ukrainian opposition gained the confirmation of Polish support for the establishment of an independent Ukrainian state. However, friendly relations between Ukraine and Poland gave hope to the Ukrainian opposition that, when the independent Ukrainian state was established, other neighbours (e.g. Hungary) would respond positively to the political transformations across their borders.

Unfortunately, an attempt to sign a similar document with the government of Belarus, which was hostile to the new political situation in Poland as well as to the intention to establish closer bilateral cooperation without the mediation of the USSR, ended in failure. During talks in Minsk the Belarusian party did not agree to the proposal to refer to the 1945 Polish–Soviet agreement concerning the national border, since Belarus claimed that it had not been a party to that agreement. Moreover, Belarus made a statement that a part of the Bialystok region (located in the territory of Poland) was ethnically Belarusian. No official territorial claims were made, although it was made clear that such a problem might occur in the future. The "two-track" policy also did not work in relations with Lithuania, since Poland treated this country differently from other republics. Lithuania expected Polish support in its conflict with the USSR; however, Polish diplomacy did not want to acknowledge the independence of Lithuania directly. Polish politics towards Vilnius was then related to the issue of increasing conflict related to the Polish minority in Lithuania, which had opposed any attempt to regain independence by the Lithuanian government.[9]

During 1991–1992 Poland's eastern policy involved establishing official contacts, as well as the implementation of the "two-track" approach. The most important element was the fact that Poland was the first state in the world to acknowledge the independence of Ukraine on 2 January 1992 and established full diplomatic relations on 8 January 1992. It was a very good beginning for new Polish–Ukrainian relations, thanks to which Poland gained a privileged position in its relations with the fledgling Ukrainian state.[10] At the same time Poland also acknowledged the independence of Belarus and Russia. The year 1992 was the beginning of a new era in diplomatic relations with its eastern neighbours. Poland signed inter-state treaties on good-neighbourly relations and friendly cooperation with Ukraine, Belarus and Russia, thus in a formal way regulating its diplomatic relations with these new states. The treaty with Lithuania was not signed until 1994. Polish diplomacy concentrated then on establishing legal and formal foundations in inter-state relations, developing political dialogue and searching for opportunities for economic cooperation. An attempt was also made to support the processes of political change initiated in those countries.

In the opinion of numerous analysts, Polish eastern policy during 1989–1992 was one of the factors that in a certain way contributed to the fall of the USSR and the establishment of good-neighbourly relations with former Soviet republics. The paradigmatic regulation of relations between Poland and Ukraine was particularly important. Poland, as the largest and strategically the most important state in Central Europe, initially occupied a special place in the plans of Ukraine. Warsaw was perceived as a regional co-leader, and presented as a model of democratic political and market transformations that could play the role of a political connection between Ukraine and the West. The idea of a "Polish–Ukrainian axis," proposed by Ukrainian Deputy Foreign Minister Boris Tarasiuk, was in the form of an announcement inviting Poland into a strategic political and military alliance.[11]

The period 1993–1995 was a time of temporary stagnation in Polish eastern policy and a weakening in the dynamics of Polish–Ukrainian and Polish–Russian contacts, as a result of changes in the Polish political arena—the creation of a coalition of a left-wing party and a peasant party after the 1993 parliamentary elections—as well as the attempts to make adjustments in Polish foreign policy towards its eastern neighbours. There were those who recommended that Polish diplomacy should withdraw from its active role in the East. There was also a belief that Poland should stop supporting the new states (Ukraine, Belarus, and Lithuania), accept the existence of the Russian sphere of influence, and maintain good relations with "any possible Russia." Attempts made in 1989–1993 to find a partner in the East within the democratic opposition were harshly criticized. The opposition was seen to be a marginal phenomenon in the realities of the former Soviet republics; they either did not gain power at all or lost it quickly. Critics pointed to the insufficient level of cooperation with Russia, in particular. With respect to security issues, the proposal was to work out a new collective security system based on the Organization for Security and Cooperation in Europe (OSCE).[12]

At that time in the monthly magazine *Dziś* [Today], which had a strong impact on left-wing circles, the idea of the so called "third road" was frequently discussed. In practice it meant a proposal to depart from the pro-Western approach and to switch to the more active eastern policy, with particular focus on Russia. Journalists from *Dzis* believed that relations with Russia are of fundamental importance for Poland. Poland would be able to maintain complete sovereignty by concurrently cultivating closer relations with the West and at least partially coordinating its economic and military policy with Russia.[13]

The fuzzy political situation in the post-Soviet area hindered the definition of a long-term political strategy and facilitated the creation of various myths, among which the most dangerous was the one of the Russian market (or the eastern market in general) as a superb opportunity for the Polish economy.[14] Some of the representatives of the coalition in power believed that the development of economic relations with the East was an opportunity for economic development and, first of all, it was supposed to be a way of strengthening the sectors which could not cope with the transformation processes (agriculture and heavy industry). Predominant opinions demanded the re-establishment of cooperation with the post-Soviet partners, mainly the Russians. An adjustment of certain sectors of the Polish economy to Russian standards by halting their structural transformations was considered. There was a common belief concerning the un-adopted opportunities related to Polish–Russian relations.

Moreover, at the turn of 1993/1994 the dispute concerning the leadership in Polish foreign policy became evident. The branches of executive power that were responsible for its performance found themselves influenced by various political environments. In a short time, differences in the evaluation of economic, political and social policy in the post-Soviet area became evident. There were also signals concerning different strategies for pursuing Polish national interests and platforms for cooperation with the eastern neighbours. Such a situation had a considerably negative impact on the form of the later dialogue with Russia, Ukraine and Belarus.[15]

The unresolved historical problems between Poland, Ukraine and Russia were also becoming increasingly visible. The Polish policy of openness towards Ukraine in 1991–1993 did not tie in with the social atmosphere concerning Polish–Ukrainian relations. The efforts undertaken by the government and political forces to normalize relations were not, unfortunately, reflected in societal feelings, which were still influenced by the negative stereotype of Ukraine from the time of World War II. The attempts to politicize the problem of national minorities and the intention to treat it as a bargaining chip in relations with Ukraine and Lithuania were also a negative characteristic of Polish eastern policy at that time.

Tensions in Polish–Russian Relations in the Mid-1990s

There were also discrepancies in Polish–Russian relations with respect to foreign policy and European security. Since Poland gained full sovereignty, relations with

135

Russia have remained one of the most crucial elements of Polish foreign policy. The integration of Poland with the democratic European institutions and the establishment of good neighbourly relations in the region, particularly with its Eastern partners, remained among the priorities of the Polish state. This stance was related to the problem of the Russian attitude towards Poland, as well as to the whole of Central and Eastern Europe. Years after the fall of the communist system there remained in Russian foreign policy the view that Central and Eastern Europe should, to some degree, remain outside the boundaries of Western Europe and at the same time the politics and economy of the area should be aligned with Russia. Therefore, the process of establishing Polish–Russian relations was difficult and frequently tense.

From the beginning, Polish–Russian relations were asymmetric. While Russia remained Poland's most important partner in the East (often at the expense of the new eastern neighbours, i.e. Lithuania and Ukraine), Poland practically ceased to exist in Russian foreign policy. Between 1991 and 1993 Russia did not have any clearly defined strategy towards Central and Eastern Europe, including Poland. There were two dominating tendencies: one was to place the region in second or even third place (after relations with the former Soviet republics and Western countries) in Russian foreign policy; the other was governed by the confused syndrome of resentment and repentance. The characteristic feature of Russian foreign policy between 1991 and 1993 towards the region was Russia's consistency in rejecting the importance of Central and Eastern Europe and the reluctance to achieve mutual understanding. Only in a few cases was the region the subject of discussion in Russian foreign policy. It was only acknowledged that Poland, Bulgaria and possibly Slovakia could be the states with the greatest importance for Russia in the region, because of their geographical locations.

An important factor contributing to the differences between the states was the differing perception of their respective "civilizing" backgrounds (historical, cultural and religious), which later became the fundamental reason for the contradictions between Poland and Russia, namely the differences in understanding and approaching the question of European security.

The increasing discrepancies between Poland and Russia in relation to their approaches to foreign policy and European security, as well as the significant asymmetry in mutual relations, were caused mainly by political, psychological and historical factors. Even the expectations of both parties turned out to be asymmetrical. Polish political elites expected that the new Russia had rejected the communist doctrine and the totalitarian regime and should immediately become a democratic country, open to the values of Western civilization and, most importantly, it should become Poland-friendly. They expected that Russian democrats would acknowledge that Poland is also an important partner for Russia and that the Polish experience in freeing itself from communism, both politically and economically, could serve as an example. However, the conviction of equal rights and the priority of Poland in Russian foreign policy had a negative impact on mutual relations.

136

For the Polish government of that time the major problem was the need to clarify the circumstances related to the so-called "white spots" in Russian–Polish history (particularly the Katyn massacre).[16] The expectation of the Polish political elite concerning the reconciliation of both nations through the final revelation of the "white spots" from the past was not realized. The principal obstacle was the approach to history, which was perceived differently in Russia and in Poland.[17] This is why Katyn soon became the subject of misunderstanding and reciprocal accusations. Members of the Russian political class almost unanimously rejected the Polish proposal for reconciliation. In their opinion there were no grounds for forgiveness on either side, since no wrong was done by either party—according to the Russian side, it was the NKVD (People's Commissariat of Internal Affairs) and Stalin who were responsible for Katyn, not Russia. The persistent requests from the Polish side to explain the issue of Katyn were received negatively in Russia. A common opinion was that the actual motivation for such actions was the will to maintain an anti-Russian mood in Polish society.[18]

The issue of the role of the Red Army in the liberation and later subordination of Poland turned out to be even more difficult. The spectacular dismantling of Red Army monuments in Poland was seen in Russia as an act of contempt and disrespect for the sacrifice of Soviet soldiers who died on Polish soil. Another disputable issue was the withdrawal of the Soviet army from Poland. Poland wanted the USSR army to leave the territory of Poland as soon as possible; on the other hand the Soviet authorities delayed the final withdrawal of their army from Poland for a considerable period of time (the last Red Army troops were withdrawn from Poland in 1993). At the end of 1992, when domestic problems and relations with the West were the priorities in Russian foreign policy, the claims and demands of Poland contributed to establishing a negative approach by Russia towards Poland, as well as the whole region of Central and Eastern Europe.[19]

The primary Polish objective of joining NATO and the EU, clearly expressed since 1992, became a new element in Polish eastern policy. In the circumstances it became clear that a serious conflict of strategic interests had occurred between Poland and Russia. But in the middle of 1993 it seemed that Poland's aspirations to join NATO and the EU were being received positively by the leaders of Russia.

The most important event in the Polish–Russian relationship of the period was the visit of Russian President Boris Yeltsin to Poland in August 1993. The visit raised hopes in Poland. President Yeltsin confirmed that the last Russian soldiers would leave the territory of Poland on 17 September 1993,[20] earlier than had been previously agreed. There was also considerable progress in discussions concerning economic cooperation. Moreover, the president of Russia handed over to Lech Wałęsa a set of secret documents from the Russian archives concerning the cooperation between the KPZR (Communist Party of the Soviet Union) and PZPR (Polish United Workers' Party) in fighting the democratic opposition. The flower-laying ceremony at the monument to the Katyn victims was also a symbolic gesture by Yeltsin.

137

However, the highlight of the visit was the joint declaration signed by both presidents, where the Russian side confirmed that Poland's joining NATO would not be contradictory to the interests of the Russian Federation.[21] It seemed that after the visit and the signing, Polish–Russian relations would normalize and, despite really difficult challenges, the countries would manage to overcome all serious differences and establish a solid foundation for a new partnership. The problems which remained unresolved were identified, and more and more often the parties showed their intention to secure a reasonable compromise.[22]

However, from that moment Russia began emphasizing that the extension of NATO would undermine the existing geopolitical situation in Europe. It was then that the alarming tendency in Russian foreign policy with respect to the whole of Central and Eastern Europe began. Opinions were bandied about concerning Russia's "historical" or "special interests" in the region. The warning voices foreshadowing Russian opposition and changes in Russia's foreign policy began when the chances of Poland joining NATO were becoming increasingly more likely. Andrei Kozyrev, Russian Foreign Minister, referred to the countries of Central and Eastern Europe as false allies of the former Soviet Union. In 1993, when the debates prior to the NATO summit of 1994 started in the West, Russian protests against the cooperation of Central and Eastern European countries with NATO also began. Additional evidence of Russian opposition came with the de facto withdrawal of the statement made by Boris Yeltsin, in Poland in August 1993, concerning the absence of Russia's objection to Poland joining NATO.[23] Almost a month later, in September 1993, President Yeltsin addressed the leaders of the US, Great Britain, France and Germany with a letter, in which he firmly expressed his objection to the countries of Central and Eastern Europe joining NATO. The Russian side also submitted a proposal that Russia and NATO could present joint security guarantees for Central and Eastern Europe. Within a short time representatives of the Russian government also started a campaign of re-interpreting Russia's consent to Poland joining NATO. Russian Defence Minister General Pavel Grachov stated that the idea of the former Warsaw Pact countries joining NATO would not be a good move for all parties. Moreover, Foreign Affairs Minister Andrei Kozyrev, along with Russian diplomats, began a concerted campaign aimed at stopping the process of NATO extension to Central and Eastern Europe countries, particularly Poland.[24] It became clear that a serious conflict of strategic interests had begun between Poland and Russia.

From 1993 the policy of objection and opposition began to dominate Russia's attitude towards Poland. It hindered initiatives and political actions in relations with the West that would lead to Poland's integration with the Euro-Atlantic system. This was done using arguments concerning the responsibility of Russia as a superpower. At all costs, Russia tried to prevent NATO's eastward extension by presenting Poland as an explicitly anti-Russian country.[25] On the other hand, Poland gave assurances that the accession of Central European states to NATO was not aimed against Russia and Ukraine.

The process of Poland's integration into the EU and NATO started to be viewed in Moscow as contrary to the Russian *raison d'état* and, therefore, it was resisted as clearly anti-Russian. The most efficient tactic was to counteract the speedy integration of Poland into NATO by creating and promoting an image of Poland as an anti-Russian country. Russian politicians wanted to create the impression that, in principle, Poles have a hostile attitude to Russia. Minor incidents were publicized disproportionately by the media, presenting an atmosphere of serious frictions. The purpose was to convince the NATO states that by accepting Poland they would accept a country in permanent conflict with Russia. Specific events and incidents were used for that purpose; they caused a crisis in diplomatic relations in 1994–1996, as well as a wave of mutual accusations.[26]

The characteristic feature for Moscow was also the conviction that Poland should be the first to take any action to improve bilateral relations by introducing adjustments in its foreign policy, since Poland was responsible for their poor condition. The Russian side did not take into consideration the arguments proposing the need to introduce a new strategy towards Poland, as well as towards the whole of Central and Eastern Europe. On the other hand, the Polish side was not able to handle the impasse and was limited only to repeating invitations and declarations of goodwill. As a result, in 1994–1996, among the Russian elites and in the media, irritation and suspicions towards Poland, as well as the old negative stereotypes, were revived; a serious crisis occurred in bilateral relations.[27]

Improved Relations between Poland and Some Eastern Neighbours, 1996–1997

Positive changes in Polish eastern policy, particularly in Polish–Ukrainian and Polish–Lithuanian relations, took place in 1996. In 1996–1997 there was a considerable increase in political cooperation and contacts between the leaders of Poland and Ukraine (Presidents Aleksander Kwasniewski and Leonid Kuchma), which was referred to as the renaissance of Ukraine in Polish eastern policy. The considerably convergent visions of Europe and the acknowledgement of common tasks in the future comprised an important premise in the development of these contacts. Polish political elites showed a growing interest in Ukraine, which resulted from its increasing importance in the European political arena, and Ukraine appreciated the importance of cooperation with Poland—a neutral and friendly neighbour. In 1996 both presidents signed the "Declaration on strategic partnership," which included a clause stating that the existence of an independent Ukraine is a factor conducive to the consolidation of Poland's independence, just as the existence of an independent Poland is conducive to the consolidation of Ukraine's independence. Additionally, an agreement was signed concerning no-visa travel, and thus Poland became the first country in Central Europe where Ukrainians could travel without visas. A year later a Polish–Ukrainian "Declaration on understanding and reconciliation" was

139

signed, where mutual references were made to the painful and often tragic history of both nations. Since then, Poland has tried, with varying success, to be an advocate in bringing Ukraine closer to European structures, and Ukraine has referred to Polish aspirations to join NATO with increasing understanding.[28]

There was also a revival of cooperation with Lithuania. After signing a treaty on friendly relations and on regulating the matters of national minorities in 1994, Poland started to be seen as one of Lithuania's major political and economic partners.[29] From that moment both states jointly followed the path to NATO and the EU.

No major improvement was recorded in Polish–Russian relations during this period, despite the intensification of political contacts, and the increasingly buoyant development in business contacts. It was only in 1996, in relationship to the presidential elections in Poland, that a group of Russian politicians enthusiastically welcomed the victory of Aleksander Kwaśniewski, hoping that the pro-NATO option of Polish policy would weaken considerably. In Moscow it was expected that Polish foreign policy would change favourably towards Russia as a result of the change of government after the elections. What is of particular importance, however, is that in Moscow it was finally admitted that the previous policy towards Central and Eastern Europe, and particularly towards Poland, was wrong.[30]

In 1996–1998 some changes were introduced in Russia's policy towards Central and Eastern Europe. The reasons for the adjustments were the dynamic processes taking place in Europe. Unofficially, Russia began a series of bilateral consultations with the countries of Central and Eastern Europe, which were motivated by a need to separate the problem of establishing bilateral relations from the issue of NATO extension. The new phenomenon in Russian policy towards Poland and the whole region was the increase in the importance of Russia's foreign economic interests in Central and Eastern Europe. At that time Poland received a number of proposals from the Russian side for business cooperation in the areas of energy and armaments, as well as in the banking sector. Apart from signing an agreement on the free trade zone, it was proposed to create joint enterprises and networks of commercial, financial and credit institutions. It was also planned to create preferential conditions for Russian power industry companies and financial institutions to operate in the Polish market.[31] If Poland had accepted such proposals for business cooperation it would have lost control over the process of transforming the power industry market and the banking/financial sector. In fact, it would have meant negating the opportunity of EU membership. It would also have contributed to the increased risk of Polish market penetration by Russian economic structures, which would remain beyond the control and standards of the market economy. Therefore, Poland rejected such a model of cooperation proposed by the Russian side.[32]

Despite all this, to a large extent Poland remained dependent on the deliveries of strategic raw materials (gas and crude oil) from Russia. In September 1996, in Warsaw, a contract with the Russian corporation "Gazprom" was signed for gas provision for a period of 25 years. It meant that Russia's participation in gas imports to

Poland would not be less than 80%. In a short period of time Central and Eastern Europe became the second (after Germany) strategic territory for gas sales to the European market. The two largest Russian corporations, "Gazprom" and "Lukoil," were becoming increasingly effective instruments of Russian foreign policy, which was evidence that it was gradually becoming less related to ideology and increasingly dependent on economic factors.[33]

The dynamic development of economic contacts did not translate into a visible improvement in political relations. The continual obstacle for their improvement was Russia's objection to the extension of NATO eastwards. Under such conditions the target of Polish policy towards Russia was to maintain friendly relations at an official level, which would serve to resolve the then current bilateral problems. After Poland's accession to NATO in 1999 and with the progress of integration with the EU, Russia started raising the issue of the possible negative effects of Poland's accession to the EU in relationship to bilateral business relations.[34]

Moreover, Russia also demanded positive solutions concerning transit traffic to the Kaliningrad Region via the territories of Poland and Lithuania after their accession to the EU. In 1995, responding to the announcement of Poland's acceptance into NATO, the Russians warned that they would locate nuclear weapons in the Kaliningrad Region.[35] Similar threats occurred a few years later, when the chances of Lithuania joining NATO and the EU became highly probable. The Russians also demanded consent from the Polish government for the construction of a special ex-territorial transport corridor across the territory of Poland to connect Kaliningrad with Belarus, which would allow for the unrestricted travel of Russian citizens to and from Kaliningrad. Also, the EU leaders were startled when during the summit of the EU and Russia in Moscow in May 2002, President Putin categorically stated that the unrestricted travel from the Kaliningrad Region to other regions in Russia was so important that the future of EU–Russia relations depended on its resolution (according to Moscow's proposal).[36] Moscow also demanded that after the EU expansion the inhabitants of the Kaliningrad Region should be able to travel freely, without visas and passports, across the territories of Lithuania and Poland, to other regions of Russia and Belarus. The opinion of Brussels was, however, very clear: each citizen of a third country entering the territory of an EU member state must have a valid travel document (passport) and a valid visa.[37]

In addition to the specific issues just discussed, psychological issues remained a considerable hindrance to Polish–Russian relations. Part of Russian society and its politicians, because a lack of historical knowledge, as well as attitudes shaped by its past totalitarian system, simply did not understand why Polish citizens voted for integration with the EU.[38] In Russia, Poland's accession to NATO and the EU was perceived as a potential threat. The situation did not change after the visit of President Putin to Poland in May 2002. It started a series of intensive Polish–Russian contacts at various levels and contributed to a temporary improvement in the political climate. However, in the long term it did not bring the breakthrough in mutual relations expected by both states. Its only measurable political effect was an open exchange of ideas concerning crucial matters of interest to both states.[39]

Polish political cooperation with Belarus did not have a partnership dimension as it did with Ukraine. In 1996 there was a considerable deterioration in bilateral relations. This was due largely to the internal political situation in Belarus, particularly the authoritarian style of power of President Aleksander Lukashenko. The continual violation of human rights and OSCE (Organization for Security and Cooperation in Europe) standards in Belarus, persecution of the opposition and the independent mass media caused a long-lasting (until now) isolation of this state in the international arena and contributed to a lowering of the importance of Polish–Belarus bilateral contacts. Therefore, Poland decided to maintain official political contacts on a lower level, and at the same time to develop contacts at lower and working levels.[40]

It should be stressed, however, that the Polish policy of isolation towards Belarus is less rigorous than the policies adopted by most EU states, where there is a dominating belief in the need to isolate the Belarusian authorities totally. It is not in the interests of the Polish authorities to isolate the Minsk regime totally not least because of the large Polish minority living in Belarus, as well as the fact that Belarus is Poland's immediate neighbour.[41]

The increase in Poland's integration with the EU was also related to the unavoidable prospect of introducing a visa requirement for the citizens of Russia, Ukraine, Belarus, as well as other post-Soviet states. For a number of years this was in actuality the only and principal problem in Polish eastern policy. Poland tried to minimize the negative consequences of the visa requirement introduction and delayed the timing of its introduction as long as possible. Among the EU accessing states, Poland was the last country to introduce visas for its eastern neighbours, at the end of 2003. The Polish–Ukrainian solution seems to be a paradigm in this case. The parties agreed that Polish citizens would be able to travel to Ukraine without visas, and Ukrainian citizens would receive Polish visas free of charge. Also Moldova and Georgia agreed to the same solution.

After Poland's accession to the EU in May 2004, the earlier concerns about the aggravation of contacts with eastern neighbours did not materialize. There was a sudden increase in the business turnover of Poland with its eastern partners, and the introduction of the visa requirement, although it limited individual traffic, did not cause any major problems during border crossing and did not transform the eastern border of the EU into another "iron curtain." Since then Polish eastern policy has become part of the eastern policy of the EU. However, a major problem is still the lack of a uniform and coordinated EU eastern policy. This was clearly illustrated during the "orange revolution" in Ukraine at the end of 2004. The Polish authorities and Poland's citizens then showed explicit support for the democratic forces of Victor Yushchenko in his struggle with the electoral fraud of Leonid Kuchma's party. Poland's president, Aleksander Kwaśniewski, along with Lithuania's president proposed mediation at a "round table." This prevented the use of force and contributed to the peaceful resolution of the dispute.[42]

While Poland and the Baltic States would like to limit the possibilities of Russian imperialism through a common EU eastern policy as well as the democratization of Ukraine and Belarus, France and Germany perceive Russia as a factor for the regional stabilization of the area to the east of the EU. Therefore, in the immediate future the most important task for EU authorities will be to define a uniform foreign policy, including a policy towards the EU's eastern neighbours. The earlier experience of new EU member states (Poland, Lithuania, Latvia, Estonia), which border the eastern neighbours of the EU, may turn out to be invaluable in this task.[43] Polish backing for democratic changes in Ukraine during the "orange revolution" led, on the one hand, to a considerable improvement in the already existing good relations between Poland and Ukraine, but on the other it aggravated Poland's already poor relations with Russia and Belarus. Currently, Russia and its president want to punish Poland for its involvement in the victory of democracy and Victor Yushchenko in Ukraine. Russia's humiliation and ignoring of Poland in the international arena have additionally influenced the determination of the Polish authorities to support the independent and pro-Western political forces in the East.[44]

For Poland, Russia was and remains very important. The pivotal theme of all Polish eastern policy is Russia and the potential threat of Russian neo-imperialism. Polish actions and strategies towards Ukraine and Belarus are motivated not only by a concern with human rights and democracy but also with a will to counteract potential Russian political and economic expansion in Central and Eastern Europe. As can be seen by twentieth-century history, such expansion is treated seriously in Poland. Therefore, a natural barrier against the Russian *reconquista* will be the independent, democratic post-Soviet states—which are viewed as Poland's natural allies.

NOTES

1. Damrosz, "Na wschod od granic Rzeczypospolitej Polskiej."
2. Skubiszewski, "Nowe sojusze, system bezpieczenstwa w Europie Srodkowo-Wschodniej."
3. Najder, "Polska polityka zagraniczna 1989–1993."
4. Pawlak (1993/94), "Polityka trakkatowa polski."
5. Nowakowski, "Polska polityka wschodnia w 1991 roku."
6. Nowakowski, "Polska pomiedzy Wschodem a Zachodem."
7. "Deklaracja o przyjazni i dobrosasiedzkiej wspolpracy."
8. "Deklaracja o zasadach i podstawowych kierunkach."; Burant, "Problematyka wschodnia"; idem, "Ukrajina i Polszcza."
9. Nowakowski, "Polska polityka wschodnia w 1991 roku."
10. Kaminski and Kozakiewicz, *Stosunki polsko-ukrainskie.*
11. Tolstow, "Ukraina geopolityczna."
12. Iwinski, "Osiem slabosci polskiej polityki zagranicznej."
13. Kossakowski, "Polska–Rosja–Ukraina."
14. Nowakowski, "Polityka wschodnia—kilka spraw oczywistych."

15. Calka, "Polska polityka wschodnia w 1994 roku."
16. During World War II, in Katyn near Smolensk, Soviet divisions of the NKVD murdered approximately 15,000 Polish POWs. Until 1991, the Soviet government had claimed that the POWs were killed by the German army. Finally, in 1991, the Russian government officially admitted that the Polish POWs were in fact murdered by Soviet soldiers.
17. Kobrinskaja, *Dlugi koniec zimnej wojny*; Magdziak-Miszewska, *Polska i Rosja*.
18. Michutina, "Tak byla li osibka?"; idem, "Tak skolko ze sovetskich vojennoplennych pogiblo v Polsze v 1919–1921 gg?"; Ivanov, "Za dolgo do Katyni"; Liebiedieva, "Katynski dzial wodny."
19. "Koncepcija vnieszniej politiki Rossijskoj Fiederacji"; Kobrinskaja, "Nowe spojrzenie na stosunki rosyjsko-polskie."
20. September 17 is a symbolic date in Poland, since on 17 September 1939 Poland was attacked by the USSR.
21. Strzelczyk, "Lech, Borys i NATO."
22. Olechowski, "Pragniemy ocieplenia stosunkow z Rosja"; Kloczowski, "Koalicja SLD-PSL wobec Rosji"; "Glowne elementy"; "Polska polityka."
23. "Dzialalnosc prezydenta Lecha Walesy"; "Urzad Prezydenta RP."
24. "Polska i Rosja"; Nowakowski, "Polityka wschodnia—kilka spraw oczywistych."
25. Bartkiewicz, "Stosunki z Rosja, Ukraina i Bialorusia."
26. Miller, "Obraz Polski i Polakow w Rosji od roku 1989."
27. Magdziak-Miszewska, "Stosunki z Rosja."
28. Fedorowicz, *Ukraina w polskiej polityce wschodniej w latach 1989–1999*.
29. Kolecka, "Stosunki z panstwami baltyckimi."
30. Pawlowa-Silwanskaja, "Ewolucja polityki Rosji wobec Polski w latach 1991–1996."
31. "Memorandum o wolnym handlu"; *Gazeta bankowa*, 27 October 1996, 12–13.
32. Calka, "Polska polityka wschodnia w latach 1989–1997."
33. *Finansovyje Izviestia*, no. 93, 1 October 1996, 6; "Miedzy potrzeba a uzaleznieniem"; Piotrowski, "Stosunki dwustronne Polski."
34. Michalski, "Stosunki z Rosja"; Najder, "Pozornie lepiej, naprawde gorzej."
35. "Obwod Kaliningradzki"; Pelczynska-Nalecz, "Siedem mitow na temat Kaliningradu."
36. Ksiazek, "Stosunki dwustronne Polski"; Piotrowski, "Obwod kaliningradzki."
37. Kurczab-Redlich, "Z Rosji do Rosji."
38. Michalski, "Stosunki z Rosja."
39. Ksiazek, "Stosunki dwustronne Polski," 302–05.
40. Piotrowski, "Stosunki dwustronne Polski," 237–39.
41. Ksiazek, "Stosunki dwustronne Polski," 318–23.
42. Kwasniewski, "Misja kijowska."
43. Cimoszewicz, "The Eastern Dimension of the EU"; idem, "Polityka zagraniczna Polski—aktualne wyzwania."
44. Podolski, "Rosyjscy chuligani polityczni."

REFERENCES

Bartkiewicz, J. "Stosunki z Rosja, Ukraina i Bialorusia." In *Rocznik Polskiej Polityki Zagranicznej* [Yearbook of Polish Foreign Policy]. Warsaw: PISM, 1993–1994.

Burant, S. R. "Problematyka wschodnia. Studium porownawcze stosunkow Polski z Litwa, Bialorusia i Ukraina." *Studia i Materialy PISM*, no. 58 (1993): 21.

——. "Ukrajina i Polszcza: do stratehicznoho partnerstwa." *Polityczna Dumka* [Political Thought], no. 3 (1997): 100–01.

Calka, M. J. "Polska polityka wschodnia w 1994 roku." In *Rocznik Polskiej Polityki Zagranicznej* [Yearbook of Polish Foreign Policy]. Warsaw: PISM, 1995.

——. "Polska polityka wschodnia w latach 1989–1997. Proba oceny, nowe wyzwania i perspektywy." In *Rocznik Polskiej Polityki Zagranicznej* [Yearbook of Polish Foreign Policy]. Warsaw: PISM, 1998.

Cimoszewicz, W. "The Eastern Dimension of the EU: The Polish View. Speech by Wlodzimierz, Polish Minister of Foreign Affairs," European Union Enlargement and Neighbourhood Policy, Stefan Batory Foundation, Warsaw, 2003a.

——. "Polityka zagraniczna Polski—aktualne wyzwania." *Zeszyty Akademii Dyplomatycznej*, no. 3 (2003b): 16–19.

Damrosz, J. "Na wschód od granic Rzeczypospolitej Polskiej." *Przegląd Powszechny*, no. 7/8 (1991): 32–33.

"Deklaracja o przyjazni i dobrosąsiedzkiej wspólpracy miedzy Rzeczpospolita Polska i Rosyjska Federacyjna Socjalistyczna Republika Radziecka." *Polska w Europie* 4 (1991): 57–59.

"Deklaracja o zasadach i podstawowych kierunkach rozwoju stosunkow polsko-ukrainskich." *Polska w Europie* 4 (1991): 60–62.

"Dzialalnosc prezydenta Lecha Walesy w sferze polityki zagranicznej. Rok 1995, bilans 1991–1995." *Rocznik Polskiej Polityki Zagranicznej* [Yearbook of Polish Foreign Policy]. Warsaw: PISM, 1996.

Fedorowicz, K. *Ukraina w polskiej polityce wschódniej w latach 1989–1999* [The Ukraine in the Polish Eastern Policy 1989–1999]. Poznan: Wydawn. Naukowe UAM, 2004.

"Glowne elementy polskiej polityki wschódniej. Wystapienie ministra spraw zagranicznych Andrzeja Olechowskiego." *Przegląd Rzadowy*, no. 3 (1994): 83–87.

Ivanov, I. V. "Za dolgo do Katyni. Krasnoarmiejcy v adu polskich konclagerej." *Vojenno-Istoriceskij Żurnal*, no. 12 (1993): 22–26.

Iwinski, T. "Osiem słabosci polskiej polityki zagranicznej." *Dzis*, no. 9 (1993): 16–17.

Kaminski, A. Z., and J. Kozakiewicz. *Stosunki polsko-ukrainskie: Raport*. Warsaw: Centre for International Relations, 1997.

Kloczowski, J. "Koalicja SLD–PSL wobec Rosji." *Arcana*, no. 5 (1996): 46–48.

Kobrinskaja, I. *Długi koniec zimnej wojny. Rosja i Europa Sródkowa 1991–1996*. Warsaw: Więź, 1998a.

Kobrinskaja, I. "Nowe spojrzenie na stosunki rosyjsko-polskie." In *Polska i Rosja. Strategiczne sprzecznośći i możliwośći dialogu*, edited by A. Magdziak-Miszewska. Warsaw: Centrum Stosunków Międzynarodowych, 1998b.

Kolecka, B. "Stosunki z panstwami baltyckimi." In *Rocznik Polskiej Polityki Zagranicznej* [Yearbook of Polish Foreign Policy]. Warsaw: PISM, 1996.

"Koncepcija vniesznej politiki Rossijskoj Fiederacji." *Diplomaticzieskij Viestnik*, no. 1 (1993): 13–14.

Kossakowski, J. "Polska–Rosja–Ukraina. Trojkat Bermudzki czy strategiczna współnota interesow." *Dzis*, no. 10 (1993): 33–36.

Ksiazek, J. "Stosunki dwustronne Polski. Federacja Rosyjska." In *Rocznik Polskiej Polityki Zagranicznej* [Yearbook of Polish Foreign Policy]. Warsaw: PISM, 2003.

Kurczab-Redlich, K. "Z Rosji do Rosji." *Polityka*, no. 26, t29 June 2002: 36.

Kwaśniewski, A. "Misja kijowska." *Polityka*, no. 51, t18 December 2004: 31–37.

Liebiedieva, N. "Katynski dział wodny." In *Polacy i Rosjanie. 100 kluczowych pojec*, edited by A. Magdziak-Miszewska. Warsaw: Biblioteka "Więz," 2002.

Magdziak-Miszewska, A. "Stosunki z Rosja." In *Rocznik Polskiej Polityki Zagranicznej* [Yearbook of Polish Foreign Policy]. Warsaw: PISM, 1996.

——. *Polska i Rosja. Strategiczne sprzecznosći i możliwosći dialogu*. Warsaw: Centrum Stosunkó Międzynarodowych, 1998.

"Memorandum o wolnym handlu miedzy Federacją Rosyjską a Rzczpospolitą Polską, Rosyjsko-polski program współpracy inwestycyjnej, Porozumienie o poparciu dla utworzenia i rozwoju ponadpanstwowych zjednoczen produkcyjnych, handlowych, kredytowo-finansowych, ubezpieczeniowych i mieszanych, Głowne kierunki partnerstwa i współpracy." *Materiały i Dokumenty Ministerstwa Współpracy Gospodarczej z Zagranica RP*. Warsaw: Ministry of Economics, 1996.

Michałski, A. "Stosunki z Rosja." In *Rocznik Polskiej Polityki Zagranicznej* [Yearbook of Polish Foreign Policy]. Warsaw: PISM, 1999.

——. "Stosunki z Rosją." In *Rocznik Polskiej Polityki Zagranicznej* [Yearbook of Polish Foreign Policy]. Warsaw: PISM, 2000.

Michutina, I. V. "Tak skolko ze sovetskich vojennoplennych pogiblo v Polsce v 1919–1921 gg?" *Novaja i Novejsaja Istorija*, no. 3 (1995): 64–69.

——. "Tak była li osibka?" *Nezavisimaja Gazieta*, 13 January 2001, 8.

"Między potrzeba a uzaleznieniem. Rosyjski gaz w bilansie energetycznym rozszerzonej UE" [Between Need and Dependency. Russian Gas in the Energy Balance of the Enlarged EU]. In *Raporty 8* [Policy Paper no. 8]. Warsaw: Stefan Batory Foundation, 2002.

Miller, A. "Obraz Polski i Polaków w Rosji od roku 1989." In *Polska polityka wschodnia*, edited by S. Miklaszewski and G. Przebinda. Krakow: Institute for Strategic Studies, 2000.

Najder, Z. "Polska polityka zagraniczna 1989–1993: bilans zaniedban." *Arka*, no. 51 (1994): 60–61.

——. "Pozornie lepiej, naprawde gorzej." In *Rocznik Polskiej Polityki Zagranicznej* [Yearbook of Polish Foreign Policy]. Warsaw: PISM, 2000.

Nowakowski, J. M. "Polska polityka wschodnia w 1991 roku." In *Rocznik Polskiej Polityki Zagranicznej* [Yearbook of Polish Foreign Policy]. Warsaw: PISM, 1992.

——. "Polska pomiedzy Wschodem a Zachodem. Szansa pomostu czy historyczne fatum." *Polska w Europie* 11 (1993): 8–9.

——. "Polityka wschodnia—kilka spraw oczywistych." *Polska w Europie* 20 (1996): 5.

"Obwód Kaliningradzki w kontekscie rozszerzenia Unii Europejskiej" [The Kaliningrad Oblast in the Context of EU Enlargement]. In *Prace OSW* [CES Studies]. Warsaw: Osrodek Studiów Wschodnich [Centre for Eastern Studies], 2001.

Olechowski, A. "Pragniemy ocieplenia stosunków z rosją." *Rzeczpospolita*, no. 41, 18 February 1994, 22.

Pawlak, S. "Polityka traktatowa Polski." In *Rocznik Polskiej Polityki Zagranicznej* [Yearbook of Polish Foreign Policy]. Warsaw: PISM, 1993–1994.

Pawlowa-Silwanskaja, M. "Ewolucja polityki Rosji wobec Polski w latach 1991–1996." In *Polska i Rosja. Strategiczne sprzecznosći i możliwosći dialogu*, edited by A. Magdziak-Miszewska. Warsaw: Centrum Stosunków Międzynarodowych, 1998.

Pelczynska-Nalecz, K. "Siedem mitów na temat Kaliningradu" [Seven Myths about Kaliningrad]. In *Punkt widzenia* [Policy Brief]. Warsaw: Osrodek Studiow Wschodnich [Centre for Eastern Studies], 2002.

Piotrowski, M. A. "Stosunki dwustronne Polski. Federacja Rosyjska." In *Rocznik Polskiej Polityki Zagranicznej* [Yearbook of Polish Foreign Policy]. Warsaw: PISM, 2001.

——. "Obwód kaliningradzki: laboratorium współpracy czy pole konfliktu?" In *Rocznik Polskiej Polityki Zagranicznej* [Yearbook of Polish Foreign Policy]. Warsaw: PISM, 2002.

Podolski, A. "Rosyjscy chuligani polityczni." *Gazeta Wyborcza*, 11 August 2005, 13.

"Polska i Rosja: partnerstwo dla transformacji." *Przegląd Rzadowy*, no. 3 (1994): 88–91.

"Polska polityka zagraniczna. Expose ministra Andrzeja Olechowskiego w parlamencie 12 maja 1994 r." *Przeglad Rzadowy*, no. 5 (1994): 60–64.

Skubiszewski, K. "Nowe sojusze, system bezpieczenstwa w Europie Srodkowo-Wschodniej." *Tygodnik Powszechny*, no. 11 (1991): 6–7.

Strzelczyk, J. "Lech, Borys i NATO." *Polityka*, no. 45, t9 November 2002, 80.

Tolstow, S. "Ukraina geopolityczna." *Eurazja*, no. 1 (1995): 8–9.

"Urząd Prezydenta RP." In *Rocznik Polskiej Polityki Zagranicznej* [Yearbook of Polish Foreign Policy]. Warsaw: PISM, 1993–1994.

The Nature of Russia's Identity: The Theme of "Russia and the West" in Post-Soviet Culture

Rosalind Marsh

The aim of this essay is to present a brief overview of the treatment in post-Soviet culture and the media, especially in literature, film and *publitsistika* on historical themes, of certain aspects of the perennial debate about "Russia and the West." I will ask whether the West is still regarded as Russia's "Other," or whether, in a period when Russia has been more open to the West than ever before, and Western and Russian tastes in historical and other fiction appear to be converging, such a polar opposition can now be seen as fundamentally outdated.

As Edward Said has argued, self-definition is an important aspect of any nation's life which not only entails defining what one *is*, but also what one *is not*.[1] In Russia this process has been central to national life in a more intense way than it has in the West, involving successive generations of rulers, thinkers and writers. The perplexing, eternal question "Russia—East or West?," and its many corollaries, such as: "Is Russia a part of Europe or Asia, or both?," "What is Russia's relation to Western civilization?," "Do Russians feel themselves to be Europeans?," have been discussed for centuries, frequently conditioning the development of Russia's political and social thought and influencing the policies of her rulers.[2]

Any judgement of comparison or contrast is usually based on some conscious or unconscious recognition of identity.[3] Thus, when Russians compare or contrast their own country with "the West," they implicitly acknowledge their affinity with Western Europe or the US. In international and cultural relations during different historical periods Russians have manifested an innate sense either of superiority or inferiority in relation to the West—a complex that some contemporary Russian scholars are now prepared to acknowledge openly.[4]

This essay focuses predominantly on the "imaginary West" perceived by Russian writers and cultural figures rather than on the historical, political and social realities of Western Europe or the US at any given time,[5] or on the concept of "an imagined political community" proposed by Benedict Anderson as the definition of a nation.[6] The term "image" is used to include beliefs, attitudes and stereotypes. For contemporary Russian writers and thinkers (as for their predecessors), the image of the West encompasses conceptions of Western culture, ideas associated with it and real or imagined experience in it, all of which are used to explore, or even to rediscover, their own country, which always remains their primary focus of interest. As in classical Russian literature, many contemporary Russian writers have internalized the idea of a "Russian West" (*russkii Zapad*)—an "invented West" that forms the counterpart of the West's long-standing representation of an "invented Eastern Europe"—which has developed into an important aspect of the Russian national consciousness.[7]

Russia's view of the West has been as stereotypical as the West's image of Russia, even in the works of Russian writers who travelled to the West, such as Fonvizin, Herzen and Dostoevsky. While Western writers have frequently emphasized the violent, tragic or apocalyptic elements supposedly endemic in Russian life, Russians (even those who admire certain progressive aspects of Western political organization and technology) tend to accentuate the alleged rationalism, coldness, egoism and soul-less materialism of Western society. Such views have been passed on from nineteenth-century classic writers such as Herzen and Dostoevsky, through the period of Soviet isolationism and Cold War hostility, to resurface in the late twentieth and early twenty-first centuries.

Just as the West constantly reinvents the idea of Russia and Central Eastern Europe, every generation in Russia discovers the West anew. In contemporary Russia, many of the key points in Russia's historical relationship with the West have been re-examined and reinterpreted, often from a nationalist viewpoint. This essay aims to present some new approaches to these vexing questions and to discuss some of the reassessments of "Russia and the West" prevalent in Russian culture at the beginning of the new millennium. My argument is underpinned by Foucault's view that discourse is "the thing for which and by which there is struggle,"[8] and of Slavoj Žižek that "facts *never* 'speak for themselves', but are always made to speak by a network of discursive devices."[9] Contemporary Russian culture and its view of "the West" present an interesting case study of how identities are constructed through discursive representation and within competing relations of power.

The Historical and Cultural Background

Since the late 1980s there has been an intensification and polarization of the debates between Russian "democrats" and "national-patriots" in Russia, both within Russia and in the émigré community. These constitute a new version of the old discussions between the "Westernizers" and the "Slavophiles," but in a more tense historical situation than the relatively stable 1840s, when there has been far more at stake. In the late and post-Soviet periods, when censorship was lifted for the first time in Russian history, the entire spectrum of opinions expressed on these issues in the nineteenth century, from Chaadaev's extreme pro-Westernism to Danilevsky's extreme anti-Westernism, has been reiterated, in new configurations, in Russian literature, thought and the media.

Russia and the West during Perestroika

During perestroika and the immediate post-Soviet period, the predominant approach to the "Russia and the West" debate adopted in literature and *publitsistika* was a pro-Western, anti-authoritarian view similar to the "new thinking" espoused by Gorbachev and his reformist associates.[10]

Although the majority of works concerned with the Russian and Soviet past published during perestroika adopted a liberal, democratic approach, by 1988–1989 a few controversies had been provoked among resurgent Russian nationalist circles by the perceived pro-Western, anti-Russian tenor of some of the newly published works. Russian nationalist critics objected, for example, to the satirical approach to Russian and Soviet history adopted in Vladimir Voinovich's *Life and Adventures of Private Ivan Chonkin* (1988) and Georgii Vladimov's *Faithful Ruslan* (1988), Andrei Siniavsky's allegedly disrespectful view of the "great Russian writer" Pushkin—and, by implication, of Russian culture in general—in the extract of his *Progulki s Pushkinym* [Walks with Pushkin] published in 1989,[11] not to mention Vasily Grossman's view in *Vse techet* [Everything Flows, 1989] that "the Russian soul has been enslaved for a thousand years."[12]

Texts published during perestroika and the immediate post-Soviet period that deal with the treatment of Stalin and Stalinism diverge along "East–West" lines according to whether the author held a predominantly "democratic" or "patriotic" viewpoint. Some "democratic" writers continued to draw comparisons between Stalin and Eastern tyrants such as Tamurlane and the Egyptian Pharaohs,[13] or to refer to him as an "Ossete,"[14] alluding to Mandelstam's underground poem on Stalin written in 1933.[15] In such anti-Stalin texts, the Orient is invested with its conventional associations of despotism and backwardness.[16] At the same time, writers of a more nationalistic persuasion traced Leninism and Stalinism to Western models such as the French Revolution[17] or to utopian Western thinkers such as Campanella, Proudhon and Babeuf.[18]

The West in Post-Soviet Culture

The presence and influence of the West (whether benign or malign) has been an enduring theme in contemporary Russian society and culture. After the collapse of communism, many contemporary Russian writers and film-makers who seek to investigate the Russian national consciousness have felt a persistent need to compare and contrast Russia with its "Other," the West. This theme features far more prominently in both Russian elite and popular culture than the representation of an "invented" Russia, Eastern Europe or the Balkans does in Western literature. Such themes are treated in only a few works of contemporary Western literature—often produced by writers of Eastern European origin (such as Tom Stoppard's dramatic trilogy "The Coast of Utopia," produced at the British National Theatre in 2002[19]).

Notwithstanding the greatly increased opportunities for Russians to travel to the West and for Western people to meet Russians, along with the availability of much

151

Russian literature in translation, stereotypes of Russia and the West continue to persist in both Western and Russian literature. Conventional views of Russia as exotic, alien and enigmatic can still be found in contemporary Western literature;[20] Russia continues to be regarded by some Westerners as the West's "Other," in the colonial sense defined by Edward Said. At the same time, some Russian writers, even those of a predominantly "democratic" or experimentalist persuasion who have spent long periods in the West, such as Tat'iana Tolstaia and Viktor Erofeyev—still retain ill-informed, simplistic views of Western ideas, most notably Western feminism.[21]

Pro-Western themes in Post-Soviet Culture

In post-Soviet Russia, émigré and democratic Russian writers and scholars still express sympathy for Western values, or try through their writings to increase understanding between Russia and the West.

In the early 1990s, attitudes to the West expressed in Russian literature and film were generally quite positive, albeit frequently superficial. In a Russian–French co-production of 1993, for example, Iurii Mamin's film "Okno v Parizh" [Window to Paris, 1993], a magical window in St. Petersburg opens onto the rooftops of Paris, and the Russian protagonists are amazed at the consumer goods on display in the sophisticated French capital. The Russian protagonist ruefully remarks: "We held off the Mongol hordes for them, so they had the luxury of developing." The film, of course, depicts not the real Paris, but the mythical Paris of beauty and freedom which exists in the post-Soviet imagination. Mamin implies a critique of contemporary Russia's misguided idealization of Western-style capitalism, but it is left to the viewer to decide whether Russian poverty or Western capitalist wealth is the most corrupting. The conclusion is patriotic: the idealistic hero decides to stay in St. Petersburg and try to help extricate the country from its current crisis.

Writers and film directors sympathetic to "democratic" values adopt a relatively balanced approach to the question of "Russia and the West" in the post-Soviet period. One such is the writer and former history teacher Viacheslav P'etsukh, who in many of his works examines the Russian character humorously and dispassionately. In *Zakoldovannaia strana* [The Enchanted Land, 1992], he suggests that there is no need for Russia to keep defining herself in relation to the West, since Russian history and geography are so distinctive. He does, nevertheless, acknowledge that the habit of judging Russia by Western standards is deeply ingrained in the Russian mind. P'etsukh's narrator ironically remarks, referring obliquely to the much-disputed tale told in the *Povest' vremennykh let* [The Primary Chronicle, *c.*1017] of the warring ninth-century Eastern Slavic tribes' invitation to the Varangian princes from Scandinavia to come and rule them:

> Zulus don't compare themselves with anyone and feel fabulous, but we, as if picking at a scab, have to say "The West has order and prosperity, whereas our only claim to fame is that we discuss the transient nature of existence while barefoot."[22]

A more ambivalent view has been expressed by Tat'iana Tolstaia, who, while some-times appearing to sympathize with the essentialist "Russian writers and thinkers" who "have often called the 'Russian soul' female, contrasting it to the rational, clear, dry, active, well-defined soul of the Western man," nevertheless acknowledges the limitations of the Russian intelligentsia's traditional approach when dealing with practical or scientific matters:

> How many scornful pages have great Russian writers dedicated to Western pragmatism, materialism, rationalism! They mocked the English with their machines, the Germans with their order and precision, the French with their logic, and finally the Americans with their love of money. As a result, in Russia we have neither machines, nor order, nor logic, nor money.[23]

Those writers of "serious literature" who have been among the most successful and popular in post-Soviet Russia, whether Vladimir Makanin in the older generation or Viktor Pelevin in the younger, have presented contemporary Russian society in a broad historical and philosophical context, stressing certain similarities between Russia and the West. In *Stol, pokrytyi suknom i s grafinom peseredine* [Baize-Covered Table with Decanter, 1993] for example, Makanin's narrator makes it clear that the long-standing association between the Table, symbolizing the authoritarian power of the bureaucratic state system, and the Cellar, emblem of the tortures inflicted by the security services throughout Russian history from the time of Ivan the Terrible to the Stalin era and beyond, is not only characteristic of Russia but of the West too:

> The association between the Table and the Cellar is substantive, unchanging, and goes back far into the depths of history, to Byzantine times, let us say. (And Roman times too, of course. I have no illusions about the Latin West.)[24]

Viktor Pelevin, who has become a "cult" writer, especially among young Russians, sets post-Soviet society, with its new market system, computer and youth culture, Westernized media and advertising, in a much longer perspective of Russian and world history and philosophy, frequently using humour to make serious points. In *Generation P* (1999) (translated as *Babylon*), a slogan ostensibly advertising the clothes chain "Gap" refers to the West's perception of Russia as uncivilized to characterize the spiritual emptiness of post-Soviet society:

> Russia was always notorious for the gap between culture and civilization. Now there is no more culture, no more civilization. The only thing that remains is the Gap. The way they see you.[25]

The perennial question of Russia's relationship with the West is reduced to a comic advertisement: "Gucci for men. Be a European: smell better"; while Tiutchev's mystical, messianic lines:

> It is impossible to understand Russia with the mind ...
> It is only possible to believe in Russia

which are much quoted in contemporary Russia,[26] are used to advertise Smirnoff vodka.[27]

However, Pelevin's work also frequently challenges the notion that Russia can be "saved" by the West. In both *Chapaev i Pustota* (1996; translated in the UK as *The Clay Machine Gun* and in the US as *Buddha's Little Finger*) and *Generation P* he explores Buddhist philosophy, emphasizing the illusory nature of both Soviet ideology and the new "ideology" of market capitalism, and suggesting that the Westernized advertising slogans prevalent in post-Soviet Russia are merely a new version of propaganda akin to socialist realism. Through irony, Buddhist concepts and imagery from Babylonian mythology, Pelevin attempts to transcend conventional Russian notions of the East–West divide.[28]

An interesting new development in the twenty-first century has been that some long-established writers of a "democratic" and "Westernizing" persuasion have turned to eighteenth-century Russian history as an appropriate means of exploring national identity. The eighteenth century is a particularly attractive period for such writers to investigate, since Russia was constantly undergoing major internal reform or upheaval under its powerful Westernizing leaders Peter the Great and Catherine the Great, while winning military battles and rising to "Great Power" status in Europe. In a period when Russia's relationship with the West has been a major political issue, contemporary "Westernizers" such as Daniil Granin, in his *Vechera s Petrom Pervym* [Evenings with Peter the Great, 2000] and Vasily Aksenov, in his *Volteriantsy i volterianki* [Voltairean Men and Women, 2004],[29] preferring to avoid didactic exhortations about the present in the fear that it may alienate their readers, choose to engage their audience by portraying engrossing historical scenes, while drawing subtle parallels with contemporary politics and society.

The Rise of Russian Nationalism in the 1990s

The resurgence of Russian nationalism in the mid-1990s can be attributed not only to the failure of Russia's market reforms but also the failure of liberal, democratic politicians to pay attention to questions of nationality, ethnicity and state building, which encouraged traditional nationalist views to move in to fill the ensuing intellectual and political vacuum.[30] Nationalism was again officially promoted in 1995 by Yeltsin's government to coincide with the patriotic celebrations accompanying the 50th anniversary of the Soviet victory in the war against fascism.[31] Yeltsin also considered it expedient to take over some of the rhetoric of his communist and nationalist opponents who challenged him in the presidential elections of 1996.[32]

The success of the nationalist revival was particularly demonstrated by the Duma's decision of 1995 to abrogate the Belovezh accords of 1991 which had ratified the break-up of the Soviet Union; the adoption of a law enshrining Russia's right to protect the Russian minorities in the "near abroad"; and subsequently, during the wars in the former Yugoslavia, the revival of traditional notions of protecting Russia's Orthodox "brother Serbs," and Russia's hostility to the expansion of NATO.

By the late 1990s (according to research conducted by Hilary Pilkington and her associates), even Russians of the younger generation, who in the Soviet period had been most open to Western influences, were renegotiating their attitudes to the West because Western cultural forms and lifestyles were coming to be increasingly perceived as an alien imposition rather than as enticing "forbidden fruit."[33] These young people continued to harbour many conventional stereotypes: in particular, they still perceived the West as materialistic and Russia as the embodiment of spirituality.[34]

The Growth of Anti-Western Feeling in Russian Culture of the 1990s

The resurgence of Russian nationalism by the mid-1990s allowed anti-Western senti-ments to surface in some mainstream Russian films on historical topics, in which foreigners or Russians subject to alien Western influences were presented either as capitalist exploiters, political enemies, or purveyors of decadent Western culture. In Nikita Mikhalkov's well-known film *Utomlennye solntsem* [Burnt by the Sun, 1994], the villain who betrays the Old Bolshevik hero is the devious Mitia, a former émigré linked with the Whites who returns from the West to collaborate with Stalin's security services.

Mikhalkov's later film *Sibirskii tsiriul'nik* [The Barber of Siberia, 1998], is even more explicit in its anti-Western bias. The Russian government reportedly contributed $10 million dollars to sponsor this $45 million film, suggesting that by the late 1990s the search for national identity and the propagation of patriotic values had now entered the mainstream of Russian culture and political thinking. Mikhalkov attempts simul-taneously to celebrate and mock the Russian national character, to assert Russia's spiritual superiority over the materialist West, and to praise traditional Russian values of collectivism and brotherhood. Although many Russian critics complained that this was a film made for the West, since 70% of the dialogue was in English and pre-revolutionary Russia was presented in a kitsch *style russe*, Western audiences could not fail to be irritated that Westerners were depicted in extremely negative terms as only exploiters, prostitutes and rogues. The film features the former prostitute Mrs. Callahan, the ruthless American capitalist Douglas McCracken who exploits Russia through his invention of an infernal machine that relentlessly mows down Siber-ian forests, and the bizarre Sergeant ("Mad Dog") O'Leary, who thinks that Mozart is a Russian girl. Some sceptical Russian critics, while recognizing the film's enormous cultural impact, acidly but cogently suggested that its main value was as a political pro-gramme and an advertising slogan[35] (since Mikhalkov, who had initially supported Yeltsin's nationalist opponent Rutskoi, temporarily contemplated standing for the presidency). With its idealized portrayal of the reactionary Tsar Alexander III (1881–1894) and young guards officers from the Russian aristocracy, it attempts to imbue its audience with pride in the Russian state and the soldiers charged with its defence. Indeed, the film is dedicated "to the honor of Russian officers." The official tsarist values of "autocracy, Orthodoxy and nationality" are much in evidence in this film, which made it an appropriate vehicle to express the essence of the new Russia and the values underpinning the Russian involvement in the second Chechen war.

One significant idea that has resurfaced in contemporary Russian culture has been the traditional messianic view that Russia is a unique country which must pursue its own path of development that is necessarily different from that of the West, and will have a special, distinctive role to play in the future. During perestroika and the early post-Soviet period there was more discussion of "how to save Russia" than "how Russia can save the world," although messianic beliefs were espoused by extremist politicians such as Zhirinovsky and Ziuganov.[36]

In the 1990s, however, Russian readers also had the opportunity to acquaint themselves with messianic notions through some of Solzhenitsyn's newly published publicistic works, notably his "Harvard Commencement Address" of 1979, which had suggested that Russia's immense suffering in the twentieth century had enabled her to experience "a spiritual schooling which has by far superseded Western experience." In Solzhenitsyn's view, "Life, repressing us in complex and mortal ways, has produced characters which are stronger, deeper and more interesting than those produced by the prosperous, regimented life in the West."[37] The implication is that the great reserves of spiritual energy imparted to the Russian people through suffering may allow their nation to play a messianic role at some time in the future.

In the works of "democratic" writers, nationalistic and messianic views of Russian history comparing Russia excessively favourably with the West were predominantly the subject of parody. In "Novaia moskovskaia filosofiia" [New Moscow Philosophy, 1989], for example, P'etsukh ironically contrasts the "old Moscow philosophy" about the backwardness of Russia propounded by Chaadaev with the ostensibly "new Moscow philosophy"—the idea that Russia "is charged with the mission of furthering spiritual development."[38] This view is, of course, not new at all, but has long been advocated by Orthodox supporters of the fifteenth-century notion of Moscow as the Third Rome and taken up by generations of Russian and Soviet nationalists. P'etsukh's comic exploration of the contradictory characteristics of his fellow countrymen in many of his works also implicitly casts doubt on Russia's capacity to "save the world." In "The Central-Ermolaevo War," for example, P'etsukh contends that Russians are always prepared for conflict, and that "the Russian soul encompasses everything ... constructiveness, negation, flair, pyromania, national pride and castles in the air."[39] While recognizing that messianism may sometimes be an arrogant illusion,[40] P'etsukh nevertheless sees it as an integral part of the "Russian theme," which, in his view, constitutes the fundamental subject of post-Soviet literature.[41] In his novella "Zakoldovannaia strana" [The Enchanted Land, 1992], P'etsukh's narrator remarks that Western Europeans should regard Russians as people returned from hell "with respect, terror, awe and rapture ... and with gratitude too, because we, like the son of God, have redeemed the sins of the world with our suffering."[42]

After Yeltsin's fruitless search for a new "idea for Russia" that could help to unite a divided, conflict-ridden country was tacitly abandoned in 1997,[43] this doomed venture was also parodied in literature. In *Generation P*, for example, Pelevin depicts a mafia bandit who instructs an advertising copy-writer to compose a Russian idea so that Russians can impress the Americans:

> "There's got to be some nice, simple Russian idea, so's we can lay it out clear and simple for any bastard from any of their Harvards ... And we've got to know for ourselves where we come from ... Write me a Russian idea about five pages long. And a short version one page long."[44]

Notwithstanding continued scepticism towards Russian messianism on the part of writers of a more "democratic" persuasion, a coherent, if sometimes unattractive and highly questionable version of Russian history has been articulated throughout the post-communist period in the three nationalist journals which continue to be published in Russia: *Moskva*, which focuses on Russian religious thought and the ideas of the "back-to-the-soil" movement (*pochvenniki*), *Molodaia gvardiia*, a supporter of the communists and the military-industrial complex, and *Nash sovremennik*, which endorses the radical national-patriots. A typical nationalist novel is "Poslednii soldat imperii" [The Last Soldier of the Empire, 1993] by Aleksandr Prokhanov (1993), the editor of the extreme national-patriotic newspaper *Zavtra*, which laments the end of the Soviet empire and the collapse of the Soviet state, displaying extreme anti-Western sentiments. Prokhanov's hero is a social scientist who refuses the blandishments of the Rand Corporation to work in the US.[45]

By the late 1990s, more extreme messianic views began to be expressed by members of the cultural intelligentsia even in mainstream, formerly "democratic" publications. In 1998, *Literaturnaia gazeta* published an article by the émigré writer Iurii Mamleev which claimed that "the vocation of Russia is to bring the world, particularly Europe, to a new and more (morally and intellectually) lofty civilization," and that "Orthodoxy is the most intact core of world Christianity." He also expressed extreme anti-Western sentiments: "In the West—and this is no secret—there is to all intents and purposes the ideology of money, the dollar, the most primitive ideology of materialism and egoism."[46] Such messianic notions and primitive denunciations of the West have, however, been ably refuted by other émigré writers, such as Vasilii Aksenov.[47]

Émigré Writers

Writings by Russian émigrés also demonstrate attitudes to the West as diverse and ambivalent as those of their compatriots in the metropolis. On the one hand, some émigré writers sympathetic to the West have used their writings to attempt to create a more realistic picture of Western society, and to increase understanding between Russia and the West.

157

Fiction can be a valuable medium for highlighting the sources of mutual incomprehension. In a novel by a Russian émigré writer who is very familiar with the West and more sympathetic to it than most, Vasilii Aksenov's *Moskovskaia saga* [Moscow Saga, 1993–1994; translated as *Generations of Winter*], a well-informed American journalist wonders "Just where did the Russians get this habit of automatically assuming they were superior to Westerners?.," while misleading his Russian interlocutor by "playing the fool, the superficial American newspaperman" so that the Russian feels that this foreigner cannot possibly understand the intricacies of Russian history and tradition: "Who among them [Westerners] could understand this, these murmurings from middle earth mixed with fifteen centuries of a people's history?"[48]

Other Russian émigrés such as Dovlatov, Zinik and Limonov have presented humorous or sensational pictures of life in the West, often describing their adopted countries from fresh or surprising viewpoints. If Russian émigré writers were better known in the West, they might enable Westerners not only to understand Russians better but also to develop a deeper understanding of themselves by demonstrating how others see them.

On the other hand, the process of initial admiration or ambivalence and subsequent disillusionment with the West reminiscent of that experienced by Russian travellers and émigrés in the nineteenth century (such as Herzen, a former enthusiastic Westernizer who adopted a more "Slavophile" position after 1847[49]) has also become apparent among the Russian diaspora in the late and post-Soviet periods. Some émigrés of the "third wave," particularly those with nationalist sympathies, have returned to Russia—most notably Solzhenitsyn, in 1994. His memoir of life in the West, "Ugodilo zernyshko promezh dvukh zhernovov: ocherki izgnaniia" [The Grain Fell between Two Millstones, 1998], expresses resentment with the West's tendency to identify Russia with communism, which he regards as bordering on Russophobia:

I no longer feel that America is such a solid, faithful, strong ally in the fight for our liberation. If only I had known! If only someone had shown me back then the American Congress's disgraceful law 86–90 (1959) in which Russians are not named among the nations oppressed by communism but Russia is named as the world oppressor.[50]

In post-Soviet Russia, writers who still choose to live in emigration are sometimes regarded as "former people" by Russian readers because, in the words of the émigré writer Boris Khazanov, "Émigré prose, like Lot's wife, cannot take her eyes off the past ... Yes, [the émigré writer] is faithful to his homeland, only it is a homeland which no longer exists."[51] Khazanov argues convincingly, however, that émigré writing should not necessarily be considered outdated, because literature based on memory is as legitimate and significant as any other form of writing. Nevertheless, such reasoning has not prevented Russian self-styled "national-patriots" from castigating émigré writers for leaving Russia and enjoying what they see as an "easy life" in the West.[52] Some prominent émigrés have retaliated by attacking what they perceive as the growing xenophobia and anti-Semitism in contemporary Russia.[53] Certainly,

158

since the mid-1990s there is some evidence that interviews with émigré writers are more likely to be published in the Russian press if they express disillusionment with the West rather than admiration for it.

New Developments in Russian Culture of the Late 1990s and Early 2000s

At the end of the 1990s and in the first decade of the twenty-first century literature continues to display a wide spectrum of opinions on the West. Some writers have depicted the wholesale transplantation of Russian values and relationships to a Western setting, as in Liudmila Ulitskaia's *Veselye pokhorony* [The Funeral Party, 1998].

Viktor Erofeyev's fictionalized memoir *Khoroshii Stalin* (2004) also demonstrates the value to Russians of travel to the West. Erofeyev generally presents a very positive view of France, showing that when his father worked as a diplomat in France during the Stalin period, his mother fully assimilated Parisian customs, and he himself gained some wonderful memories. He also emphasizes the support he and his colleagues obtained from France during the *Metropol'* affair of 1979, and even publishes long extracts from a review of the almanac in *Le Monde* (in French).[54] Nevertheless, Erofeyev also revisits some old stereotypes of the materialistic West—especially France as a country where people do nothing but eat: "Paris is composed of food. It is completely permeated with the smell of food. The French do nothing but eat."[55]

Moreover, in one of his numerous articles attempting to explain Russia to the West, Erofeyev has also revived the conventional notion that Russian culture is "so totally different from Western culture" and emphasizes the alleged distinction between "Western civilization" and "Russian culture":

> Western civilization is largely determined by the mass media, commerce and so on . . . In Russia there is virtually no civilization, we don't know how to keep the streets clean, but we have a deeper understanding of culture, at least in the spiritual sense. We live in a world caught midway between Europe and Asia. We don't know how to organize society—and so we have a more direct experience of life.[56]

Here, Erofeyev comes close to Pushkin's (highly questionable) statement that "Russia never had anything in common with the rest of Europe. Her history demands a different thought and a different formula."[57]

In the twenty-first century the perennial theme of East–West relations has also been explored in the extraordinary film *Russkii kovcheg* [The Russian Ark, 2003] by Aleksandr Sokurov. In a single take, perhaps symbolic of the director's notion of Russian historical continuity, the camera pans over figures from Russian history as they roam through the magnificent rooms of the Hermitage in St. Petersburg, decorated by Western architects and hung with Western paintings, under the watchful eyes of a representative of the West, the black-clad "Marquis." He is evidently an embodiment of the Marquis de Custine, the famous traveller who described Russia in 1839 as a "prison" permeated by police informers, arbitrary government and slavish adulation of the tsar.[58] Sokurov seems to be suggesting that different historical periods exist in Russia side by side, and that some features of Custine's backward Russia still survive today. As he said in an interview:

> There's no doubt that several periods of time are existing in parallel in the life of Russia today. Elements of feudalism and elements of early Russian capitalism and continuing socialist habits ... Yes, Russia is distinguished by the fact that in one temporal plane, a multitude of historical epochs are in existence. And despite the fact that we live in the twenty-first century, we are also living in the eighteenth, nineteenth and twentieth centuries.

The Marquis, who, in Sokurov's words, is not merely an incarnation of Custine but is also intended to represent a "composite, universal European,"[59] makes scathing remarks about Russia's lack of indigenous talent and its constant need to imitate the West. However, at the end of the film he decides to join the ball (the last Great Royal Ball ever held in the Winter Palace in 1913) and expresses the desire to stay for ever dancing the mazurka with lovely ladies. Yet even in his change of heart the Westerner once again shows a lack of understanding of Russian history, ignoring the director's voice which warns him to hold back and laments the passing of so many lives. Ultimately a thick mist descends and the Hermitage is left to float away into the unknown while the narrator makes the mournful pronouncement "Goodbye, Europe!" It is possible to interpret the conclusion in a pessimistic light, as a prophecy of the birth of the Soviet regime destined to destroy Old Russia and its European heritage, but an alternative view is that Sokurov is simply posing Gogol's famous question "Whither Russia?," while demonstrating that Russia may be able to select and conserve the most valuable aspects of its past history and culture as it moves on into the future. This is a conclusion similar to that in Chaadaev's "Second Philosophical Letter,"[60] which argued that Russia's unique history could be regarded not as an impediment but an advantage.

Nationalist and Anti-Western Writings

By the beginning of the twenty-first century nationalist and messianic ideas were also being expressed with increasing frequency in Russian literature and the media, although opinion polls held at different times differed in their findings about whether the majority of the Russian people agreed with such views.[61]

At the end of the 1990s and the beginning of the twenty-first century, a new genre of nationalist fiction emerged which came to be known as the "imperial novel," since it advocated a strong state and imperial expansionism. One prominent example is Pavel Krusanov's *Ukus angela* [The Bite of an Angel, 1999], winner of the prize sponsored by the journal *Oktiabr'*, which adapted to the contemporary political and cultural situation by combining fashionable fantastic and esoteric themes with imperialist ambitions. Krusanov describes an alternative world in which, at the end of the twentieth century, Russia, instead of shrinking to its smallest size for about 200 years, has extended its empire to China and the Balkans, and is waging a world war to annex more territories. The novel depicts the rise to supreme power of the dictator Ivan Neki-taev (whose name literally means "not-Chinese"), who is presented as an Antichrist figure, with demonic powers. Nekitaev stops at nothing in his ruthless pursuit of dic-tatorial power, and at the end of the novel, when he begins losing the war he had started, he unleashes his "Hounds of Hecate" to hasten the Apocalypse. Krusanov's novel proved popular among Russian readers because it successfully catered to the post-imperialist nostalgia engendered by a failed superpower. As the perceptive Russian critic Vsevolod Brodsky has stated:

> *Bite* plays on the subconscious hopes and fears of the post-Soviet reader, oppressed by
> the transformation of his country from a world superpower to a slightly embarrassing
> European country with poor municipal services.[62]

Hostility to the West has been articulated more openly in Russian culture and the media since the late 1990s, although these feelings have been predominantly anti-American or anti-Semitic rather than anti-Western in general. The experience of the 1990s encouraged "national-patriots" focusing on contemporary Russian society to attack so-called "Western" values on three main grounds: the proliferation of Western commercialism and the threat of US-led globalization; the growth of porno-graphy and violence in society and the media; and the enormous wealth and power of the oligarchs, regarded as predominantly Jewish, which fuelled anti-Semitism, something never far below the surface of Russian life.

All these elements are present in Aleksandr Prokhanov's national-patriotic bestseller *Gospodin Geksogen* [Mr Hexogen, 2002],[63] winner of the "National Bestseller Prize" in 2002, which marks the growing appeal of a new kind of anti-Western, politically com-mitted Russian nationalist literature in the twenty-first century. Prokhanov's novel satirizes many of Russia's major politicians of the last decade, including Yeltsin ("The Idol") and Putin ("The Chosen One"). It is suggested that Gorbachev and Reagan conspired together at the Reykjavik summit of October 1986 to dismantle com-munism and the USSR; the Belovezh accords signed by Yeltsin in December 1991 which "destroyed the great Soviet Union" are presented unequivocally as "criminal," and the Yeltsin regime is depicted as totally corrupt and decadent, dominated by two powerful Jewish oligarchs, Astros and Zaretsky, who bear a strong resemblance to Gusinsky and Berezovsky (granted political asylum in London in 2003).

This novel, which displays extreme anti-Semitism, anti-Western feeling and Stalinist nostalgia, was greeted with some enthusiasm, even in liberal publications: Aleksandr Ivanov, the director of "Ad Marginem," the intellectual publishing house which printed several hundred thousand copies of Prokhanov's novel, particularly praised its exposure of Russia's "banal" enthusiasm for capitalism in the 1990s: "There was adolescent joy over supermarkets, Coca-Cola, *foie gras*, and Beaujolais. It was puppy love." Similarly, Mikhail Kotomin, the chief editor of "Ad Marginem," claims "Prokhanov has the energy of social hatred. After reading the novel, when you see a Mercedes you want to throw stones at it."[64]

Prokhanov's text is certainly permeated by revulsion against contemporary Russian capitalism, presented as typical of egoistic "Western" values and embodied by rich Russian Jews and the corrupt traders "of Caucasian nationality" who have inundated Moscow. Prokhanov makes constant reference to the oligarchs' scorn for Russia, their love of luxurious foreign goods and the "international Jewish network" that allegedly connects them to Israel and the US. He also exploits many conventional anti-Semitic ploys, emphasizing, for example, Zaretsky's allegedly perverted sexual practices (such as masturbation) and hinting that he had an affair with Yeltsin's daughter Tat'iana Diachenko.

Some critics regarded Prokhanov's work as an example of an antidote to the boring, politically correct prose of the post-Soviet period and a return to the socio-political commitment of classical Russian literature. However, a better analogy might be that Prokhanov's text—for all its fashionable esoteric and cabbalistic elements—to some degree represents a throwback to the extremist anti-Western, anti-Semitic political novels produced by the neo-Stalinist writers Viacheslav Kochetov and Ivan Shevtsov from the 1950s to the 1970s.[65]

Prokhanov's bestseller is devoted to an extraordinary worldwide conspiracy called "Project Swahili," which at first seems to be concerned merely with domestic Russian politics—replacing the corrupt Yeltsin regime with "the Chosen One"— but is eventually revealed to be a mad, megalomaniacal plan for world domination, in which the Russian and American security services will collaborate to further US global power. The complex web of the plot is gradually disentangled, finally exposing the central conflict between the political security service, the FSB, which is presented as pro-Western, and the military intelligence service, the GRU, which believes that Russia should follow its own path of development. Prokhanov claims that these two secret societies, or "orders," date back to the Stalin period (when Russian nationalism was revived to unite the country against Nazi Germany).[66]

The main bearer of positive values in the novel is a traditional Russian "holy fool" (*iurodivyi*), who sacrifices himself for Russia by crashing on Red Square in a home-made aeroplane bearing a picture of the Virgin Mary on one side, and of Stalin on the other. When he dies, the baton is passed to his daughter, a reformed prostitute reminiscent of Sonia in Dostoevsky's *Crime and Punishment*, who is about to fly with the troops to Chechnya to expiate her sins.

Anti-Western bias has also sometimes been evident in Russian television adaptations of popular novels. The serialization of Boris Akunin's novel *Azazel'* (1998) (translated as *The Winter Queen*) on the television channel ORT from 2002 largely omitted the interesting section of the novel set in an authentically re-created Victorian London, and introduced references to a "Jewish-Masonic conspiracy"—an interpretation that is specifically rejected in the novel as "anti-Semitic ravings"[67] (although in both versions an aristocratic Englishwoman, head of an ostensibly philanthropic international organization, is exposed as the main villain).

Anti-Western feeling is even more evident in contemporary Russian mass culture such as the thrillers of Viktor Dotsenko and the wave of recent works eulogizing the Russian security services. In Ilia Riasnoi's recent bestseller *White Legion*, for example, Gorbachev's reforms are presented as a CIA plot, and the chaotic post-communist society is saved from complete ruin by a secret network of former KGB officers.[68] Such works can be regarded as post-Soviet equivalents of Western "Cold War" thrillers such as Ian Fleming's "From Russia with Love." Perhaps they should not be taken too seriously—although mass culture is often a better indicator of popular opinion than "elite literature."

The formula "Russia for the Russians," for example, was initially espoused by extremist fascist groups and youth subcultural groups such as the *skinkhedy*, whose punk group "Terror" produced a series of threatening, xenophobic tapes entitled "The Skinheads are Coming" which voiced such extreme anti-Semitic expressions as "Gotta keep down the Kikes," "the Jewish conspiracy to control the world" and "the myth about the Holocaust."[69] However, according to opinion polls held in 2005, fear and dislike of immigrants are sentiments now expressed by the majority of the Russian population.[70]

Commercialism

The extreme distaste felt by Russian writers of a nationalist persuasion for the influx of commercialism, popular culture and pornography, which they attribute to an undifferentiated "West," is evident in many works of the 1990s and early twenty-first century.

Some literary works of the twenty-first century provide insights into psychological attitudes that are becoming more prevalent in Russian society: for example, in Liudmila Ulitskaia's *Kazus Kukotskogo* [The Kukotsky Case, 2002] the nationalistically minded Toma and her husband make a point of refusing to buy Western goods. The more Westernized Zhenia comments scornfully:

> "[Toma] and Mikhail Fedorovich don't use shampoo, can't stand foreign goods. They are patriots. They won't have [foreign] soap, medicines or clothes. And they embellish everything by saying it's ours, made in our own country. What mediocrity!"[71]

This trend has been noted by some sociologists, and by the twenty-first-century advertisers that have capitalized on the new mood, largely exchanging the predominantly Western images of the early 1990s for names and images that appeal more to Russian and Soviet values, and making increasing use of anti-Western slogans. One prominent example is an advertising campaign for "Zolotaia Yava" cigarettes, which are actually produced in Russia by the Western company British and American Tobacco. The brand's billboard advertising campaign shows the cigarettes "invading" US territory. One advertisement depicts a US astronaut on the moon recoiling backward from a giant pack of Zolotaia Yavas lodged in a moon crater, and the campaign's slogan reads "*Otvetnyi Udar*" (Counter Strike).[72]

Some nationalist writers continue to attribute the excesses of Russian television to "the West." In an interesting and well-written work by a nationalist author, Vladimir Krupin's story "Stalinskaia dacha" (2002), for example, the narrator, who claims that he "rarely watches television," flicks through the Russian television channels and complains:

> Whichever channel I switched on, everywhere was filth, depravity, smut and vulgarity. From the cloudy lens of the blue screen drunkenness, violence, sex and shooting were squeezed out in great profusion . . . If I had been cast down from another planet, I would honestly have decided that the inhabitants of the Earth were animals flecked with dandruff that spent their time chewing, cleaning their teeth three times a day, wearing sanitary towels on some kind of critical days, destroying the smell of sweat, washing with powders, cleaning wash-basins and drinking beer in barrels. In short, all the achievements of the West, which has no conscience [*svobodnogo ot sovesti*] poured onto me from the television screen.[73]

In this curious passage, Krupin's narrator refers to a strange amalgam of what to a Western observer seem to be unexceptionable Western products ensuring personal and domestic cleanliness (toothpaste, deodorant, washing powder and household cleaning products), and demonstrates a certain degree of misogyny (the mocking reference to products of feminine hygiene needed on "some kind of critical days"). Of course, during most of the Soviet period, such essential products were not only not advertised, but were not available to Russian women. These goods are, however, linked with other, less attractive Western consumer goods such as chewing gum and beer (a product by no means limited to the West). Krupin goes on to link the West with the growing sexual licence permitted on Russian television: "Have you tried being unfaithful to your husband? "Try. It will change your life," and with a disrespectful attitude to Russian history: "And everywhere leaders were depicted, Russian history was mocked."[74]

Krupin may well be polemicizing with the lighter, more humorous approach adopted to such phenomena in Pelevin's novel *Generation P*, which had acknowledged that advertisers were increasingly exploiting images from Russian history and politics to attract the consumer. Ironically, Pelevin's protagonist also conceives the idea of using the slogan "critical days" to advertise tampons, without the misogyny implicit in Krupin's story, but with what nationalists would no doubt deem a mocking approach to the tragic events of Russian history, since his advertising copy is designed to recall Yeltsin's violent conflict with the Russian Parliament in 1993: "Critical days—blood may flow. Tampax—your shield against excesses."[75]

Conclusion

Since 1991, Russia has been more open to the West than in any other period of the twentieth century, there have been increasing opportunities for Russians to assimilate

164

Western culture, and, as sociologists have shown, "the West" has been constructed by Russians in more complex and diverse ways than ever before. Young Russians are now able to differentiate more clearly between the US and various countries of Western Europe[76]—"the West" is no longer simply seen as a homogeneous whole, as in the past. It could also be argued that in the late twentieth and early twenty-first centuries Russian and Western culture have been drawn closer together by their shared condition of postmodernity created by the collapse of all "grand narratives,"[77] including the former "dreamworlds" of American capitalism and Soviet communism.[78] However, despite the growing convergence between Russia and the West on certain levels, post-Soviet culture and the media still frequently attest to the persistence of conventional, undifferentiated views of "the West"; as in the nineteenth century, it is "more the imagined West than the real West" that Russian writers either adore or deplore.[79]

The search for a new national identity in Russia after the collapse of communism has once again brought to the fore a wide spectrum of views familiar from classical nineteenth-century literature and thought. On the one hand, émigré and democratic Russian writers and scholars still express sympathy for Western values, or try through their writings to increase understanding between Russia and the West. On the other hand, it is possible to trace a significant shift from the expression of pro-Western sentiments in Russian culture of the late 1980s and early 1990s to an increasing manifestation of Russian nationalist and anti-Western sentiments in the late 1990s and the early twenty-first century. This closely reflects the changing political situation: whereas Gorbachev expressed the aspiration that his country would join "the common stream of world civilization,"[80] and such views continued to be voiced during Yeltsin's first term of office, they have become much more muted among the Russian elites at the beginning of the new millennium. In 2005 political debates were still raging on questions such as "Is Russia on the path toward Europe or is it heading its own way?"[81]

Along with the resurgence of traditional notions of Russia's uniqueness, asserted in speeches by Vladimir Putin[82] and taken up by some nationalist writers, there has been a heightened awareness of the presence (often the malign influence) of "the Other" (whether in the form of Westerner, Jew or "person of Caucasian nationality"). Contemporary Russian culture suggests that conventional views of a homogenized West as Russia's "Other" are by no means outdated—indeed, they are becoming more prevalent in the twenty-first century, at a time, ironically, when the idea of "the West," especially "Western Europe," is becoming increasingly recognized as a highly mobile and provisional concept.

During Putin's second term in office, Russia continues to forge an autonomous foreign policy, largely abandoning messianic rhetoric and maintaining close relations with individual European countries (particularly Germany and France). At the same time, Russian literature, culture and thought constantly strive to define what is Russian, in both individual and national terms, while also exploring what is human. It is probable that the West—in all its previous meanings, and in those yet to be invented—will continue to be an important part of that process in the twenty-first century.

165

In contemporary Russian literature and film, attitudes to the West remain as varied and as ambivalent as they have always been. At the beginning of the twenty-first century, Russian writers and cultural figures are once again, as throughout history, attempting to combine and recombine contemporary Western influences with their native traditions—from both the Soviet past and its pre-revolutionary precursor. This is true both of "high culture" in Russia and of popular and youth culture.[83] Post-Soviet literature and cinema display a complex blend of influences from pre-revolutionary Russia, Soviet Russia, Western Europe and the US—hence its great and enduring fascination.

NOTES

1. Said, *Orientalism*.
2. For perceptive discussions of these issues, see Berlin, "A Remarkable Decade"; Wheeler, *Russia*; and the articles in *Slavic Review*, 1964; and Malia, *Russia under Western Eyes*. See, in particular, Roberts, "Russia and the West," an admirable attempt to provide a logical methodology for tackling this question. This subject does, of course, have an enormous bibliography, and can be addressed only briefly in this essay.
3. This has been pointed out by Marc Raeff, "Russia's Perception of her Relationship with the West."
4. For recent examples, see Shlapentokh, "The Changing Russian View of the West"; Paramonov, "Historical Culture."
5. Some Russian writers have been acutely aware of this distinction: see, for example, Annenkov, *Literaturnye vospominaniia*; Tynianov, "O slonenke."
6. Anderson, *Imagined Communities*, 6.
7. On Western attitudes, see Wolff, *Inventing Eastern Europe*; Cross, *The Russian Theme in English Literature*; Todorova, *Imagining the Balkans*.
8. Foucault, "The Order of Discourse," 372.
9. Žižek, *The Sublime Object of Ideology*, 11.
10. The sources of this Westernizing "new thinking" are discussed extensively by Robert D. English, *Russia and the Idea of the West*, esp. 193–228.
11. For an ultra-nationalist attack on Siniavsky as a "Russophobe" and a comparison of his *Progulki s Pushkinym* with Salman Rushdie's *Satanic Verses*, see Shafarevich, "Fenomen emigratsii," 5.
12. Grossman, *Forever Flowing*, 157. On the critical reaction to the publication of the works by Grossman, Voinovich and Vladimov in Russia, see Marsh, *History and Literature in Contemporary Russia*, 120–23, 204.
13. Leonov, *Piramida*, 608.
14. P'etsukh, "Zakoldovannaia strana," 83.
15. Cited in Mandel'shtam, *Hope against Hope*, 13.
16. Discussed at length in Said, *Orientalism*.
17. See Korolev, "Golova Gogolia."
18. See Mozhaev, "Muzhiki i baby."
19. Other reasons for Western writers to focus on Russia include an interest in left-wing politics: see, for example, Tariq Ali and Howard Brenton's play "Moscow Gold" (1990). Other Western writers have simply become fascinated with Russian history: see, for example, Helen Dunmore, *The Siege*, and her interview with Robert McCrum, "The Siege is a Novel for Now."

20. See, for example, Fallowell, *One Hot Summer in Saint Petersburg*; Guillaume, *La Tour Ivanov*; Shulze, *33 Moments of Happiness*. The views of Russia and Russian writers of these authors are discussed in Anne Thomas, "The Portrayal of Russia and the Russians in Works by Three Contemporary Western Writers."
21. See, for example, Erofeev, *Muzhchiny*, 81–82; Tolstaya, "Notes from Underground," 4–5; idem, "Women's Lives," 1–13. Tolstaya has, however, pointed out that some Western feminists are themselves guilty of colonial attitudes to Russian women.
22. P'etsukh, "Zakoldovannaia strana," 75.
23. Tolstaya, "Women's Lives," 6, 24–25.
24. Makanin, "Stol, pokrytyi suknom i s grafinom peseredine," 29.
25. Pelevin, *Generation P*, 85.
26. Likhachev, *The National Nature of Russian History*, 18.
27. Pelevin, *Generation P*, 201, 77.
28. For another positive vision of what contemporary Russians can learn from Eastern spirituality, see Vladimir Khotinenko's film *Musul'manin* [The Muslim, 1995].
29. Granin, *Vechera s Petrom Velikim*; Viktor Aksenov, *Volter'iantsy i volter'ianki*.
30. See Brudny, *Reinventing Russia*, 259–65.
31. See Davies, *Soviet History in the Yeltsin Era*, 73–75.
32. The real threat this represented was demonstrated by the fact that Ziuganov stood as representative of the "nationalist–communist alliance" and won 40% of the vote.
33. Pilkington et al., *Looking West?*, 206–11.
34. Ibid., 226.
35. See Kichin, "Aristokrat," 8.
36. See the discussion of the views of these two politicians in Remnick, *Resurrection*, 88–92, 295–316.
37. Solzhenitsyn, *Sobranie sochinenii*, Vol. 9, 290. Such views recall Sir Isaiah Berlin's remark (in "A Remarkable Decade," 181) about the "combination of intellectual inadequacy and emotional superiority" evident in Russia's feelings about Europe.
38. P'etsukh, "Novaia moskovskaia filosofiia," 112.
39. P'etsukh, "The Central-Ermolaevo War," 237.
40. See P'etsukh, "Nagornaia propoved' i Rossiia," 269–70.
41. P'etsukh, "Russkaia tema," 3–7.
42. P'etsukh, "Zakoldovannaia strana," 72.
43. An essay competition was announced in "Konkurs 'Rossiiskoi gazety,'" 1. For further discussion, see Service, *Russia*, 183–85; Smith, *Mythmaking in the New Russia*, 158–72.
44. Pelevin, *Generation P*, 137–38.
45. Prokhanov had previously written works praising the Soviet invasion of Afghanistan and lambasting Gorbachev.
46. Mamleev, "Rossiia—mezhdu vechnost'iu i liubov'iu," 3.
47. Aksenov, "Nostalgiia ili shizofreniia."
48. Aksyonov, *Generations of Winter*, 7, 9.
49. On Herzen's disillusionment with the West, see, in particular, Alexander Herzen, *Letters from France and Italy, 1847–1851*. Other Russian travellers (predominantly male), such as Fonvizin and Dostoevsky, were simply repelled by what they perceived as the egoism, materialism and spiritual emptiness of Western society. See Fonvizine, *Lettres de France (1777–1778)*; Dostoevsky, *Winter Notes on Summer Impressions*.
50. Solzhenitsyn, "Ugodilo zernyshko promezh dvukh zhernovov," 132. For articles agreeing with Solzhenitsyn, see, for example, Kozhinov, "Solzhenitsyn versus Solzhenitsyn," 4; Kublanovsky, "Solzhenitsyn in Exile," 4–6.

51. Khazanov, "Lotova zhena," 10.
52. *Den'* (1992).
53. Voinovich, "Fashisty i kommunisty v odnom stroiu," 1.
54. Vernet, in Erofeev, *Khoroshii Stalin*, 17.
55. Erofeyev, 2004, 17.
56. Cited in Reynolds, "Translator's Introduction," xviii.
57. Pushkin, Review of "Vtoroi tom 'Istorii Russkogo naroda' Polevogo," Vol. 11, 127.
58. de Custine, *La Russie en 1839*, 233.
59. Sokurov, Interview with John Hartl, 2.
60. Chaadaev, *"Philosophical Letters" and "Apology of a Madman,"* 166–67.
61. Shevtsova, *Putin's Russia*, 169, 212.
62. Brodsky, "Letter from Russia."
63. Prokhanov, "Poslednii soldat imperii."
64. See Kishkovsky, "Russian Novelist Scoffs at Post-Soviet Leaders."
65. For further discussion, see Marsh, *Soviet Fiction since Stalin*.
66. See Brandenberger, *Stalinist Mass Culture and the Formation of Modern Russian National Identity*.
67. Akunin, *Azazel'*, 99–100; Akunin, *The Winter Queen*, 75.
68. For further discussion of this new fashion, see Finn, "In Russia, a Pop Culture Coup for the KGB," CO1.
69. Gilichensky, "The Tip of the Iceberg (Russian Neo-Nazis in Israel)."
70. "Majority of Russians Fear Immigrants." Citing an opinion poll held in April 2005 by the All-Russia Public Opinion Centre (VTsIOM) which showed that 63% of the 1,500 Russians polled believed "the presence of immigrants increases the level of crime and corruption."
71. Ulitskaia, *Kazus Kukotskogo*, 454.
72. Feifer, "Emergent Marketing."
73. Krupin, "Stalinskaia dacha," 70–71.
74. Ibid., 71.
75. Pelevin, *Generation P*, 258.
76. Pilkington et al., *Looking West?*, 220.
77. Lyotard, *The Postmodern Condition*.
78. Buck-Morss, *Dreamworld and Catastrophe*.
79. Barghoorn, "Some Russian Images of the West," 576.
80. Gorbachev, "The Crimean Article," 119.
81. The title of a conference organized by the Heinrich Böll Foundation in Germany, May 2005.
82. One example was Putin's speech to the Bashkortostan People's Assembly, 6 October 2001, when he asserted: "Russia is a unique country hosting a great variety of nations, nationalities, ethnic groups, cultures and epochs." For an alternative view, comparing the Russian empire to other historical empires, see Lieven, *Empire*.
83. For further discussion see Pilkington et al., *Looking West?*, 222–26; Goscilo, "Russian Culture of the 1990s."

REFERENCES

Aksenov, Vasilii [Aksyonov, Vassily]. *Generations of Winter*. Translated by John Glad and Christopher Morris. New York: Vintage Books, 1994.
——. "Nostalgiia ili shizofreniia." *Moskovskie novosti*, 9 November 1997.

Aksenov, Visilii. *Volter'iantsy i volter'ianki: starinnyi roman*. Moscow: Eksmo, 2004.

Akunin, Boris. *Azazel'*. Moscow: Zakharov, 2002.

——. *The Winter Queen: An Erast Fandorin Mystery*. Translated by Andrew Bromfield. London: Weidenfeld & Nicolson, 2003.

Anderson, Benedict. *Imagined Communities: Reflections on the Origin and Spread of Nationalism*. New York: Norton, 1991.

Annenkov, P. V. *Literaturnye vospominaniia*. First published in 1880. Leningrad: Akademiia, 1928.

Barghoorn, Frederick C. "Some Russian Images of the West." In *The Transformation of Russian Society*, edited by Cyril E. Black. Cambridge, MA: Harvard University Press, 1960.

Berlin, Isaiah. "A Remarkable Decade" In *Russian Thinkers*, edited by Henry Hardy and Aileen Kelly. London: Hogarth Press, 1978.

Brandenberger, David. *Stalinist Mass Culture and the Formation of Modern Russian National Identity*. Cambridge, MA: Harvard University Press, 2002.

Brodsky, Vsevolod. "Letter from Russia." Translated by Keith Gessen. *Context*, no. 9 (2001). Online Edition, < http://www.centerforbookculture.org/context/no9/brodsky.html > (accessed 1 August 2005).

Brudny, Yitzhak M. *Reinventing Russia: Russian Nationalism and the Soviet State, 1953– 1991*. Cambridge, MA: Harvard University Press, 2000.

Buck-Morss, Susan. *Dreamworld and Catastrophe: The Passing of Mass Utopia in East and West*. Cambridge, MA: MIT Press, 2000.

Chaadaev, P. Ia. *"Philosophical Letters" and "Apology of a Madman."* Translated by Mary-Barbara Zeldin. Knoxville: University of Tennessee Press, 1969.

Cross, Anthony. *The Russian Theme in English Literature*. Oxford: William A. Meeuws, 1985.

Davies, R. W. *Soviet History in the Yeltsin Era*. London: Macmillan, 1997.

de Custine, Marquis Astolphe. *La Russie en 1839*. First published Paris, 1843; *Journey for Our Time: The Journals of the Marquis de Custine*. Edited and translated by Phyllis Penn Kohler. London and Portland, OR: George Prior, 1953.

Den', no. 1 (1992). Cited in A. Latynina. "Ia tebe vlepliu odin beze. . .." *Literaturnaia gazeta*, 8 January, 2.

Dostoevsky, Fyodor. *Winter Notes on Summer Impressions*. Translated and introduced by Kyril Fitzlyon. London, Melbourne and New York: Quartet Books, 1985.

Dunmore, Helen. "The Siege is a Novel for Now." Interview with Robert McCrum. *The Observer*, 10 June 2001.

——. *The Siege*. London: Penguin, 2002.

English, Robert D. *Russia and the Idea of the West*. New York: Columbia University Press, 2000.

Erofeyev, Viktor. *Muzhchiny*. Moscow: Podkova, 1999.

——. *Khoroshii Stalin: roman*. Moscow: ZebraE, 2004.

Fallowell, Duncan. *One Hot Summer in Saint Petersburg*. London: Vintage, 1995.

Feifer, Gregory. "Emergent Marketing." *The Moscow Times*, 6 June 2000.

Finn, Peter. "In Russia, a Pop Culture Coup for the KGB." *Washington Post*, 22 February 2005.

Fonvizine, Denis. *Lettres de France (1777–1778)*. Traduites du russe et commentés par Henri Grosse, Jacque Proust et Piotr Zaborov. Paris: CNRS Editions; Oxford: Voltaire Foundation, 1995.

Foucault, Michel. "The Order of Discourse." In *Untying the Text: A Poststructuralist Reader*, edited by Robert Young. London: Routledge & Kegan Paul, 1981.

Gilichensky, Zalman. "The Tip of the Iceberg (Russian Neo-Nazis in Israel)." <www.pogrom.org.il/The%20Tip%20of%20the%20Iceberg.htm> (accessed 18 November 2006).

169

Gorbachev, Mikhail. "The Crimean Article." In *The August Coup: The Truth and its Lessons*. New York: HarperCollins, 1991.

Goscilo, Helena. "Special Issue on Russian Culture of the 1990s." *Studies in Twentieth-Century Literature* 24, no. 1 (2000).

Granin, Daniil. *Vechera s Petrom Velikim: soobshcheniia i svidetel"stva gospodina M.* St. Petersburg: Istoricheskaia illiustratsiia, 2000.

Grossman, Vasily. *Forever Flowing*. Translated by Thomas P. Whitney. New York: Harper & Row, 1972.

Guillaume Lyane. *La Tour Ivanov*. Paris: J.-C. Lattès, 2001.

Herzen, Alexander. *Letters from France and Italy, 1847–1851*. Edited and translated by Judith E. Zimmerman. Pittsburgh and London: University of Pittsburgh Press, 1955.

Khazanov, Boris. "Lotova zhena." *Literaturnaia gazeta*, 4 February 1998.

Kichin, V. "Aristokrat." *Izvestiia*, 5 April 2000.

Kishkovsky, Sophia. "Russian Novelist Scoffs at Post-Soviet Leaders." *New York Times*, 24 August 2002, <www.freeserbia.net/Articles/2002.Scotts.html> (accessed 1 August 2005).

"Konkurs 'Rossiiskoi gazety': ideia dlia Rossii." *Rossiiskaia gazeta*, 30 July 1996.

Korolev, Anatolii. "Golova Gogolia." *Znamia*, no. 7 (1992): 7–66.

Kozhinov, Vadim. "Solzhenitsyn versus Solzhenitsyn. Literary Scholar and Historian Vadim Kozhinov Talks with Viktor Kozhemiako." *Sovetskaia Rossiia*, 3 December 1998.

Krupin, Vladimir. "Stalinskaia dacha." *Literaturnaia ucheba*, no. 5 (2002): 65–74.

Kublanovsky, Iurii. "Solzhenitsyn in Exile." *IU*, 9 December 1998, 5. Translated in *Current Digest of the Post-Soviet Press* 50, no. 50 (1998), 4–6.

Leonov, Leonid. *Piramida*. Moscow: Golos, 1994.

Lieven, Dominic. *Empire: The Russian Empire and its Rivals from the Sixteenth Century to the Present*. New Haven: Yale University Press, 2000.

Likhachev, Dmitri. *The National Nature of Russian History*. New York: Harriman Institute, Columbia University, 1990.

Lyotard, Jean-François. *The Postmodern Condition: A Report on Knowledge*. Translated by Geoff Bennington and Brian Massumi. Minneapolis: University of Minnesota Press, 1984.

"Majority of Russians Fear Immigrants." *RIA Novosti*, 23 May 2005, <www.barentsobserver.com/index.php?id=249199> (accessed 1 August 2005).

Makanin, Vladimir. "Stol, pokrytyi suknom i s grafinom peseredine." *Znamia*, 1993, no. 1: 9–53. Translated by Arch Tait as *Baize-Covered Table with Decanter*. Columbia, LA and London: Readers International (1995).

Malia, Martin. *Russia under Western Eyes: From the Bronze Horseman to the Lenin Mausoleum*. Cambridge, MA: Belknap Press, 1999.

Mamleev, Iurii. "Rossiia—mezhdu vechnost'iu i liubov'iu." *Literaturnaia gazeta*, 28 January 1998.

Mandel'shtam, Nadezhda. *Hope against Hope*. Translated by Max Hayward. London: Penguin, 1975.

Marsh, Rosalind J. *Soviet Fiction since Stalin: Science, Politics and Literature*. London: Croom Helm, 1986.

——. *History and Literature in Contemporary Russia*. London: Macmillan, 1995.

Mozhaev, Boris. "Muzhiki i baby." *Don*, nos. 1–3 (1987).

P'etsukh, V. [Pietsukh, Viacheslav]. "Novaia moskovskaia filosofiia." *Novyi mir*, no. 1 (1989): 54–124.

——. "Nagornaia propoved' i Rossiia." In *Tsikly*. Moscow: RIK "Kul"tura," 1991.

——. "Zakoldovannaia strana." *Znamia*, no. 2 (1992): 67–107.

——. "Russkaia tema" [Essay]. *Druzhba narodov*, no. 7 (1993): 3–7.

170

——. "The Central-Ermolaevo War." In *The Penguin Book of New Russian Writing*, edited by Victor Erofeyev. Harmondsworth: Penguin, 1995.

Paramonov, Boris M. "Historical Culture." In *Russian Culture at the Crossroads: Paradoxes of Postcommunist Consciousness*, edited by Dmitri N. Shalin. Boulder: Westview Press, 1997.

Pelevin, Viktor. *Generation P*. Moscow: Vagrius. Translated by Andrew Bromfield as *Babylon*. London: Faber and Faber, 2000.

Pilkington, Hilary et al. *Looking West? Cultural Globalization and Russian Youth Cultures*. University Park: Pennsylvania State University Press, 2002.

Prokhanov, Aleksandr. "Poslednii soldat imperii." *Nash sovremennik*, nos. 7–9 (1993): 7–46, 15–16, 10–50.

——. *Gospodin Geksogen: roman*. Moscow: Ad Marginem, 2002.

Pushkin, A. S. Review of "Vtoroi tom 'Istorii Russkogo naroda' Polevogo." In *Polnoe sobranie sochinenii*, by A. S. Pushkin, 14 vols. Vol. 11. Moscow-Leningrad: Akademiiamauk SSSR, 1935–1949.

Raeff, Marc. "Russia's Perception of her Relationship with the West." *Slavic Review* 23, no. 1 (1964): 13–29.

Remnick, David. *Resurrection: The Struggle for a New Russia*. New York: Vintage Books, 1998.

Reynolds, Andrew. "Translator's Introduction." In *Life with an Idiot: Stories by Victor Erofeyev*, by Victor Erofeyev, translated by Andrew Reynolds. London: Penguin, 2004.

Roberts, Henry L. "Russia and the West: A Comparison and Contrast." *Slavic Review* 23, no. 1 (1964): 1–11.

Said, Edward W. *Orientalism*. London: Penguin, 1955.

Service, Robert. *Russia: Experiment with a People*. London: Macmillan, 2003.

Shafarevich, I. "Fenomen emigratsii." *Literaturnaia Rossiia*, 8 September 1989.

Shevtsova, Lilia. *Putin's Russia*. Translated by Antonina W. Bouis. Washington, DC: Carnegie Endowment for International Peace, 2003.

Shlapentokh, Vladimir. "The Changing Russian View of the West: From Admiration in the Early 1990s to Hostility in the Late 1990s." In *Is Russia a European Power? The Position of Russia in a New Europe*, edited by Tom Casier and Katlijn Malfliet. Leuven: Leuven University Press, 1998.

Shulze, Ingo. *33 Moments of Happiness*. Translated by John E. Woods. New York: Vintage International, 1998.

Slavic Review 23, no. 1 (1964): 1–29.

Smith, Kathleen E. *Mythmaking in the New Russia: Politics and Memory during the Yeltsin Era*. Ithaca, NY and London: Cornell University Press, 2002.

Sokurov, Aleksandr. Interview with John Hartl. *Seattle Post Intelligencer*, 2 February 2003, 2, <www.russianart.spb.ru/eng/interview_full.php?int_id=14> (accessed 1 August 2005).

Solzhenitsyn, Aleksandr. *Sobranie sochinenii*. 20 vols. Vol. 9. Vermont and Paris: YMCA Press, 1978–1991.

——. "Ugodilo zernyshko promezh dvukh zhernovov: ocherki izgnaniia." *Novyi mir*, no. 11 (1998), 95–153.

Thomas, Anne. "The Portrayal of Russia and the Russians in Works by Three Contemporary Western Writers." Unpublished paper, University of Bath, 2005.

Todorova, Maria. *Imagining the Balkans*. New York and Oxford: Oxford University Press, 1997.

Tolstaya, Tatiana. "Notes from Underground." *New York Review of Books*, 31 May 1990, 4–5.

——. "Women's Lives." In *Pushkin's Children: Writings on Russia and Russians*, translated by Jamey Gambrell. Boston: Houghton Mifflin, 2003.

Tynianov, Iurii. "O slonenke." *Peterburg*, no. 1 (1922).

Ulitskaia, Liudmila. *Kazus Kukotskogo*. Moscow: Eksmo, 2003.

Vernet, Daniel. *Le Monde*, 25 January 1979. Republished in Viktor Erofeev, *Khoroshii Stalin: roman*. Moscow: ZebraE, 2004.

Voinovich, Vladimir. "Fashisty i kommunisty v odnom stroiu." *Literaturnaia gazeta*, 23 December 1998.

Wheeler, Marcus. *Russia—East or West*. Belfast: Queen's University of Belfast, 1969.

Wolff, Larry. *Inventing Eastern Europe: The Map of Civilization on the Mind of the Enlightenment*. Stanford: Stanford University Press, 1994.

Žižek, Slavoj. *The Sublime Object of Ideology*. London: Verso, 1994.

Index